Clarence C. Dill

Clarence C. Dill

THE LIFE OF A WESTERN POLITICIAN

KERRY E. IRISH

WSU
PRESS

Washington State University Press
Pullman, Washington

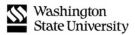

Washington
State University

Washington State University Press
P.O. Box 645910
Pullman, Washington 99164-5910
phone: 800-354-7360
fax: 509-335-8568
e-mail: wsupress@wsu.edu
web site: www.publications.wsu.edu/wsupress
© 2000 by the Board of Regents of Washington State University
First printing 2000

Library of Congress Cataloging-in-Publication Data

Irish, Kerry E., 1954–
    Clarence C. Dill : the life of a western politician / Kerry E. Irish.
        p. cm.
    Includes bibliographical references (p.) and index.
    ISBN 0-87422-190-0 (pbk.)
        1. Dill, Clarence C. (Clarence Cleveland), b. 1884. 2 Legislators—United States—
Biography. 3. United States. Congress. House—Biography. 4. United States—Politics and
government—1901–1953. 5. Washington (State)—Politics and government—1889–1950.
I. Title.

E748.D552 I75 200
328.73'092—dc21
[B]
                                                                99-088359

Contents

To Vickie

Acknowledgments

A S WITH ANY WORK of scholarship this book rests on the foundation provided by dozens of other scholars. Without the contributions of the works listed in the bibliography my version of Dill's life would not have been possible. I am particularly grateful to the people who have written about Grand Coulee Dam. Though my views on important elements of the Grand Coulee story differ from some writers, the work of scholars like Paul Pitzer and George Sundborg was instrumental in developing my own understanding of how the dam was built. Nor does my debt to Pitzer end there. For it was Pitzer who, having viewed my manuscript, suggested to WSU Press, his publisher, that my biography of Dill was worth a look. Pitzer's action epitomized the search for truth that we in the academic community so value; for as the reader of this work will discover Paul and I disagree on much concerning Clarence Dill.

I am also in debt to all of the archivists who assisted me in acquiring the various documents which form the backbone of the research for this work. I am particularly indebted to Laura Arksey at the Eastern Washington State Historical Society in Spokane, Washington. Mrs. Arksey was generous to a fault with her time and even allowed me to extend my working hours in the library beyond business hours.

I would also like to thank my colleagues, and former teachers, at George Fox University for their continued counsel and encouragement. Ralph Beebe, Lee Nash, and Mark Weinert were consistent in their inquiries about my work and exhortations to complete it.

Two men guided the dissertation from which this work has been drawn. Without their patience and insight the dissertation would not have been written.

Robert E. Burke had been trying to persuade someone to work on Dill for a number of years. Thus it was at his suggestion that I took up the challenge of Dill's long and varied life. Much to my regret Dr. Burke retired from active teaching just as I was preparing to work diligently on Dill. Nevertheless he remained on my committee, devoted a great deal of time to my work, and provided irreplaceable comment and correction. My respect and affection for Robert Burke is deep indeed.

With Burke's retirement I was required to choose a new chair for my committee. Robert Stacey suggested I ask Richard S. Kirkendall to fill that role. I could not have made a better choice and was indeed grateful when Kirkendall assented to perform the task. His deft hand as an editor improved my writing considerably. I believe that my work on Dill was much improved because I had two men of such intelligence and erudition devote so much time and energy to my work. Of course whatever errors of fact or interpretation remain in this account are my own.

In producing the first draft of the dissertation I was fortunate to have the fine assistance of one of my students, Matt Clemons, whose patience with my changes was exceptional and whose talents as a writer and typist were indispensable. I am also grateful to Becky Ankeny, chair of the writing and literature department at George Fox. Ankeny made countless stylistic suggestions which vastly improved the readability of this work.

My mother, Lois Mizell, and stepfather, Ken Mizell, provided both encouragement and financial support during my long years of graduate study. I am deeply indebted to them for their many kindnesses.

This book would never have been produced without the influence of my father, Ralph E. Irish. He imparted to me a love of history which has culminated in a career as a historian. He was an avid reader of the history of ancient Rome, World War II, and the United States.

When I graduated with the Ph.D. degree in the spring of 1994 the poet Tess Gallagher spoke at commencement. Her remarks included the observation that in achievement there is loss or sacrifice. Her words were full of wisdom and spoke powerfully of my own family's sacrifice in my (our) achievement.

I had been in school for twelve years when I graduated. My wife had worked to support us during that time, frequently working more than fifty hours per week. Our daughters, Kelly and Jenny, grew from pre-schoolers to high schoolers in that time. I do not know what kind of life we would have had had I not been in school during that time, but I know that Kelly and Jenny would have seen more of their mother.

Vickie D. Irish has been my wife and best friend since we were both eighteen years old. I cannot conceive of life without her, and certainly would not have been able to choose the path in life I have trod without her sacrifice, encouragement, and spirit of perseverance as an example. Not only would there be no biography of Dill without her; I do not know who I would be without her. So it is that I dedicate this book to her.

Introduction

CLARENCE DILL'S LONG LIFE had a significant impact on American society in the second through fourth decades of this century and profoundly affected his adopted home, the Pacific Northwest. As a congressman from Washington's Fifth District in the years before the United States entered World War I, he worked tirelessly to persuade Americans that Europe's misfortunes were not ours. In the teens and twenties he was instrumental in changing the face of politics in Washington state. Because of the political realities in his adopted home, which was a haven for conservative Democrats and Republicans, while also containing a large number of progressives of both parties, Dill—a progressive Democrat—was forced to become something of a political maverick. He could never afford to identify too closely with the conservative element of his party for fear of alienating the progressive Republicans upon whose crossover votes he depended for election.

During the twenties, Dill deftly gauged the prevailing wind of public opinion concerning prohibition, emphasizing his dry stand when it served his purposes and minimizing his commitment when times had changed. However, his skills as a politician were never more evident than in the 1928 Senate election when he convinced a number of leading conservative Republicans that he was the better choice, rather than their own candidate, if their primary goal was a protective tariff for logs and lumber. Dill's political skills, which featured an ability to gain cooperation from those of diverse interests, were further tested in his work for the federal regulation of radio.

In the twenties and thirties, when radio became a national phenomenon, Dill was that medium's authority in the Senate. In radio's early days, a number of entrepreneurs would have liked nothing better than to gain ownership of the airwaves to create a monopoly. On the other hand, there were groups that strove equally hard to see radio become government owned. Dill opposed both sides, preferring a system of regulation that would preserve the access of many voices to radio while retaining the vitality of private ownership. In the trying times of the thirties, radio, by virtue of the fact that Americans from east to west heard many of the same programs and heard their president speak words of assurance, was a unifying force in American life. Clarence Dill had no small hand in creating that force.

Dill's greatest regional accomplishment was his work on Grand Coulee Dam. Grand Coulee began the transformation of the Pacific Northwest from a virtual economic colony of the eastern portion of the nation to a full-grown member of the American union. Dill's work for the development of the Pacific Northwest did not end with the building of Grand Coulee. For twenty-five years after his retirement from the Senate he strove to create a system of storage dams in Canada that would control flood waters, enhance dam efficiency, and provide cheaper power for the public utility districts he had so long supported. In all these endeavors Dill exemplified the cooperative spirit and builder's mentality so common amongst Americans of the West.

In exploring and explaining Dill's belief in cooperation and compromise, it is not my purpose to reopen the long argument between Frederick Jackson Turner and Bernard Devoto and their disciples. Today's historians generally believe that Devoto's interpretation allows for a deeper, more complex, understanding of the West. My work on Dill clearly supports that consensus. It is my purpose to remind Westerners that cooperation and compromise are still necessities if the diverse western peoples, who are currently struggling with a number of important issues, are to live in harmony with one another and the land.

Dill possessed many of mankind's weaknesses, and not a few human strengths, especially as they manifested themselves in the West of the early twentieth century. Unfortunately, the task of recreating Clarence Dill was difficult because he did not keep his congressional papers, nor were his personal papers much help. Consequently, this biography relies a great deal on other manuscript collections, newspapers, government records, and secondary sources. The result is a biography that sometimes prompts questions in the reader that are simply unanswerable. Unquestionably, more should have been written about Rosalie Jones Dill, Dill's first wife; but there is not much information about her. Then too, I often wondered what Dill himself thought about this or that subject, but there were often only public pronouncements to guide me. Dill did write an autobiography very late in life, *Where Water Falls,* which has been of some value. However, Pacific Northwest historians have long considered this work self-serving at best and often flatly in error. It is a self-promotional book and I have thus used it cautiously, primarily for those human details that help reveal Clarence Dill. I have not used it as the primary evidence for my major arguments.

All of the above aside, I tried to capture the essence of Clarence Dill. I hope the reader will find his story as interesting as I have.

U.S. Senator from the state of Washington, Clarence C. Dill. *#L93-66.42, Cheney Cowles Museum/Eastern Washington State Historical Society, Spokane, WA*

CHAPTER ONE

T𝐇𝐄 M𝐀𝐊𝐈𝐍𝐆 𝐎𝐅 𝐀 W𝐄𝐒𝐓𝐄𝐑𝐍𝐄𝐑

CLARENCE DILL WAS BORN into a family with a rich American heritage. Several of his ancestors fought in the Revolutionary War.[1] Theodore, Clarence's father, fought for the Union in the Civil War, but somehow escaped becoming a Republican, a fact which would have a profound effect on his son.

Theodore toiled as a tenant farmer on a 223-acre farm just outside Fredericktown, Ohio. Clarence's mother was a devout Christian and hard working farmer's wife, who attended the nearby Methodist church.[2] The Dills were poor even by the standards of the day. Because the Republicans had maintained a firm lock on the White House since the Civil War, Theodore may have favored the politics of the Democratic Party out of a spirit of protest. Certainly the Dills were a family zealous for the party of Andrew Jackson.

Amanda Dill gave birth to her son Clarence on September 21, 1884, the height of the Gilded Age.[3] This, combined with the fact that Ohio was the political hotbed of the nation during this period, made an indelible mark on the younger Dill. He would always be torn between a career in politics and the desire to make money. The family's poverty and political involvement profoundly influenced the young man as well.

When Clarence was twelve, William Jennings Bryan captivated him with his "Cross of Gold" speech. In emulation of his hero, Dill set out to master the art of oratory. The young man would go out to the barn, his collie for an audience, and practice Bryan's great speech. Two years later he had the opportunity to hear Bryan speak at Mansfield, Ohio. In awe of the Great Commoner, Clarence went through the reception line twice to shake Bryan's hand.[4] There was little chance now that Clarence would become anything but a Bryan Democrat.

Dill spent many hours behind a plow and doing chores late into the evening. One hot summer afternoon, after having spent the day turning furrows, Dill made a decision. He did not want to be a farmer; he wanted to go to Congress. While plowing on that sultry afternoon, the reluctant farm boy realized that a career in Congress would allow him to combine his love for oratory with his passion for politics.[5]

Dill made no secret of his desire for a congressional career. He so boldly proclaimed his ambitions that friends often teased him.[6] But Fanny Ball, the wife of his father's landlord, encouraged young Clarence in all his aspirations. Mrs. Ball was selling tickets one day to a box social, but Dill could not afford the twenty-five cent ticket price. Mrs. Ball offered to loan him the money, but he replied, "I don't know when I can repay you." She said, "I'll take your note, payable when you make your first speech in Congress."[7] The ambitious and hungry young man wrote the note.

Dill graduated as valedictorian of his high school class and took a job as a country school teacher. While teaching, he worked on his debating skills and saved money for college. He taught school for two years before he had enough money to enroll in Ohio Wesleyan University, his mother's choice, in the autumn of 1903.[8]

At Ohio Wesleyan, Dill came under the influence of Robert Fulton, one of the nation's most prominent teachers of public speaking and forensics.[9] In an effort to expose his students to various speaking styles, Fulton invited well known speakers and celebrities to address the class. On one occasion, Fulton persuaded William Jennings Bryan to make an appearance. It was one of the highlights of Dill's college career. Bryan instructed the young debaters to train their voices so that the audience would never have to listen, they could not help but hear. Bryan also advised the students to learn when to stop. He said, "Never talk too long. Leave your audience hungry rather than overfed. So they can be saying to themselves, 'I wish he had gone on,' instead of, 'Thank God he quit.'"[10]

In 1905, while working as a part-time reporter, Dill was assigned to travel to Marion, Ohio, to investigate the murder of a Cleveland man. He took the interurban thirty miles north to Marion. Arriving in the city, Clarence questioned a police officer. The policeman suggested the best place to learn about the murder was probably the office of the publisher of the local newspaper. Entering the dingy, paper-strewn office, Dill apologized to the editor and publisher of the *Marion Star* and proceeded to explain his dilemma: he did not have any idea how to write the murder story. The kindly editor told him to take the news story that his reporter had already written and use it in whatever way suited him. The editor also gave Clarence some names of people to contact. Elated, Dill offered to pay for the information but the editor refused saying, "No, no. I'm really glad if I've helped you." Dill thanked the editor again and said, "I hope I can write you a story some day to help you become governor." Warren G.

Harding responded, "I'm afraid it will be a long time before I am so honored."[11]

Dill graduated from Ohio Wesleyan in 1907 with a bachelor of letters degree. He decided to take advantage of his newspaper experience and so secured a job on the *Cleveland Press*.[12] But few of the rookie reporter's stories found their way to print. A few weeks later the editor fired him. Clarence asked him why; the editor replied, "You just don't know news."[13]

The young college graduate refused to give up. Such perseverance was a trait that would serve him well in the years to come. He landed a job with the *Cleveland Plain Dealer*. Unfortunately, he had the same problem working for that paper. But he stumbled onto a story about a girl who had been a barroom dancer since the age of ten, and at the age of seventeen, was suing for back wages. Even a reporter fresh out of college could not miss the human interest angle. The story sold papers and taught Dill how to write news. Not long after, the *Cleveland Press* offered Dill his old job at a higher wage. He took it, and with it came the opportunity to cover Tom Johnson's campaign for mayor of Cleveland.[14]

Dill learned a great deal covering Johnson's campaign. He noticed how Johnson used humor to deflect pointed questions until the questioner was willing to accept almost any answer.[15] The young reporter also observed that Johnson had the ability to actually convert opponents. On one occasion, Johnson met with more than one hundred preachers who were upset that he had failed to close saloons in the big hotels and city clubs on Sundays. Johnson responded that he had closed the saloons along the waterfront on Sundays first because the families of the men who frequented those saloons were most in need of the money spent there. Johnson went on to explain that he lacked policemen to close all the saloons at once, but if reelected, he promised to close them all. Whether or not Johnson's selective closing of saloons on Sunday represented manpower realities as he claimed (his sympathetic biographer admits Johnson was not above twisting the truth) or was an example of how progressivism targeted the lower classes for reform, the ministers left saying, "Tom's alright."[16]

In covering Johnson's campaign, Dill's predilection toward progressive political opinions could only have been reinforced, taken as he was with Johnson's campaign style and oratorical ability. Tom L. Johnson was perhaps the foremost proponent of urban progressivism in the early twentieth century. Lincoln Steffens believed Johnson was the "best mayor of the best governed city in the United States."[17]

Johnson championed the cause of the common man, advocating measures such as a three cent street car fare and municipal ownership of utilities. But Johnson had also earned great wealth, taking advantage of his Gilded Age opportunities. He carefully protected his own wealth and even argued publicly that he felt free to profit from his investments in monopolies as long as monopolies were legal. Then, ironically, in the next breath, he lambasted the existence of monopolies.[18] Clarence Dill came to be very much like Tom L. Johnson: able to get along with a wide spectrum of people, progressive in political ideology, but determined to make money along the way.

When Dill went to work in Cleveland, he knew that it was only temporary. He had told professor Fulton that he intended to move to the Pacific Northwest at some point. Fulton asked him why, and Dill responded, "Because it is a new and developing country and it has had a lure for me for several years."[19] A cousin who had visited the region had written home extolling the pristine virtues of Oregon's Willamette Valley in particular and the Pacific Northwest in general. Dill was impressed. Fulton shook his hand and said, "I'm sure you'll be able to go to Congress from that country..."[20] Dill had retained the dream throughout his college years and now was about to embark on a search for a place in which the dream might become reality, a place "with freedom, an active outdoor life, a place with the excitement of something mighty to be built."[21]

Dill soon discovered that reality has a way of setting in before one expects. For various reasons, especially financial, he spent the winter of 1907-08 teaching school in Dubuque, Iowa.[22] After completing the school year, he decided to attend the Democratic National Convention in Denver, where his hero, William Jennings Bryan, became the Democrat's standard bearer for the third time. From Denver, he intended to continue his journey to the Pacific Northwest.

After the convention, the would-be congressman took the Union Pacific down the Columbia Gorge; standing at the rear of the observation car, he looked at the great river for the first time. The wild white water of the Columbia fascinated the young man, as did majestic Mt. Hood and Mt. Adams. But Portland failed to impress the adventuresome Dill. It was a beautiful city; that was not the problem. Or, in a way, it was. Dill sought a frontier city; but Portland was already old. Dill later described it as "more like an Eastern, than a Western city." He decided to go north to Tacoma and Seattle, but those cities disappointed him as well. He later wrote that he could not see the future possibilities for development in either of the two cities on the Sound. This, of course, implies that he was looking for a city with which to grow, a city that would provide an opportunity for an ambitious young man to make his way in politics.

Portland, Seattle, and Tacoma surprised Dill, who expected to discover frontier opportunities. Brick buildings several stories high, paved streets, mass transportation, and street lights, all spoke of well established societies. A builder at heart, Dill could see no future in cities that appeared to be already built. Moreover, a power structure three generations old would make it difficult to crack the political establishments of these cities. Hence Dill's disappointment with these "Eastern" metropolises. The young man, pioneer blood in his veins, turned his eyes toward Spokane, hoping that eastern Washington city contained the frontier-like opportunity that he longed for. If not, he would head east to Minnesota and take the newspaper job a friend had offered him.[23]

Sun bathed the city on a July morning in 1908 when Dill left the Northern Pacific depot and headed for downtown Spokane. He wrote in his autobiography, *Where Water Falls:* "I thought I had never seen such white sunlight, nor breathed such invigorating air. After eating my breakfast, I walked through the business section to the bridge overlooking the falls of the Spokane River, and talked to a policeman and some other people on the streets, I decided here was where I wanted to live and go to Congress."[24]

Dill had gone West in search of the frontier and was disappointed when he did not find it in Portland or Seattle. Spokane, less developed than the western cities, though clearly well past the frontier stage, more readily suited Dill's purposes. Nevertheless, it must have taken some self persuasion—lost to his memory in the intervening years—that Spokane would offer the future he dreamt of. For Spokane was already the Queen of the Inland Empire when Clarence Dill arrived. Railroads—the lifeblood of many western towns—had made the city a booming service center: marketing, transportation, jobbing, shopping, medicine, and education were all available in abundance.[25]

The men and women who had built the city were very much like the young man who had jumped off the train that July morning. Though the city by the falls was two to three decades behind the Puget Sound cities, it had a core of boosters and builders possessed of great ambitions for its economic growth and aesthetic beauty. The most important and influential of Spokane's creators was William H. Cowles, editor and publisher of three of Spokane's daily newspapers. Cowles had arrived in Spokane in 1891 as a partner in, and business manager of, the *Spokesman*. He gradually bought out his partners and in 1894 purchased *The Review*. He would merge the two into the *Spokesman-Review*. In 1897 he was able to gain control of the *Spokane Chronicle*. As the last years of the nineteenth century passed, Cowles emerged as the most powerful man in eastern Washington: "Politicians sought his endorsement, businessmen his blessing, and publicists his cooperation."[26]

Cowles, Aubrey White, and other Spokane leaders were not just concerned with the city's economic future. They were determined that Spokane be a beautiful city, highly livable as well as economically prosperous. When it was obvious that land in the city was growing both scarce and more expensive, Cowles and White led an effort to purchase land for city parks. In addition, White—president of the Park Board—hired the Olmsted brothers, well known landscape architects, to plan the city's park system. He also persuaded the city council to plant 80,000 trees in the city.[27] Cowles and White typified the men and women of Spokane who were cooperating to build the leading city in eastern Washington: "Newspapers called them 'progressive' men, and every town that would amount to anything had them."[28]

Clarence Dill had decided to make Spokane his home, but did Spokane want him? The unemployed reporter applied for work at the various newspapers and visited them nearly every day. No one seemed interested, but he was able to strike up a friendship with the assistant editor of the *Spokesman-Review*, Charley Hart. The two men had a mutual acquaintance that Dill embellished to win Hart's favor (Dill was adept at selling himself and would become more so). Days went by, and still Clarence remained without a job. He made plans to use his return ticket to get to St. Paul and to work in a wheat field for a week to raise traveling money. The day before he was to go to work shocking wheat, he received a phone call from Hart. The editor asked the nearly desperate young man if he still wanted a job. Dill replied, "I most certainly do." Hart told him to get down to the office right away.[29]

Elated, Dill virtually flew down to the newspaper office. Hart wanted him to work as the *Spokesman-Review*'s police reporter. Based on his previous experience, Clarence believed he could do the job. A few weeks later, Malcolm Glendenning, editor of the paper, asked him to do a story on how the saloon men of Spokane intended to vote in the upcoming gubernatorial election. Whoever the saloon men favored would draw the wrath of the prohibitionists—including W.H. Cowles. Glendenning suspected that the saloon men would not recognize Dill as a *Spokesman-Review* employee, and thus gave him the assignment and five dollars to be used to provide liquid refreshments in hope the libations would loosen the tongues of the saloon men. Dill slaked the thirst of the saloon men, and his own, so thoroughly he had to go home and lie down for a few hours before he could write the story.[30]

Dill's "research" revealed that the saloon men favored Republican Henry McBride, a former governor of the state. The young reporter's story landed on the front page of the *Spokesman-Review* on August 27, 1908, nearly two weeks before the primary election. McBride lost.[31] In addition to canvassing local drinking establishments, Dill's work for Cowles eventually included writing some of the latter's editorials. [32]

In the fall of 1908, Dill accepted a position as an English teacher and debate coach at South Central High School in Spokane. In his spare time, he read law under the instruction of J.W. Graves, a Spokane lawyer and fraternity brother. Dill spent most of his evenings and Saturdays studying law.[33] Obviously, he not only dreamed about going to Congress, but also worked hard to prepare himself to go there. But Clarence did not forget about the people he left behind in Ohio. His mother told a *Spokesman-Review* reporter in July 1937 that her son had faithfully written her a letter once a week.

In 1910 Dill felt ready to pass the bar exam. He journeyed to Olympia where he took the written exam on the first day. Shocked to find his name missing from the list of those who had passed, and afraid that the bar exam now represented a serious barrier on his road to Congress, he asked the chief examiner just how poorly he had performed. The examiner replied, "I'm sure you passed. I graded your papers." The chief examiner looked again at the official list of those who had passed. The list had been folded at the top, and whoever had copied it for posting had not seen Clarence Dill's name at the very top; far from failing, the former school teacher posted the highest score of the day.[34]

Soon after settling in Spokane, Dill involved himself with the local Democratic Party. This choice of parties placed him on the opposite side of the political fence from his employer, influential Republican William Cowles. It also meant that he had chosen the hard route to political success, for the Democrats were decidedly the minority party in eastern Washington. However, Dill's Democratic roots were long and deep. There is no indication that he ever vacillated. His work with the party paid off soon after he passed the bar. As a young lawyer in private practice, Dill made little money. Fortunately, the elected chairman of the Democratic County Committee, Thomas A. Scott, appointed Dill secretary of the committee with the responsibility of managing the county campaign. The young lawyer at first declined, but when Scott informed him that the position carried a $150 a month salary, the pragmatic Dill immediately accepted.

It was a good match for both Clarence and the party. For the first time in many years the Democrats elected four county officials, a prosecuting attorney, and a county commissioner. New prosecuting attorney John Wiley made Dill an assistant at $175 a month. Aware of his own inexperience, Dill asked for responsibilities he knew something about: police court attorney. He felt confident that his reservoir of experience as a police reporter would stand him in good stead. Moreover, his new position provided him the opportunity to inform newspaper reporters about human interest cases he would be handling in court. He later wrote, "This enabled me to get more publicity about myself than anyone else in the prosecutor's office."[35]

The gregarious Dill rose quickly in the Democratic Party. At the Jefferson-Jackson Day Celebration of 1912, he made a "bang-up corking good Jacksonian and Jeffersonian spiel."[36] The speech impressed more than newspaper reporters. The party's central committee asked him to be the temporary chairman of the State Democratic Convention to be held in the spring.[37] Dill went into the year favoring Woodrow Wilson for the presidency and even helped form Washington's Wilson League. But Speaker of the House Champ Clark, who was favored to win the nomination, had strong support in Spokane. Dill backed away from Wilson in favor of William Jennings Bryan.[38] The Wilson and Clark forces were all but irreconcilable, especially in Washington state, but neither side considered a Bryan man a foe. Dill had positioned himself to avoid making enemies.

Petty conflict marred the convention, held in Walla Walla. Dill, as temporary chairman, gave a speech which for a moment united the convention forces against the real enemy—insurgent Republican Teddy Roosevelt. Dill had a reputation for oratory and his speech at the convention did nothing to damage that reputation. In his oration, he fired broadsides at Roosevelt and the Republicans. He accused Roosevelt of being long on words and short on action, possessed of incredible egotism in his desire for a third term, and a tool of big business. Then Clarence trumpeted the heritage and strengths of the Democratic Party:

> Never before since the Civil War has there been so general an agreement as to leaders, issues and opportunities of and in the Democratic party as there is today. The Democratic party is the only party that was born with the nation and it will survive as long as the nation endures. It has survived every defeat and recovered from every disaster, because it has always had a great ideal. That ideal has been a government that would permit special privileges to none and guarantee equal rights to all. The insurgent Republicans should join the Democratic party. Until

they do they can be no more than a Red Cross brigade to stanch the political wounds caused by a system of special privilege in the form of a high protective tariff and obedient allegiance to big business.[39]

Impressed with Dill's oratory, and previously unable to agree on a permanent chairman, the Clark and Wilson forces settled on Clarence in that position. The fact that he was perceived as a Bryan advocate smoothed the way for his ascension.[40]

After clearing away minor issues, it did not take long for the more numerous Clark forces to gain the upper hand at the convention. Apparently facing defeat, Charles Heifner, leader of the Wilson forces, attempted to stampede the convention for Bryan. He narrowly missed his goal.[41] What role the convention chairman played in the attempted stampede can only be guessed, but it is at least conceivable that Heifner and the Wilson forces wanted a man in the chairmanship sympathetic to their candidate. Dill, before his change of heart, had been a Wilson man.

Dill went to Baltimore to attend the Democratic National Convention. While there he wrote notes of his experiences, the most interesting of which were his comments concerning William J. Bryan's speech nominating John W. Kern of Indiana. Bryan whipped the crowd to a frenzy with the words, "He never sold the truth to save the hour. Those words were spoken of the hero of Monticello, and I could not feel myself worthy to claim to be a follower of his, if I today were willing to sell the truth to save the present hour." He continued, "I appeal to you as delegates, let the commencement of this convention be such a commencement that the Democrats of this country may raise their heads among their fellows and say 'the Democratic Party is true to the people.'"[42] Dill believed, as did several reporters he spoke to, that if Bryan had quit speaking at that moment, the convention might have gone as he wished. But Bryan had lost his touch. He continued to speak until the crowd deserted him. Dill learned a valuable lesson, a lesson Bryan himself had stressed to Clarence as a young college debater, but had apparently forgotten himself: know when to quit.[43]

Dill returned home and worked for various Democratic candidates. A competitive field vied for the Democratic Party's nomination for governor in 1912. Ernest Lister of Pierce County took the front-runner's position, while W.W. Black, a judge from Snohomish County, mounted a vigorous challenge. Five other candidates sought the nomination. As the September primary drew near, most of the candidates attacked Lister, resulting in Black's victory.[44] However, the state supreme court declared that Black was ineligible to serve as Washington's governor because the

Washington State Constitution prohibited a sitting judge from running for political office. Lister took Black's place on the ballot.

The *Seattle Post-Intelligencer* considered Lister an amiable fellow, but did not give him much chance in the general election since the Democrats had so completely bungled the selection of a candidate through their "ignorance of the State Constitution."[45] Nevertheless Lister won the election with a plurality of fewer than 700 votes.[46] In the presidential election, Teddy Roosevelt swept the state—making Lister's election all the more remarkable.

Clarence Dill had provided Lister with at least a modicum of prominence at the state Democratic Party Convention back in May when he had appointed Lister sergeant at arms. Lister, in need of a private secretary with well-developed diplomatic skills, chose Dill for the post. The new governor remembered how the young man had so skillfully handled his duties at the convention. In Olympia the Democrats would be substantially outnumbered. If Lister were to get anything done he could not afford to antagonize the opposition unnecessarily. Dill was an excellent choice.[47]

The 1910 census mandated the creation of two new congressional districts in the state of Washington. Dill, of course, hoped that one of those districts would include Spokane. Obviously the Republicans could not draw the districts so as to place a Republican incumbent in each one—there were not enough Republican incumbents to go around. Hence they strove to create districts which had a solid record of Republican strength. Spokane had never sent a Democrat to the nation's capital. Pliny Allen and Ed Sims, the Republican leaders of the house and senate, liked Dill. The governor's secretary had gone out of his way to create a cordial relationship between the legislature's leaders and the governor's office.[48] Consequently, they agreed to draw Washington's new Fifth District so as to leave it without an incumbent. Of course they were confident the Republican candidate would defeat Dill. Besides, the real fighting over the re-districting legislation was over the form of Seattle's new congressional district, and over the state legislature's lines. This fight was bitter, and did not follow party lines as much as it resembled urban/rural antagonisms.[49] The issue was not decided until the last night of the legislative session: the Fifth District survived as Dill hoped.[50]

When Dill came to Olympia to serve as Lister's secretary, it was with the understanding that he would serve only for a few months. With the passage of the redistricting legislation, Dill—the builder and aspirant to Congress—had what he really wanted: a clear shot at a congressional seat. Shortly after the legislative session, Dill informed Lister of his intent to return home in order to prepare for the congressional campaign of 1914. In the meantime, he intended to support himself with his private law practice.[51]

As a party organizer, chairman of the state Democratic convention, and governor's secretary, Clarence Dill had demonstrated the ability to reconcile opposing groups while positioning himself for advancement. His talents were widely recognized within the state; so much so that Jim Ford, a columnist with the *Spokesman-Review*, wrote of them in less than flattering terms, making those abilities sound like character flaws. Ford recalled how Dill had possessed the audacity to say nice things about some Republicans, had waffled between Champ Clark's forces and Wilson's in the early stages of the presidential campaign, and essentially argued that Dill cared for nothing except his own political advancement. Ford's point was to cast Dill as absurdly trying to create harmony amongst those of all political persuasions. But in order to win the Fifth District's congressional seat, Dill would need all of the diplomatic skills and charisma Ford so uncharitably criticized in order to persuade enough Republicans to vote for him.[52]

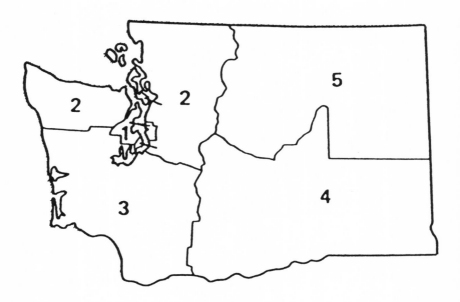

U.S. congressional districts in the state of Washington, 1915.

CHAPTER TWO

Go East, Young Man

DILL SPENT THE LAST HALF of 1913 in private law practice in Spokane, but took every opportunity to speak at ladies' clubs, business clubs, social functions, and political gatherings. The twenty-nine-year-old, would-be congressman had long been a student of elections. He had seen Tom Johnson handle crowds and Ernest Lister maneuver colleagues.[1] Campaigning effectively in the huge Fifth District would require physical stamina; but Clarence was prepared to endure ceaseless work to make his dream come true. Winning the fall election would also test Dill's ability to appeal to a cross-section of Americans: farmers, laborers, city dwellers, women, Republicans, and Democrats; he would need votes from all these groups to defeat his challengers.

The congressional district Dill hoped to represent consisted of Chelan, Okanogan, Douglas, Ferry, Lincoln, Pend Oreille, and Spokane counties—essentially the entire northeastern corner of Washington. Its farmers, loggers, and small businessmen often lived in—or depended on—small towns that grew slowly in the valleys, largely isolated from the outside world. The largest city, Dill's hometown of Spokane, sported a fashionable new residential district on the west side where many of the town's leaders, almost all conservative Republicans, lived. The region had never sent a Democrat to Washington, D.C.

Though William La Follette, the Republican incumbent, was now in the Fourth District, Clarence faced other obstacles besides the sheer size of his chosen home.[2] Other political aspirants shared Dill's excitement about a new congressional district with no incumbent. Sixteen men filed as candidates in the Fifth District; Clarence faced three other attorneys from Spokane in the Democratic primary, and two minor party candidates and ten Republicans also sought the seat.[3]

Dill kicked off 1914 with a speech dedicating Newport's city hall. He argued that the small towns of America were the backbone of the country and urged his listeners to support local businesses and education and to become involved in local politics. In these sentiments, Dill sought to tie the people of Newport emotionally to his personality and candidacy. But he was doing more than fishing for votes. He had fond memories of his childhood, and though he had come west to build a life and contribute to a region, he also hoped to recreate for himself the kind of home he had known in his youth. That home included more than family, friends, and familiar surroundings. It extended to the activities Dill had enjoyed as a boy: hunting, fishing, and in general, the outdoors.

Dill formally announced his candidacy on April 30, 1914:

> There are just two conceptions of government. One is based on the idea that the power to perform public service comes up from the great common people; the other, on the idea that it comes down from a superior authority. The public official who believes that society is built up from the bottom will always be found fighting for the interests of the masses of mankind, while the public official who believes society is suspended from above, will work primarily for the interests of the well-to-do, and then wait and hope for the benefits to sift through to those below.[4]

Dill was identifying himself with the tradition of Jefferson and Jackson and with the president, Woodrow Wilson. In this effort, he sought to benefit from and support the political philosophies of the great men of the Democratic Party.

As much as he admired these men and their achievements, Dill desired to see the Democratic Party become the party of progressivism. Progressivism was practically inbred in Clarence Dill. William Jennings Bryan had been a boyhood hero, and Tom Johnson, the renowned progressive mayor of Cleveland, had profoundly affected the young man. For Dill, progressivism both explained and offered solutions to the nation's problems. Clarence and millions of other progressives saw American society in rather simplistic terms. Progressives, usually motivated by a combination of evangelical Protestantism, the new natural and social sciences, and the conviction that a once egalitarian America was slipping away, believed that the forces of compassion and justice were in conflict with those of greed and reaction. The former were those who possessed fewer of the world's goods, generally farmers, laborers, and small merchants, along with their more educated advocates, while the latter were the wealthy, or at least prosperous, owners and managers of business. Because wealth so clearly provided political power, it naturally followed that achieving political equality necessitated a narrowing of the range of economic diversity. At the same time, it seemed obvious to progressives that because the nature of society was beyond the control of the individual, only government could wield enough power to produce a more equal distribution of wealth and thus political power.[5]

One might say progressives rejected the philosophy of *laissez faire* for what they believed was a more humane pragmatism. However, progressives were not socialists, much to the chagrin of the socialists of the day and some later observers. Rather, "they hoped to restore social harmony without overturning the foundations of private property or family life."[6] Progressives favored limiting the power of trusts and enhancing the power of the working man and consumer. They worked to rid cities and states of corruption, advocated prohibition, were often pacifistic and anti-imperialistic, and believed in giving women the vote. They were also paternalistic, nationalistic, and, especially in the South, racist. Even in the North, however, their efforts to help immigrants were based on the belief that the Anglo-Saxon middle-class way of life was the American way of life. Progressivism also carried forth the essence of populism: a concern for farmers. Indeed, the Great Commoner, William Jennings Bryan, symbolized the continuity of the two movements as he was a leader of both. To understand Clarence Dill, then, it is crucial to keep his concept of progressivism in mind. Even after the progressive era had clearly passed, he consistently referred to himself as a progressive.[7]

Dill took careful note of the work of the suffragist leader of the Inland Empire, May Arkwright Hutton. Instrumental in bringing the vote to women in Idaho in 1896, Hutton repeated her work in Washington in 1910. In 1914 she was a respected member of the Democratic Party and an advocate for women's issues.[8] Aware of his need for every conceivable vote, Dill sought to profit from the new element in Washington State politics—women.

Early in 1914, Dill was dating Helene Morrissey, a Spokane schoolteacher. He sought her advice on how he might best impress women voters. Reluctant to instruct the young candidate, Morrissey claimed to know nothing about politics. Slightly miffed, Clarence said, "I'm disappointed in you. You're Irish and the Irish take to politics like a cat to cream and you're a woman and women know things by instinct, yet you plead ignorance." Dill's comment triggered Morrissey's Irish temper, "All right, I'll tell you one thing. A woman does not like a man who is conceited and she won't vote for him. Now don't you forget that." Dill replied, "But I am conceited or I would not be running for Congress before I am thirty years old." Helene finished him off, "I know it. That's why I said that."[9]

Dill took his friend's advice and made a concerted effort to avoid appearing conceited. Moreover, he deliberately set out to garner the women's vote and to enlist women as workers in his campaign. In his effort to gain those votes, Dill often went door to door. He would introduce himself and apologize for bothering the "lady of the house," then proceed to explain that because women were eligible to vote for the first time that year, he wanted to make himself well known to them. He went on to tell how he had been born on a farm in Ohio, worked his way through college, and studied law at night while teaching school during the day. He finished by saying that the newspapers, being Republican in sympathy, gave him little coverage, forcing him to depend on personal appearances and private contacts. His strategy worked wonders; everywhere he went, he left women who were intending to vote for C.C. Dill.

In June Dill took his campaign on the road. He preferred to travel on the train and avoid the rough roads of northeastern Washington. When trains were not available, he took whatever means of transportation he could find. He sometimes speculated on which would give out first: man or machine. As the wheat fields rolled by, he must have often wondered if all his efforts would pay off or if his dream of going to Congress would disappear like wind-driven chaff.

The young politician had a strategy to gain the votes of men as well as women. In Marcus, Washington, Dill asked the hotel keeper if he knew who might be persuaded to introduce him to the men in the business district. The hotel keeper responded, "Go alone. You'll get more attention then." Dill followed the man's advice and later noticed that when someone introduced him to a friend, invariably the conversation centered on the two acquaintances and not on the prospective congressman. He made it a point to introduce himself whenever possible.[10]

Dill devoted a great deal of time to the outlying areas of the district. After he had spoken in Hillyard to Democrats organizing a club to support Wilson's policies and other Democratic candidates, the *Inland Empire News* reported favorably on his speech. Dill was distancing himself from his competition. As June turned to July, he toured the northern portion of the district, following his separate strategy for men and women. He reported at a meeting of the Spokane Democratic Central Committee, "People up there who have taken no part in politics for ten years tell me they are going to vote the Democratic ticket this year."[11]

In August, half a world away, the outbreak of World War I had an almost immediate effect on the congressional campaign in the Fifth District. In keeping with his campaign theme of support for President Wilson, Dill argued Americans were indeed fortunate that a man of peace occupied the White House.[12]

Dill excelled at getting people involved in his campaign. Asked to speak to a group of firemen's wives, he instructed the women on how to be sure they could vote for the Democratic candidate in the primary election. Then he encouraged them to persuade one or two friends to vote for him as well. Excited to be involved in the political process, many of the women promised they would deliver substantially more than one or two friendly votes. Dill warned the women that the task might be more difficult than they suspected, but they were undaunted. They not only proceeded to influence friends to vote for Dill, they assisted converts in registering and voting.[13]

As a result of his strenuous campaigning and his facility for organization, not to mention his success with female voters, Clarence went into the primary election favored to win the Democratic Party's nomination to Congress.[14] There were no surprises. Dill defeated his challengers and now faced Republican Harry Rosenhaupt and Progressive Thomas Corkery in the general election.[15]

Having won the primary, the would-be congressman repeated his successful strategy in hopes of winning the general election. In this contest, however, Dill would be a decided underdog: Rosenhaupt had the advantage of the region's track record of supporting Republicans and a significantly larger party structure. In addition, the ten Republican candidates had polled five thousand more votes in the primary than the four Democratic candidates. To win, the Democratic nominee would have to convert a massive number of Republican voters.

Dill did not waste any time, nor did he overlook any opportunity to speak. He appeared at the Inter-State Fair on September 20, spoke at luncheons, and advanced his candidacy at women's clubs and business meetings. Towns like Foothill and Kiesling, whose residents might have thought themselves safe from the onslaughts of a congressional campaign, had to put up with the orations of Clarence Dill.[16]

The congressional election of 1914 presented clear choices to the voters of Washington's Fifth District. Dill ran first and foremost as a Woodrow Wilson supporter. Harry Rosenhaupt sought to capitalize on the recession that had gripped the country in 1913 and still lingered in the Inland Empire. He advocated a return to the high Republican tariff of the pre-Wilson period and the building of a merchant marine that would free American trade from foreign dependency. Thomas Corkery championed a non-partisan tariff commission, child labor laws, and low interest loans for farmers.[17]

In October, Dill made another swing through the rugged northern half of the Fifth District.[18] His speeches on this trip featured an attack on his opponent's tariff position. He argued:

Republicans and Progressives in this campaign are fighting a straw man when they try to make the tariff one of the leading questions of the campaign. The tariff is not, and cannot be made an issue. The European war destroyed the tariff issue so far as this campaign is concerned. Those who defend a high tariff do so on the theory that American manufactures are thereby protected from the competition of foreign manufactured goods. The people of Europe are so busy killing one another and making powder and armaments that they have no time for anything else, and, even if they could make them, they could not ship them across the seas. The best proof of this is found in the fact that the tariff duties no longer produce revenue and we are forced to levy a war tax. If we were still depending on the old high tariff duties, the war tax would necessarily be much higher.[19]

Dill seemed to make valid points concerning the tariff; many were persuaded.

While the Democrat attacked Rosenhaupt's tariff stance, he fought a rear guard action against Corkery's progressivism. Corkery threatened to capture enough progressive votes to defeat Clarence and hand victory to the Republicans. Dill deftly responded to the Corkery threat by emphasizing his approval of the heart of Corkery's program: child labor laws and a rural credit law that would provide low interest loans to farmers.[20]

The campaign, hectic and exhausting, nearly ended in tragedy. After finishing a speech in Entiat, Dill apparently lingered too long with voters. Made aware his train was about to leave on its up-river run, the candidate hurried to the station. The train slowly chugged out of Entiat as Clarence attempted to leap aboard. But he missed the train's platform and sprawled underneath the moving cars. Two bystanders jerked him off of the tracks, saving his life. Fearing the worst, the engineers stopped the train, but were relieved to find only a badly shaken would-be congressman and a couple of quick-thinking townsmen.[21]

Although the tariff issue defined the campaign, Dill had not forgotten women. As the election approached, many observers believed women were supporting Clarence in huge numbers. This phenomenon even attracted the attention of old-time politicians who had been confident that granting the vote to women would not substantially alter political demographics. These sages were sure that men "did all the voting."[22] Nor was this lack of respect for the role of women limited to old-timers; a reporter for the *Colville Examiner* theorized that women supported Dill in such large numbers because "he is clean, capable, courteous, and is the possessor of a winning personality."

The reporter had no excuse for his patronizing tone as the article went on to quote a woman on the reasons she supported Dill: "I am...working to help elect C.C. Dill...because I think he is the proper man for us to send to Congress and help uphold President Wilson's policies...not only Democratic women but all women should get out and help elect Dill."[23] Of course, Dill's amiable personality did not hurt him.

On October 11, Dill attracted a large crowd in Colville. He knew the tariff issue might hurt him. Many people in the district believed the lower Democratic tariff had adversely affected them. Reiterating his support for Wilson, he charged the Republicans with deceiving the people on the tariff issue. The Democratic candidate went to great lengths to demonstrate that the election of a Republican congressman could not possibly affect the country's tariff policy, as Wilson would most assuredly be able to sustain any veto.[24]

While canvassing the district, Dill had not lost sight of the fact that the campaign would be won or lost in Spokane. He had visited his hometown consistently throughout the campaign and intended to devote the last week of the race to the city. His opponents, equally aware of the importance of Spokane, also focused their efforts there as the race came to a close. According to pollsters, Rosenhaupt entered the last stage of the campaign with the lead. Republicans across the state, confident of victory in other races, focused their attention on the Fifth District. Indeed, the newly created Fifth District captured the attention of the entire state because it featured a close race among fervid campaigners.[25]

In the last days of the campaign, Rosenhaupt continued to hammer away at Dill's tariff position. The *Spokesman-Review* came to the Republican's aid with an editorial that exposed holes in Dill's tariff argument. The paper argued that the war had not interrupted trade to the extent the Democrat claimed, in fact, quite the opposite. The European nations were now dumping goods in American ports because many of their European trading partners were unreachable. The paper quoted statistics from New York where drygoods imports for the week ending October 3, 1914, were the highest in eight years. Hence the American tariff, had it still been high, would have been producing significant revenue.[26]

Rosenhaupt and the *Spokesman-Review* made points, but Dill defended the Underwood tariff in terms appealing to many and hammered home the point that electing anyone other than a Democrat to office was a waste of the district's congressman. Corkery, the Progressive, argued that neither of the candidates from the larger political parties was fit for office.[27]

Though the district's newspapers generally supported Rosenhaupt, at least one editor admitted that he liked C.C. Dill despite his membership in the wrong party. "If fate and the voters ordain that Mr. Dill is to represent this district in congress we do not know of any Democrat whom we would rather see in the office."[28]

But Anna McCue, a suffrage and labor leader representing the Congressional Union, a national woman suffrage organization, could think of several. Apparently unaware of the political realities in the Fifth District, McCue was touring the state campaigning against Democratic candidates because the national Democratic organization had not supported national woman suffrage. It was only days before the election. Dill could not afford to lose the women's vote. In a bold move, he decided to confront McCue when she spoke at a meeting of the civic and legislative committees of the City Federation of Women's Clubs of Spokane. McCue spoke to the women for twenty-five minutes, "flaying the national democratic organization for spurning suffrage as a nation-wide institution." When she had finished, the uninvited Dill rose and asked chairperson Sara Flannigan for five minutes of rebuttal. Clearly astonished at Dill's request, Flannigan put the question to a vote. The ladies agreed to hear the intruder. The progressive Democrat repeated his stance on woman suffrage; the ladies applauded. Encouraged, he suggested that Miss McCue's time would have been better spent in a state where anti-suffrage Democrats were running for office. Though newspapers considered Dill's behavior to be lacking in chivalry, to tell the story, they had to mention his response, which was exactly what he wanted. Dill could not afford to let McCue go unanswered. Moreover, the entire episode demonstrated to thinking voters how important Dill considered women and their support to be.[29]

On the eve of the election, Dill relaxed, knowing he had done all humanly possible to secure his election. He predicted that the district's support for Wilson would minimize the number of progressive Democrats willing to vote for Corkery, leaving enough votes to carry him into office. Moreover, he hoped Corkery's candidacy would hurt Rosenhaupt: a significant number of progressive Republicans might vote for Corkery. Dill confidently broke down just how the various counties would come in: "I shall come to Spokane county with a lead of 1,500 to 2,000 votes and will carry this county by at least 1,500, which will make my plurality between 3,000 and 4,000 in the district."[30]

Dill's prophecy came true. He carried the district, polling 24,410 votes to Rosenhaupt's 20,033. Corkery took 15,509 votes, the majority of which had probably been Republican supporters before the Progressive Party came to be.[31] The one county the Democrat thought he might lose, Chelan (Wenatchee), he lost, but by only a few votes. Dill's victory was a stunning upset and a significant achievement.[32]

Republicans were surprised the Democrat had won because not a single daily newspaper in the district had endorsed him.[33] In fact, many had done their best to ignore him in the last few weeks of the campaign. The *Spokane Press* characterized the opposition in colorful language:

> We were willing, last September, to admit that Boston had a chance to win from the Athletics, that Pinchot might be defeated by Penrose in Pennsylvania, that Uncle Joe Cannon might go back to Congress, and that the Kaiser might take Paris. Mind you, we were willing to admit all these possibilities a short time ago; in fact, we'd admit anything almost: but we would never have admitted that any man, much less a Democrat, could go out and be elected to Congress without the support of a single daily newspaper in his district. Why, it simply couldn't be done; that's all! But it was done, and right here in our own little Fifth Congressional District.[34]

Dill's triumph amazed political observers for other reasons as well: Republicans garnered more than 5,000 more votes in the primary than the Democrats; northeastern Washington had a long tradition of Republican dominance; and finally, Republicans dominated Washington State, especially when it came to national office.[35] The state had not sent a Democrat to the lower house of Congress since 1899.[36] The Republican victories in all of the other races for national office in the state contributed to the shock of Republican defeat in the Fifth District and to the significance of Dill's victory.[37]

Dill's victory began a transformation, though a very slow one, in Washington State politics. It gave Democrats throughout the state hope (which had received precious few infusions since the Democrats had mustered the power to give the state's electoral votes to William Jennings Bryan in 1896) that they might one day control the state's delegation to the national capital.[38]

There were other significant ramifications to Dill's victory. It raised the possibility, which many in the party shuddered to think of, that the future of the Democratic Party in Washington State lay in identifying itself with workers and farmers. Dill had polled majorities in all of his district's rural counties except one and had won in the city of Spokane despite the opposition of that city's newspapers, most of which were staunchly conservative in editorial policy.

Though Dill's strategy and style were impressive, Thomas Corkery played an important role in the Democrat's victory. Had Corkery not run, a significant number of his supporters would have returned to the Republican Party despite Dill being politically closer to Corkery than Rosenhaupt.

In the second decade of the twentieth century, American political parties were in a state of flux, searching for an identity. Ideology was but one factor among many that determined the allegiance of voters.[39]

More importantly, Dill's overt effort to gain the women's vote and to include them in his campaign marked a distinct and lasting change from the past. Unless Dill committed a catastrophic political mistake, anyone who hoped to unseat him would have to take women seriously as a political force. There is no way to demonstrate that the women's vote turned the election to Dill in 1914, but it is instructive to remember that the candidate gambled the campaign on his challenge to Anna McCue before the City Federation of Women's Clubs.

In celebration of Dill's victory, the Women's Democratic Club put on a dinner, which the new congressman attended. A letter from May Arkwright Hutton was read (Hutton had predicted in 1912 that Dill would be the next congressman from the Spokane area) and Dill spoke briefly, thanking the women "for the aid they had given him in the campaign and assuring them that he would be loyal in representing their interests in Washington."[40]

While the Europeans rained death and destruction over most of their continent, Clarence Dill fulfilled his dream to be a congressman from Washington. Strange as it may seem now, his services were not required in the nation's capital until December 1915, when the new Congress convened. On his way to Washington, D.C., Dill stopped in Ohio to pick up his parents and Professor Fulton, who wanted to attend the inauguration. The solemnity of the occasion impressed everyone in Dill's party, but they were surprised at the brevity of the ceremony.[41]

On January 31, 1916, the young congressman made his first speech in the House.[42] Back in Ohio, Fanny Ball, an old woman now, received the news with a great deal of pride. But Dill had completely forgotten that he owed her money. She wrote him a letter reminding him, and he promptly paid in full—70 cents, including interest.[43]

Dill devoted most of his first term as a U.S. congressman to two issues: opening the Colville Indian Reservation to white settlement and securing more mail routes for his rural constituents. Fortunately, he soon found a powerful friend in Congress.

Soon after the session opened, Champ Clark, the speaker of the House, called the freshman congressmen together to explain the rules of the game. Clarence recorded the instructions of the revered Speaker:

> Starting as a member of Congress is like the spelling bee, you must spell-up from the foot of the class. The secret of success here is hard

work, loyalty to your party, and more hard work. Remember that every request from a constituent is important—big to him and therefore important to you, no matter how small it may seem. Your biggest job is to get reelected.

If you get licked, don't let that end your career if you want to become a statesman. I got licked. Uncle Joe got licked [Joe Cannon]—licked twice. La Follette got licked. Bryan got licked. The question to decide is, will you stay licked.[44]

Dill never forgot Clark's admonition.

Dill had gone quietly about his business for several weeks when he happened by Clark on his way to the House Office Building. Clark hailed the young man and asked him, "Why don't you ever come to see me?" Dill answered, "I haven't had any particular business to discuss with you, and knowing how busy you are, I didn't think I should bother you." The Speaker told Dill, "Come in and see me, I want to talk to you." Dill presented himself at the Speaker's office at ten o'clock the next day. Clark wanted to know whether or not Dill planned to run again. Dill responded that he did, but his chances for reelection seemed slim because the Bull Moose Party had reconciled with the Republican Party. Clark informed Dill that he was interested in helping the young man in whatever way he could. Because Dill was the only Democratic congressman from the Pacific Northwest, Clark did not want to lose him. Indeed, Clark hoped to build the Democratic Party in that region through Dill's accomplishments in conjunction with those of the Wilson administration. When Clark asked Dill what could be done to help ensure his reelection, Clarence explained the importance of opening the Colville Indian Reservation to white settlement.[45]

Conflict between Indians, the Indian Bureau, and whites over the Colville Indian Reservation in north-central and eastern Washington had been ongoing for decades. The Colville reservation was one of the pristine remnants of the American frontier. Thousands of people hoped to settle on the rich land. Even those who had no interest in settling the land, men like Dill, possessed a romantic view concerning inhabiting new land. The early twentieth-century builders of the West considered themselves the rightful heirs of their predecessors' pioneer spirit. The Colville frontier consisted of more than a million acres of land, rich in timber and minerals, with farm land, grazing land, and water resources. The *Wenatchee Daily World* described the reservation:

> The agricultural lands are best adapted to stock raising, fruits, and grains. The forest will yield hundreds of millions of feet of lumber. Although

sufficient investigation had been conducted to reveal the presence of gold, silver, copper, nickel, and lead, lack of transportation facilities has prevented mining on a large scale.[46]

Agricultural lands on the reservation were expected to yield up to $2,000 of produce per acre. Whites looked upon the Indians' domain with great longing.[47]

Dill's primary objective in his first term was to see to the opening of the reservation.[48] He did not see this endeavor as a contradiction of his progressivism. Progressives did not necessarily espouse the equality of all Americans as one of their ideals. In the South, the popularity of progressivism depended in part upon the exclusion of blacks.[49] Moreover, progressives often had a paternalistic attitude toward others.[50] Then, too, many whites who were truly concerned about Indians believed integration with white society was best for them. Dill followed this line of thinking. Thus his effort to open the reservation did not occasion a crisis of conscience. Of course, success in opening the reservation would immensely help his re-election prospects.

At first glance, Dill's mission would not seem overly difficult. The conditions that led to the controversy began in 1872 when President Grant's administration created the Colville Indian Reservation and settled nearly 4,000 Indians of various tribes on it. Several years later, a portion of Chief Joseph's Nez Perce band was put on the reservation as well. In 1891 a federal commission purchased the northern half of the reservation, about 1.5 million acres, for eventual sale to settlers and businesses. This left the Indians the southern half of the reservation, which the United States government decided to open to white settlement in 1906. The Colville Indians approved the latter decision. On December 1, 1905, 350 of the estimated 551 adult Indians signed the McLaughlin Agreement, conceding their claims to the reservation and accepting individual allotments of eighty acres per man, woman, and child and 1.5 million dollars for their reservation rights. Any unclaimed land was to eventually revert to Indian ownership. The desire to wriggle free from the paternalistic control of the federal government motivated many of the Indians. But this freedom did not occur within the lifetime of most of the signers of the McLaughlin Agreement.[51]

The Opening Act of 1906 provided that the secretary of the interior dispose of the lands not taken by individual Indians by selling land to buyers chosen by lot. So the matter rested from 1906 until 1914. By 1914 it was obvious the Indian Bureau had no intention of facilitating the opening of the reservation. Secretaries of the interior had come and gone, and the matter had slipped between the cracks. The Indian Bureau preferred the status quo, for if termination of Indian reservations became national policy, termination of the Indian Bureau would soon follow.

The Indian Bureau used any means of delay it could devise. Even after it was obvious Congress was taking a renewed interest in opening the Colville Reservation, and that the Washington delegation had some political clout, and after an agreement opening the reservation in the summer of 1916 had been reached, Commissioner Cato Sells of the Indian Bureau continued to obstruct the opening.[52]

Dill and the other members of Washington's congressional delegation now attempted to push the Indian Bureau toward opening the Colville land.[53] Speaker of the House Clark instructed Clarence to call on House Majority Leader Claude Kitchen and tell him to bring up the Washingtonian's resolution to open an investigation of the Indian Bureau.

Next, Dill went to see Secretary of the Interior Franklin K. Lane. The secretary claimed he knew nothing about the delay in opening the Colville Reservation. Lane called Clark to see what was going on. Dill listened to the conversation as he sat in Lane's office. Dill probably embellished his version of that conversation. According to Dill, Clark dressed Lane down in no uncertain terms, telling the secretary if you do not "do something about this reservation, we will pass it [the resolution investigating the Indian Department] and investigate [the] Indian Department."[54] Lane promised to call Sells and get the Indian Bureau moving. In a conversation with Dill, Sells promised to be ready to conduct the drawings for settlers by July 1, 1916, and to open at least six more townships to settlement.[55]

Meanwhile, Dill and the other members of the Washington delegation were busy. The resolution calling for the investigation of the Indian Bureau was discussed in the House.[56] Dill now argued the greatest danger American Indians faced was the probability of becoming permanent wards of the state. In fact, he claimed, such a result seemed to be the inescapable fate of Indians on reservations. Ultimately, he envisioned complete integration of reservation Indians with white society as the best solution, what he would have called a progressive solution, to this dependency.

In his speech, Dill presented numerous instances of Indian Bureau malfeasance, ineptitude, and corruption. He explained how the Indian Bureau arrogated unto itself the power to spend tribal funds without congressional approval. Dill hammered the department:

> Of course they spend this money [tribal money], as they say, for the benefit of the Indian, but the trouble is they, the officials, are the judges of when, where, and how the Indians shall be benefited and how much

of his money shall be spent. The practical result has been that the expenditures for salaries and employees in the department have increased by leaps and bounds, and it seems they increased fastest on those Indian reservations where the Indians have tribal funds which can be so used. The general increase in expenditure, for salaries, and employees in the Indian Department in the last five years has been one hundred and fifty percent, while on some of the reservations the increase has been two hundred fifty percent to three hundred percent.[57]

Dill further delineated how the Indian Bureau had acted in bad faith specifically in reference to the Colville Reservation. The Opening Act of 1906 instructed the bureau to open the reservation. Instead the Indian Bureau built a new Indian agency on the reservation in 1914 in the middle of land most likely to go to white settlers. The new agency featured homes for Indian Bureau employees, a magnificent water system, and tennis courts all paid for by Indian money for the "benefit of the Indians."[58]

Dill's public castigating of the Indian Bureau, his behind the scenes maneuvering, and the efforts of the other members of Washington's delegation—especially Senator Miles Poindexter—led to the Indian Bureau moving quickly to follow the dictates of a Congress ten years past.[59] Moreover, on May 3, 1916, President Wilson signed additional legislation that facilitated the opening of the Colville Reservation. When he finished, he turned to Dill and handed him the pen; Clarence cabled a telegram home: "I saw the President sign the Colville proclamation at 10:25 today."[60]

Though Dill tellingly blasted the Indian Bureau's self-interest, the congressman and his constituents were not without self-interest of their own. In a letter to Arthur Gunn, Dill proved he was anxious to help anyone interested in vying for a portion of the Colville Reservation. Dill's letter serves as a reminder of white civilization's hope to profit from Native American lands.[61]

Dill himself apparently hoped to profit from the opening of Colville lands as well. Though the details are very sparse, it seems Dill took advantage of his position as a congressman to profit from the sale of the reservation. His activities came to the attention of the authorities who were considering prosecution when William Humphrey, another congressman from Washington State, intervened on Dill's behalf. Humphrey persuaded the authorities that: "such action [the action is not specified] on your part [Dill's] carried no moral turpitude and that you were innocent of any intentional wrong doing, that you were a young man and it would tend largely to discredit you and would be a disgrace through life—and that I would not consent to it."[62]

Whether Dill was simply naive or unethical cannot be determined; however, he was forever grateful to Humphrey and would later help him gain a seat on the Federal Trade Commission despite Humphrey being a Republican.[63] The incident at least suggests the possibility that Dill's judgment could be overcome by avarice.[64]

Regardless of who might profit or lose, the opening of the reservation went forward. Those interested in securing reservation lands registered for the drawing in one of six eastern Washington cities.[65] Officials estimated 1,500 homesteads would go to those whose names were drawn.[66] Dill had succeeded in meeting his first term's primary goal.

Moreover, the opening of the Colville Reservation constituted only one of his accomplishments. Dill also delivered on his promise to his rural constituents. As he visited the small towns and large farms in his district during the campaign, he had promised to establish new rural mail routes. In his effort to make good on this promise, he secured the help of Jack Garner, a congressman from Texas. The wily Texan's instructions were to take only one request at a time to the clerks in the Postmaster General's Office, and treat the clerks with extreme courtesy while explaining the importance of the new route. Garner added, "Follow it up so it doesn't get pigeonholed somewhere." Finally, he told Dill to be sure the request got to Dan Roper, the assistant postmaster general and a good South Carolina Democrat, and then to visit Roper personally to explain the necessity of the request. As Dill later wrote, "We secured more rural mail routes that first year than any district had ever won."[67]

Dill's impressive accomplishments were largely based on his ability to make friends with powerful men like Champ Clark. His friendly manner and charm helped. The young Democrat also benefited from the fact that his party controlled both houses of Congress. Dill also knew that the Speaker's help had a price tag; he was expected to "spell up" as Clark put it. Back in the Fifth District, Dill could run for reelection, claiming that he knew how to get things done in Washington, D.C., that he had been an effective bird dog for his constituents. In the election of 1916, Dill would argue that his efforts were helping to build the West, making life better there. It was an impressive argument, for Westerners occasionally felt that they were not treated with quite the same respect back East as other Americans.[68] But Clarence Dill seemed to be doing just fine both for himself and his district in the nation's capital.

Dill won election as Washington's Fifth District Representative to Congress in 1914 and again in 1916. *#85-030, Washington State University Libraries, Pullman, WA*

CHAPTER THREE

REELECTION, REFLECTION, AND WRATH

I N THE FALL OF 1916, Clarence Dill and Woodrow Wilson stood for re-election. Though Dill opposed the president's preparedness program, the two men agreed on the role the country ought to pursue in regard to the war: neutrality. Ultimately both men became casualties of the war's vicissitudes and tribulations. Indeed, Wilson's role in the "war to end all wars" eventually overshadowed his domestic accomplishments, significant as they were; while Dill found the war profoundly vexing. The young congressman made decisions concerning the war that separated him from Wilson and ultimately led to his defeat when he ran for reelection in 1918. In addition, Dill's war-related votes and speeches forever imprinted upon the minds of some influential Washingtonians that he was a dangerous radical.

The European war had bogged down in the mud of eastern France. Americans increasingly sought either to prepare for eventual belligerency or to find a way to stay out. Clarence Dill's heart was with the latter, though he was willing to compromise with those of the former opinion, given certain conditions.

No sooner had the war begun than Dill, in keeping with his affinity for the political views of William Jennings Bryan (a noted opponent of the war), announced his antipathy to it—a common American response in the summer of 1914.[1] Even Teddy Roosevelt agreed with Dill's stance. Gradually, many Americans came to favor entering the war, but Dill remained opposed.[2] He was a member of the "progressive-pacifistic movement." These people saw America in the role of savior to a decadent Europe, but they believed America could only fulfill that role if it were itself "triumphant over social and economic injustice" at home and unmarred by the stain of war abroad.[3]

Inevitably, however, the issue of preparing for the possibility of war arose, and when it did, the congressman favored what he considered common sense precautions. Dill advocated preparedness to justify government intervention in the private sector. He believed that if the government purchased weapons from the private sector, war materiel manufacturers would make enormous profits, as many of them had during the Civil War. Like John Dewey, he believed the war provided the opportunity for the federal government to regulate, and in some cases even operate, key war industries. He believed that government involvement in the private sector in this fashion would result in greater efficiency and savings to American taxpayers. In May 1916, he urged his congressional colleagues to follow his thinking:

> If I had my way the government would, as soon as facilities could be provided, build every ship for its Navy and make all its own munitions. I am in favor of the government manufacture of all the necessary equipment for national defense, first because it will remove the sinister influence of the war trust in the determination of our policy of national defense; and, second, it will enable us to secure a dollar's worth of preparedness for a dollar, instead of 60 or 70 cents worth of preparedness for a dollar.[4]

But even his position on preparedness represented something of a compromise, for in his heart, he believed that American participation in the war would be a tragic mistake. Dill canvassed his entire district on war-related issues in the spring of 1916. More than 12,000 people tallied votes. He asked his constituents if they favored doubling appropriations for the Army and Navy: by a three-to-two margin the residents of Spokane favored the increase, while the rural people of his district barely approved. Asked if they favored Wilson's war policy, Spokane residents approved four to one. The rural voters approved only two to one; other questions in the survey implied that those who opposed Wilson's policy thought it too provocative, rather than too timid. Dill even asked if voters would support a Jeffersonian style embargo—refusal to ship munitions and foodstuffs in an effort to remain neutral. Spokane rejected such an idea two to one; the rural portion of the district rejected the proposal, but by the narrower margin of roughly seven to five. Finally, Dill asked voters if they favored compulsory military service. Spokane residents were evenly split, while citizens in rural areas rejected such a policy at a three-to-two ratio.[5]

Dill's survey provides significant insight into American public opinion in the West in the spring of 1916. It is even more valuable because Dill's staff broke the poll down into counties, then into rural and urban figures. Though historians have long been aware that rural America in general, especially the Midwest and West, had greater isolationist feelings than more populous regions in the East, Dill's survey demonstrates that isolationist sentiment, even in the West, was centered in rural areas. Dill followed his lifelong hero William Jennings Bryan concerning the war, and thus was sympathetic to rural people.[6]

As the war rumbled into 1916, the Wilson administration, buckling to pressure from interventionists like Teddy Roosevelt, pushed for preparedness measures that alarmed Dill.[7] In February 1916, Wilson prudently advocated increased expenditures for the Army and Navy. But in the middle of the month, Dill and more than fifty other Democratic congressmen, combined with Republicans, succeeded in torpedoing Wilson's preparedness plan for the Army. It would have been easy for Dill to vote for the president's preparedness program. His constituents, according to his own survey, approved of preparedness. Moreover, his president and party would expect him to vote in favor. But Clarence followed his own conscience and supported an alternative plan.[8]

Back home the *Spokesman-Review* raged over Dill's "befogged" position on preparedness. The newspaper pointed out that Dill had campaigned in 1914 as a supporter of the president, but had now betrayed him. It went on to criticize Dill for his arrogance concerning developing the Army: "Mr. Dill…has a program that is altogether his own, with no resemblance to the program proposed by the general staff, or the original of the President and his secretary of war."[9] However, the paper exaggerated when it called Dill's plan "his own." Dill was but one of a number of congressman, largely from the West and South, men dependent upon farmers and labor for support, who were against the administration's plans for creating the so-called "Continental Army."

Dill agreed with Majority Leader Claude Kitchen who proposed simply to increase the number of soldiers in the National Guard.[10] This plan had several advantages: first, the recruits would not be sent long distances from home at great expense; second, the National Guard, so increased, would retain its defensive nature; and third, the nation would be spared the specter of a huge force the disposal of which—according to Dill—was at one man's whim.[11] It was this plan, after Congress forced Wilson to compromise, that became the nation's strategy for expanding its Army in 1916.[12] Clearly, Clarence Dill, the "Woodrow Wilson man," was quite willing to separate from the president and follow his own judgment.

Just as controversial as the preparedness measures was the method of paying for the arms Congress approved. In 1916 the tax structure of the United States clearly favored the rich. Most of the nation's revenue came from the tariff and consumer taxes on alcohol and tobacco. Conservatives, along with the Wilson administration, wanted to sell bonds and raise consumer taxes to pay for preparedness. Progressives, including Dill, fought this with great vigor. A group of Democrats, Dill among them, threatened to desert Wilson on preparedness issues unless measures requiring "the burden of expenses for whatever increases are made in the Army and Navy will be borne by those who receive large incomes, rather than by those who toil from dawn to dark to provide sufficient clothes for themselves and their families." Specifically, the Democratic opposition to Wilson's increased military expenditures demanded raising the income tax on the wealthy.[13] The progressives prevailed. The Revenue Bill of 1916 taxed high incomes, estates, and the gross receipts of munitions manufacturers.[14]

In his reelection effort, Dill realized he had to appeal to even more Republicans than he had in 1914 now that he faced a reunited Republican Party with a significantly larger registered electorate. Hence, he decided to appear as non-partisan as reasonably possible. Dill de-emphasized his association with the state Democratic Party even more than he had in his first run for Congress. He reasoned that Democrats would vote for him regardless of his method, but his reelection depended on appealing to Republicans.

The first manifestation of Dill's strategy occurred at the state Democratic convention in early May 1916. He simply didn't attend. He wrote an apologetic letter from Washington, D.C., explaining he was unable to attend due to his congressional duties. At the convention, state Democrats moved in a conservative direction, reinforcing Dill's decision to separate himself from the party. Governor Lister felt the same course of action politic and followed Dill's example. Thus did Washington's Democratic Party alienate its only two successful major candidates from 1914.

Dill did not launch an early campaign. He felt very comfortable about his position in the primary and expected congressional business to keep him in the capital through July. He ran unopposed in the Democratic primary and faced Republican Thomas Corkery, his Progressive opponent from 1914, in the general election. Playing the part of the prodigal son, Corkery had returned to the patriarchal GOP upon the demise of the Bull Moose Party.[15]

Two progressives, Dill and Corkery, now battled for Dill's congressional seat. Corkery attacked as insufficient the farm legislation Dill had voted for and the Wilson administration had passed. Corkery advocated credit to tenant farmers so as to enable them to purchase land. The Republican also championed national prohibition "with both feet" as he put it.[16] But neither position distanced him from Dill, nor did they provide him an opportunity to show how the Democrat had moved from his pro-Woodrow Wilson stance. Corkery could have pointed out Dill's differences from Wilson on prohibition and woman suffrage, but he did not. The president preferred local option; Dill supported national prohibition, which put him in direct alignment with the majority of the Democratic Party in Washington State. Wilson preferred state option for woman suffrage; Dill supported national woman suffrage.[17] Thus Corkery allowed Dill to campaign as a "Woodrow Wilson Man," while the congressman continued to advocate two major policy differences with the president. Dill had the best of two worlds: popular positions on two important issues, and identification with a popular president.

In the fall, Dill toured his district, but with less intensity than he had shown in 1914. Dill campaigned on President Wilson's accomplishments and his own, especially his work in opening the Colville Reservation and securing rural mail routes. Speaking in the opera house in Harrington, Washington, Dill said of Wilson: "I have supported him consistently...and I expect to continue to do so." Dill went on to explain to his Harrington listeners that he believed, should the country one day face war, the proposition should be put to a vote of the people. Those voting in favor, Dill argued, should be the first drafted. He added, "I will never vote for war until I am willing to go myself." Dill finished his speech with his customary humor, "I never paid an income tax until I went to Congress and I like it so well that I would like to continue to pay it."[18]

In the last three weeks of the campaign Dill intensified his reelection efforts, revisiting all the little towns and lonely farms he had come to know so well in 1914. The political sages and part-time bookies down at the cigar stores put odds on the election that indicated Wilson, Poindexter (one of Washington's Republican senators), and Dill victories.

Eastern Washington newspapers were not thrilled with the prospect of the latter's victory. The *Okanogan Independent* took a shot at Dill for wearing out the "I" on his typewriter. Dill was a great letter writer, or at least he required his clerks to be. Upon the slightest provocation, he wrote letters that trumpeted his accomplishments; hence the *Independent's* criticism. Such a practice was shrewd politics, even essential considering the attitude of the region's newspapers toward Dill.[19]

In addition to writing letters, Dill returned to his successful 1914 strategy of seeking both the support and votes of women. He sent government pamphlets on baby care to the new mothers in his district. Women loved his thoughtfulness. He said at the time, "a great many mothers wrote to tell me of their appreciation of these booklets...mothers in country localities seemed to find the treatises especially valuable."[20] Dill did not miss opportunities to speak to women. On one mid-October day he spoke to the women of the Woodrow Wilson League and then delivered a speech at the Grand Army of the Republic Ladies' Dance. Corkery well knew Dill's strength with women and attempted to attract as many of their votes as possible. Late in the campaign, the Republican, apparently feeling the election slipping away, decided to make an emotional appeal. He reminded voters of his support for a bill in the state legislature that provided state aid to mothers who had been left destitute through the death or desertion of their husbands. The speech was effective: women were seen with tear-filled eyes, and the paper predicted Corkery had found an issue that would change votes.[21]

Only days before the election, there was little Dill could do to respond to Corkery, especially since the newspapers were not friendly. He hoped the voters were sophisticated enough to recognize Corkery's tactic for the "me too" plea it was.

Dill continued to campaign as a "Woodrow Wilson Man" and repeated his promise to oppose American entry into the European war should it come to a vote. The results of the campaign were predictable; the Republicans swept the state's major offices just as in 1914, with two lone exceptions: Lister and Dill. The two Democrats who had distanced themselves from the conservative mood in the party had been the only Democratic winners.[22] Indeed, the one thing most of the victorious major candidates had in common was their progressivism, regardless of party affiliation.[23] The *Seattle Daily Times* complained bitterly that Dill's letter writing efforts had won the election.[24]

Dill's work on rural mail routes, the opening of the Colville Reservation, and concern for rural women, had provided a core of support in the more remote areas of northeastern Washington. He clobbered Corkery in Douglas and Ferry counties; beat him decisively in Lincoln, Okanogan, and Pend Oreille counties (the latter had been very close in 1914); and won in a close vote in Spokane County.[25]

Dill's victory depended also on women. Candidates of both parties expressed their views in women's clubs, tailoring their messages in recognition of women's political power. Corkery's last minute plea for the women's vote is a good example. Dill's promise to vote no on a war resolution, often especially poignant to women, is another. Furthermore, on the Saturday before the election, the Democrats organized a parade in Spokane. Dill rode in a car followed by a dazzling white "peace" float and six women on foot.[26]

The war between the Democrats and Republicans had gone to the Democrats on the national level, to the Republicans in Washington State, and to Clarence Dill in Washington's Fifth District. But unbeknownst to the political combatants of 1916, the war in Europe would decide the fate of all parties.

Though Dill had worked for popular causes and allied himself with a popular president, his consistently expressed isolationistic sentiments began to cost him his support at home. As the fateful spring of 1917 drew near, Dill's separation from the president's policies became evident in the Fifth District. In March, when Germany delivered on its threat to sink American shipping, opposition to him arose. One newspaper declared, "The first thing the people of this district ought to do is recall congressman Dill, or keep him quiet until the war is over."[27] Mounting criticism from home did not deter Dill. As Germany and the United States drifted toward war, he repeated his unpopular views:

> I am opposed to this country's entrance into the European war. I am so opposed to our entrance into that war that if I were sure that by voting against this bill peace would be certain to continue until the end of that war I would vote against it. If I were sure that by voting for it peace would be ensured I would vote for it. If I were sure that by any amendment whatsoever peace would be certain I would vote for the amendment. But, Mr. Chairman, we cannot be sure of anything in times like these. We must act according to the information we have and the judgment we have.[28]

But the President of the United States, whose knowledge of history far exceeded Dill's, and whose perspective on world affairs had been informed through far more diverse sources, had slowly—agonizingly—arrived at a different conclusion. The American decision for war rested solely upon Wilson's shoulders. Winston Churchill later wrote: "The action of the United States with its repercussions on the history of the world depended, during the awful period of Armageddon, upon the workings of this man's mind and spirit to the exclusion of almost every other factor."[29]

Wilson feared for those who would be asked to fight and die and for those who would be asked to live in a different America. The president knew his decision would mark "a turning point of the twentieth century."[30] Through this ordeal, Wilson came to believe with all of his being that America's future, indeed democracy and freedom throughout the world, were in greater jeopardy from a German victory than from American participation in the war.[31] Arthur Link wrote that the primary reason behind the president's decision for war was "his conviction that American belligerency now offered the surest hope for early peace and the reconstruction of the international community." Thus Wilson weighed the actions of the Imperial German government against the interests and future of the United

States and found Germany to be a threat that could no longer be tolerated. For this cause, on April 2, 1917, Woodrow Wilson appeared before the combined houses of Congress and, in an eloquent oration reminiscent of Lincoln, asked that Congress recognize the state of war Germany had thrust upon the nation.[32]

Wilson's address had no effect on the congressman from Washington's Fifth District. On April 6, having also agonized for months over the war, Dill rose from his seat on the floor of the House to deliver his own views on America's crisis. He had promised that he would vote no should America arrive at the precipice of war; he now came to his own moment of self discovery. His words on that day provide valuable insight into the man and the time:

> Mr. Chairman, during the two years that I have been in this House I have heard Members repeatedly on important occasions say that we were face to face with a great crisis. But to-day, while nobody had talked particularly about that phase of it, I think everybody realizes that this is the greatest crisis that this Nation has ever faced, and probably one of the greatest crises of the world....
>
> We have been told here that this is a war to establish democracy throughout the world. Well, it may be, but I have no faith in establishing democracy by joining my country's resources and its armies and navies with the...monarchical government of Italy, with the government of England, call it what you will, a nation whose 500 years of history has [sic] left a bloody trail on every continent in the world; and I for my part will not take the step which this resolution proposes, and go into the war on the side of the allies. This is a war upon the part of the allies for trade and territory. We have no interest in that. Our only interest is in our protection of our own rights.
>
> So far as interfering with our rights are concerned, both groups are guilty. England created a war zone, filled it with submerged mines, and warned us to keep our vessels out. We protested, but we submitted. Germany created a war zone, filled it with submarines, and warned us to keep our vessels out. We protested and sent our vessels in. They were destroyed. Had we sent our vessels into the English war zone they would have been destroyed....
>
> Gentlemen, I have thought about this as I have never thought about anything else in all my life. For nights I have been unable to sleep upon it. I have tried to bring myself to stand by the President's demand, thinking that possibly I was wrong. I thought how I might be able to go home and explain my vote for this resolution in some way or other. I thought I might say that the country had gotten into this situation, that it was every member's duty to show a united front, and that I had to be patriotic, but I knew that if I did that I would know in my own

heart it was a lie. We are not into it. The test of unity of the nation is not before we go in; it is after we get in. This is the time when the Members of this Congress as representatives of the American people are to say whether or not we shall go in. For my part I am opposed to going in. [Applause]

I have no illusions as to the consequences of my action. Newspapers and those who let the newspapers think for them will cry out "Traitor!" and "Poltroon!" no doubt. Many who have been my political supporters in the past will now oppose me, but that does not matter. I am a young man. Few, if any, members of this House have had fiercer struggles to reach here than I have had. If I must leave public life because of my action to-day, I shall go, but it will be with head erect, able to look every man and woman in the face, because I have kept faith. I do not know what the future holds for me, and I do not care. I refuse to do a thing which my conscience revolts against. I refuse to do a thing which in my judgment is the greatest crime ever perpetrated upon a free people, namely, drag them into this hell of a war by joining with the allies.... [Applause]

But let me say this, gentlemen, that when this resolution passes, as it probably will, my opposition is over. I am an American from Revolutionary days, and I shall vote for every measure which is designed to help in winning this war. I believe that even though we go to war, the hope of civilization and freedom will remain with the American continent.[33]

Rain cleansed the streets of Washington, D.C., in the early morning hours of April 6, 1917. The House had been in session throughout the night when the time for voting finally arrived. At three in the morning the House voted 373 to 50 in support of Wilson's war resolution. Both Clarence Dill and William La Follette (Republican congressman from Washington's Fourth District) voted against American entry into the Great War. The most difficult period in Clarence Dill's life was at hand.[34]

Hours before the vote Dill spoke to Wilson; he explained to the president his campaign promise to vote no on the war, and that a straw vote of his district indicated his constituency disapproved of U.S. entry into the war. Wilson responded that he believed that the people had changed. Dill said to the president, "Not in my district." Wilson then asked Dill if he would support the war once the country entered it. Clarence responded that, "when the boys were drafted and taken across the ocean the people would support them, and that I would vote to help win the fight. He arose, thanked me, and said 'We are going into the war.' I left his office and never saw him again."[35]

There was considerable opposition to American entry into the Great War. Leadership of that opposition came predominantly from midwestern and western progressives. Senator George Norris of Nebraska, Senator Robert La Follette of Wisconsin, Representative Jeannette Rankin of Montana, progressive peace advocate Jane Addams of Illinois, and President of Stanford University David Starr Jordan all vociferously opposed American involvement in the war.[36] These leaders had in common a progressive ideology tinged with a larger dose of pacifism than most progressives. Moreover, they tended to be more concerned with the lower classes, farmers, and labor than with the middle class. Dill fit this description perfectly. It is little wonder, then, that he opposed the war. Nevertheless, most progressives followed Wilson and helped him make the war a progressive crusade for democracy.[37] Dill could have easily gone along with mainstream progressives throughout the country and supported the president's war resolution. Instead, he sided with Wilson's opponents—men like George Norris, whose speech on the floor of the Senate was remarkably similar to Dill's.[38]

Even such stalwart antiwar leadership could not overcome congressional fear of an electorate energized, or at least resigned, to war: both Dill and Norris told stories about colleagues who had said to them that they wished they possessed enough courage to vote against the war.[39] However, once the war had been declared, Dill followed Norris, Jordan, and Bryan in supporting the war effort.[40]

In his reelection campaign of 1918, Dill faced the accusation that his support of the war after American entry was merely a campaign claim. Though this accusation was not accurate, there were substantial reasons for believing the charge.[41] First, Dill introduced a bill calling for publication of income tax returns.[42] With this bill he hoped to expose profiteering amongst manufacturers of war goods. Though there is no reason why munitions makers should reap inordinate profits from American wars, the propagating of such legislation placed Dill—in the public mind—in the antiwar camp.[43] Secondly, Dill gained the admiration of the People's Forum, an antiwar group, for his antiwar vote in Congress. Unfortunately, this support came well after the vote had been taken, giving the impression that Dill persisted in thwarting American efforts to prepare for and wage war.[44] Most importantly, Dill opposed the administration's plan to institute conscription.[45] In opposing the draft, Dill again aligned himself with the more radical elements of Congress exemplified by La Follette. But opposition was not confined to radicals; Speaker of the House Champ Clark, among others, also found the conscription act distasteful.[46] Dill believed the draft violated the principles of democracy and that a volunteer army could meet the military needs of the nation.[47]

Though Dill believed a slim majority of his constituents approved of his no vote, the mood of the people changed once war was declared. The politically expedient thing to have done would have been to support Wilson's war program. But Dill, true to his principles, did not do that.[48]

An inferno of criticism awaited Dill upon his return home. His prediction that the word "traitor" would be employed to describe his actions was prescient, yet he underestimated the hostility awaiting him. Rufus Woods of the *Wenatchee Daily World* wrote: "May the Lord forgive this district for electing to office a man so ignorant, if he is ignorant, or a man so unsafe, dangerous, seditious, if he is not ignorant." William Cowles's *Spokesman-Review* lost no opportunity to flay Dill as a pacifist and moral reprobate.[49] The Democrat Club of Republic, Washington, attacked Dill in much the same vein, and called him too stupid to represent the district in Congress.[50] In short, Dill made so many powerful political enemies in 1917–18 it seemed his political career was over.[51]

In an effort to deflect criticism at home, Dill led a congressional junket to Europe, ostensibly to discover why American troops were being treated poorly. Ten congressmen left for the front in October 1917, crossed the Atlantic in a camouflaged transport ship, and were wined and dined in both London and Paris. They found that whatever problems had caused American troops discomfort had been corrected, though some of the Doughboys complained of not seeing any action.

On their way to the front, the travelers went through the Marne battlefield. Women, old men, and children worked fields where once thousands of dead soldiers had lain. Except for the cemeteries and an occasional bombed-out dwelling, little sign of the battle remained. Dill—amazed—observed silently. The people reclaimed the fields so faithfully that errant German shells sometimes took crops instead of Frenchmen—sometimes both. The battlefield of Verdun, where outnumbered French forces had turned back the German onslaught at a cost of 400,000 men, also impressed Dill.[52]

Dill would have made better use of his time had he spent it actually furthering the war effort and explaining his policies to his constituents, rather than touring Europe. The trip's real purpose of deflecting criticism did not work on the newspapers back home. One paper made light of the minimal danger Dill faced while in the trenches, remarking that whatever German shells were fired near the Washingtonian were no doubt fired in honor of his antiwar work in the United States, not in anger.[53]

In December 1917, Clarence returned home to explain himself, albeit late and on a limited scale. In a speech at a Lutheran church, perhaps chosen because the congregation might be less hostile to Dill's policies, he regaled the crowd with tales of his trip to the front. He had brought several souvenirs home with him, and one—a saber—he waved above his head at certain emotional points. The *Spokesman-Review* made the saber-waving congressman appear ridiculous. Nearly everything Dill tried backfired. Digging his own political grave, he received plenty of unneeded help. Newspapers falsely accused him of revealing the position of American troops and speaking to German officers. Less hot-headed citizens denied that Dill was a traitor; to them he was simply without a sense of moral right or wrong. In a letter to the editor of the *Spokesman-Review*, W.H. Canfield, a Spokane area resident, was both right and wrong about Clarence Dill, neatly exemplifying why Dill was being so vilified. Canfield argued that all the Democrat cared about was getting reelected, hence his trip to Europe. Canfield was right that the trip was a campaign ploy; he was wrong in stating that all Dill cared about was reelection. Dill knew his lukewarm support of war measures was politically dangerous. Canfield was right, however, when he wrote, "the simple truth is that it is the people, not Mr. Dill, who have changed."[54] Woodrow Wilson had said the same words to the young congressman in April 1917.

Dill returned to his district in July 1918 to face a challenger in the primary, V.T. Tustin of Spokane—a highly regarded attorney. Tustin attacked Dill personally rather than focusing on his war votes, and he took advantage of the fact that the Democratic Party's leaders had repudiated the congressman. Newspapers reported that crowds clearly favored Tustin over Dill.[55] However, some of Dill's supporters remained loyal. Dan Drumheller, one of the early pioneers of Spokane and a fellow "builder," told Dill one day that he had just told a group of Republicans that though Dill would lose this one, he was sure Dill's popularity would return and he would "be sent back to Washington to help build the Pacific Northwest."[56]

Dill had lost none of his political gall. He appeared before Spokane Democrats in July and argued that he ought to be the party's nominee because he had the best chance of being elected. More importantly, he would be the best choice to ensure the adoption of President Wilson's policies. He based his argument on his growing seniority on various committees and his demonstrated bullheadedness: "No clique of big businessmen, newspaper editors, or politicians ever have or ever can control me, and I shall go back to Washington as free to serve all the people as I have always been." Wilson, however, did not personally endorse Dill's candidacy.[57]

Over the previous four years, Dill had developed a corps of support-ers impervious to anything the newspapers might say about him. This corps, made up of farmers, women, and progressives of all walks of life, stuck by him in his battle for reelection. Dill defeated Tustin, no doubt shocking many, and prepared to battle former state Supreme Court Judge Stanley Webster for his seat in Congress. In the Fourth District, Republican William La Follette, who had also voted against the war, lost in the primary.[58]

In fall 1918, an outbreak of extremely virulent influenza raged across Europe. Those returning from the continent brought the pestilence home, where it killed thousands of Americans, especially the old and young.[59] The disease struck Clarence Dill shortly after the primary election and forced him into a hospital for nearly a month. His doctor believed the sickness would have killed him had he not generally abstained from alcohol.[60]

Though Dill recovered, Webster too came down with the flu and was forced to remain in bed; he did, however, draw the support of many influ-ential Democrats.[61] Julius Zittel, former Democratic Party state chairman and adviser to Governor Lister, threw his support behind Webster saying: "His [Dill's] continued opposition to the policies of President Wilson, his impossible speeches in Congress, and his general misrepresentation of American ideals call for his retirement to private life." Zittel, former Sena-tor George Turner, and ninety-two other leading Democrats in Washing-ton state signed a petition repudiating Dill. Then, too, Dill's opposition stooped to irrelevancies such as impugning his patriotism because his cam-paign manager's name, Frank Funkhouser, was of German origin.[62]

The campaign drew national attention because both national con-gressional committees gave aid. The Democrats hoped to hold their only seat in the state, while the Republicans hoped to reestablish their supremacy in northeastern Washington. The Democrats flooded the district with cam-paign literature; the Republicans relied upon favorable press. The two can-didates could not have presented a clearer choice to the voters. Webster was a "radical pro-war Republican," while Dill opposed many of the nation's war measures.[63]

When Dill's opponents were not impugning his war-vote record they were reveling in the inhospitable treatment he received as he went from town to town. In one rural hamlet a professional man, though a Demo-crat, ordered him out of his office and advised him to go to Germany where he would be welcomed. In another town, a Democratic committee-man, having received Dill's card, tossed it into the nearest cuspidor. At least one Washington newspaper grew weary—if only for a moment—of the Republican campaign, describing it as little more than a "flag raising ceremony." Essentially the contest came down to whether one believed the war was waged for trade and territory, as Dill had said in his speech in Congress before the war vote, or whether one believed the war was being fought to preserve "civilization, Christianity, and humanity" as Judge Webster declared.[64]

Americans were still dying in the far-off fields of France when the voters of the Fifth District went to the polls on November 5, 1918. Many of them had relatives fighting the Germans, and everyone knew someone involved in the war effort. Furthermore, George Creel's propaganda committee had ignited Americans with a white-hot patriotism and infected them with a black intolerance.[65] Under such conditions there was little doubt as to how the vote would turn out. Webster won.[66] Clarence Dill's lifelong dream was dead.

Chapter Four

RESURRECTION

C LARENCE DILL HAD LONG SINCE resigned himself to defeat, so when it
arrived in November 1918, he was not crushed. Of course there was
a transition period from public to private life, but soon the still young ex-
congressman decided to rebuild his political career. Though Dill could not
possibly have predicted in early 1919 how the nation would respond to the
end of the war and the Versailles peace treaty, that response would help
him revive his dream. By the fall of 1922, he found himself involved in one
of the more interesting Senate elections in Washington State history.

But first, Dill had to earn a living. He and fellow war opponent Ed
Keating of Colorado agreed to start a weekly newspaper designed for railroad men. The purpose of the paper, christened *LABOR*, was to "provide
uncensored news of the activities of Congress regarding labor legislation."[1]
Keating became editor while Dill sold subscriptions to railroad unions
around the country and lectured in support of the Plumb Plan—which
called for outright nationalization of the railroads, which had come under
government operation as a war measure. In addition to his work for *LA-
BOR*, Dill opened law offices in Washington, D.C., and Spokane. In Washington Dill specialized in persuading members of Congress to pass bills
concerning reclamation, a long-term Dill interest.[2]

Though Dill appeared politically dead after the election of 1918, he
remembered Champ Clark's advice: "Don't stay licked." He began working in local politics just as he had earlier. The comeback trail was not easy.
Newspapers refused to forget the past. In March of 1920, he wrote a letter
to the *Seattle Post-Intelligencer* (*P.I.*) in which he castigated the paper's coverage of remarks he had made to the Democratic State Committee. The
paper had quoted Dill as saying he found, "the so called reds, I.W.W.'s, and
Bolsheviki most reasonable people to talk things over with and [he] believed they could be talked into the Democratic column."[3] Dill's letter set
the record straight: he had admonished the radicals that the Democratic
Party had no use for any method of reform beyond the ballot box. He also
anticipated the *P.I.*'s defense and pointed out that though he believed the

nation's working people were reasonable and could be persuaded to vote the Democratic ticket, his use of the term "working people" could not fairly be held to be synonymous with "reds, I.W.W.'s, and Bolsheviki."[4] Dill concluded by warning the paper that he intended to avail himself of the protection of the law should any further libelous statements be made about him.[5]

Despite his ongoing battle with the newspapers, Dill was determined to resurrect his political career. He recognized that a significant opportunity lay in becoming a delegate to the 1920 Democratic National Convention in San Francisco. Inspired by resentment of Dill's antiwar votes, V.T. Tustin, who had opposed Dill in the 1918 primary, led a determined effort to keep him from becoming a delegate.[6] Nevertheless, Dill's political strength in Spokane County secured him a position.[7]

In San Francisco, Dill used his friendship with many Democratic leaders to rise to the head of Washington's delegation. In addition, he helped select a chairman for the state's steering committee. Edward M. Connor had been the favorite, but opposition to him arose in part because he was not in favor of prohibition. Dill maneuvered to have Mrs. J.M. Simpson, a dry, named chair of the steering committee. He even made a seconding speech for the vice presidential nominee, Franklin Delano Roosevelt, thus beginning a relationship that would later have a profound effect on the development of the Pacific Northwest.[8]

While Dill was busy rebuilding his political career, the course of events in the nation and Europe provided a helping hand. The war had been disruptive to American life and institutions. The federal government had inserted itself into the private sector in a manner heretofore unimaginable. Indeed, contemporaries of Dill, like John Dewey, had hoped for just such an insertion of government into American life to enhance social justice. However, the war ended abruptly after "only" seventeen months of American belligerency. Consequently, state intrusion into the nation's social and economic structure was not well established when the war ended; and because war production had been sluggish at best, most Americans did not see that insertion as a success.[9] In 1920, there was a distinct move to the right as Warren G. Harding won the presidency vowing a return to "normalcy."

At the same time the United States shifted to the right at home, developments at the Versailles Peace Conference ensured an unfavorable American reaction. The peace without victory Wilson sought escaped him. Europeans appeared to have learned little from four years of carnage. Secret agreements and vengeance ruled the "peace makers," rather than Wilsonian mercy and justice.[10]

Disillusionment with the peace hammered out at Versailles coincided with, and perhaps exacerbated, the American response to an apparent Soviet threat, primarily manifested in the form of radical labor and intellectuals sympathetic to the communist movement. Thus, the United States endured the phenomenon known as the Red Scare. Many Americans became convinced the effort to make the world safe for democracy had been a mistake.[11] A few Washingtonians even remembered Clarence Dill's warning that the Europeans were all equally guilty of barbarous behavior and none were worthy of American help. By the early twenties, Americans had grown disillusioned with their foreign crusade and wary of foreign philosophies (communism) and now concentrated on saving at home what had been lost abroad. Though the country became more conservative in this effort, those who had voted against the war became less despicable, their words now appearing almost prophetic. Of course the rightward lurch the nation experienced after the war presented different challenges to Dill's progressivism; but the isolationism and xenophobia that was a part of that turn to the right helped provide him a door to political resurrection.

Other developments helped Dill as well. A sharp recession hit the United States in 1920–21 and lingered through the decade for farmers and Washington's lumber men, making the reelection of Republican congressmen and senators in the state problematic in 1922.[12] Moreover, national prohibition split rural areas from urban and became the dominant political issue of the roaring twenties. Historian Alan Dawley captured this rural-urban split:

> Samuel Gompers described prohibition as a class law against workers' beer, and in the same vein, one urban Congressman undoubtedly spoke for the majority of wage earners in denouncing the howls of malicious joy issuing from rural America in "inflicting this sumptuary prohibition legislation upon the great cities. It preserves their cider and destroys the city workers' beer."[13]

Washington was no less affected by this rural-urban split over Prohibition than any other part of the country.

The state also mirrored the nation in its opinion as to how energetically prohibition ought to be enforced. Sentiment for repeal of prohibition in Washington was not strong in the early and mid twenties, but sentiment for strict enforcement wavered as well. In other words, the nation "firmly decided for ambiguity."[14]

Though prohibition was the law of the land, it owed its existence more to the fervor of patriotism than to the popularity of abstinence. In addition, those who opposed prohibition were rapidly gaining political power. Cities from 1922 on voted Democratic and wet consistently and were gaining in political strength. Moreover, historian David Burner has noted that, "At one time the prohibition movement had received support from all classes—both urban and rural; by the twenties it was rural and fundamentalist."[15] Nineteen-twenty is generally regarded as the year in which more Americans came to live in cities than in rural areas. In Washington state, that bench-mark had been reached in 1910.[16]

As 1922 began, Dill believed that incumbent Republican Senator Miles Poindexter was vulnerable. Consequently he thought about challenging Poindexter. A successful campaign would require a considerable expansion of his constituent base both ideologically and geographically. Though the state generally voted Republican, the potential for Democratic victory in the cities lay close to the surface. The trick lay in retaining the dry vote of the rural areas while securing the generally wet Democratic vote of the city—no easy assignment. It would take the shrewdest of politicians to define the election so as to accomplish that task. In Washington state, however, even uniting the disparate rural-urban Democratic vote would not be enough to secure victory. A significant number of Republican cross-over votes would have to be snatched for a Democrat to win office. Then too, an eastern Washingtonian such as Dill faced the added obstacle of obtaining sufficient western Washington support to win a statewide election. Separated geographically by the Cascade mountains and psychologically by both distance and varying interests, the two regions eyed each other suspiciously. Parochialism was virulent and there was even occasional talk of dividing the state. Few politicians from eastern Washington, the less populous region by far, had been able to win office in a statewide election. Republican Wesley Jones from Yakima was one of the few who had accomplished the feat. Jones still held his Senate seat in 1922, thus making victory for another easterner even more difficult.

Dill, then, faced a daunting political challenge if he hoped to unseat Miles Poindexter in 1922. There were, however, some rays of hope. The 1922 election was far from being an election that would be decided in an era of normalcy, regardless of President Harding's trumpet call; rather, there were serious undercurrents of unrest related to issues such as prohibition, labor unions, and Americanism versus Bolshevism. The feeling in America was one of nervousness, not normalcy.[17]

Though not officially a campaign speech, Dill's address to Jackson Day banqueters at Colfax, Washington, in early 1922 certainly did not hurt his senatorial aspirations. He supported Harding's and Secretary of State Charles Evans Hughes's effort to restrict naval arms while he carefully avoided associating himself with those who believed the country should unilaterally disarm. He had learned well. He concluded his remarks attacking the Republican handling of the economy, particularly the Republican call for patience while many Americans were losing jobs and homes.[18]

Two months later in an address before another Jackson Day gathering in Tekoa, Washington, Dill sought to energize his fellow Democrats for the coming campaign. He called their attention to the rule of political history dating back to the Civil War that the party that elects the mid-term Congress elects the next president. Then he turned his attention to the case of Truman H. Newberry, a senator from Michigan who had been elected with the help of enormous private funds. Now openly a candidate, Dill spent the balance of his address lambasting Newberry and Poindexter's vote to seat the notorious Michigan senator. The Newberry issue would be a constant theme in Dill's campaign.[19]

Newberry had spent well over $250,000 in his bid to win the 1918 Republican primary in Michigan. The Senate debated whether or not to seat him because he had been convicted of violating the Corrupt Practices Act, a federal election law that capped campaign expenditures in both primary and general elections. However, the Supreme Court overturned his conviction, ruling Congress had no authority to regulate state primaries. Poindexter had voted to seat Newberry because Republicans in the Senate were in the midst of attempting to thwart President Wilson's League of Nations. The Republicans needed every vote they could muster, and Newberry represented another vote against the League. In considering the Newberry case, the Senate could not help but condemn his campaign expenditures, declaring such disbursements to be "contrary to sound public policy, harmful to the honor and dignity of the Senate, and dangerous to the perpetuity of a free government." However, the authors of this indictment voted to seat Newberry in spite of the above. Dill vilified such hypocrisy.[20]

Opposition to Poindexter took more than one form in 1922. The Farmer-Labor Party decided at its convention to oppose Poindexter through the third party method, rather than uniting with Democrats or progressive Republicans. The senator had angered the Farmer-Labor Party through his alignment with the Harding administration on such issues as the extension of federal regulation of business, tax policy, and government assistance to farmers. But the Farmer-Labor Party's decision failed to gain the support of significant farm and labor groups. The Washington State Federation of Labor, Washington State Grange, various railroad brotherhoods, and other groups opposed the Farmer-Labor Party's strategy, preferring to work with either of the two main parties. Moreover, the grassroots organization of the Farmer-Labor Party lacked strength; the party was able to field a full slate of candidates for local and state legislative offices in only two counties. Nevertheless, the party's animosity toward Poindexter symbolized a growing statewide disenchantment with the senator, especially among progressives. In the face of such animosity, Poindexter felt the best policy was to ignore the mounting criticism and stress his achievements, especially his successful sponsoring of legislation providing for survey work on the Columbia Basin Project.[21]

Poindexter had experienced a long and interesting career. He had come from Virginia to Washington, opened a law office, and was active in politics through the 1890s. After Bryan's campaign in 1896, he switched parties, forsaking the Democrats. In the early twentieth century he became a Roosevelt progressive and was elected to Congress in 1908. He supported federal regulation of railroads, the income tax, and progressivism in general. In 1910 he was elected to the Senate seat Dill hoped to deprive him of in 1922. In 1912 he was the only senator in the nation to declare himself a member of the Bull Moose Party and as such supported Theodore Roosevelt for president. Though Woodrow Wilson defeated Roosevelt, Poindexter supported Wilson's progressive legislation.[22]

Howard Allen, Poindexter's biographer, argues the senator's progressivism stemmed from his desire to support the middle class against big business, large financial institutions, trusts, and railroads while protecting that class against the challenges from labor unions, socialists, the urban working class, and immigrants. The basis of Poindexter's progressivism, then, was not humanitarianism or egalitarianism, but an effort to forestall radical social reform with moderate reform while protecting the middle class from the onslaught of the groups at either end of the social scale. If the social and economic conditions that pressured the middle class changed, or were perceived to have changed, Poindexter could be expected to change as well. World War I transformed how the middle class in America regarded itself and its enemies. Consequently, during and after the war, Poindexter moved to a more conservative political position, arguing that America's greatest enemies were the socialists and Bolsheviks, rather than unrestrained capitalism.[23]

Poindexter's new conservatism angered many in his own party. He might have been defeated in the primary if Republican moderates and progressives could have agreed to run one candidate against him, but the anti-Poindexter movement splintered amongst several candidates, thus playing into the senator's hands.

The results of the primary surprised few. Despite the opposition of Lyman Seelye of Bellingham and James Longstreet of Port Townsend, Dill won handily, as did Poindexter. James Duncan of the Farmer-Laborites advanced that party's cause. However, neither Dill nor Duncan had captured the minds of the voters. Only 10,548 people bothered to vote for Dill, and fewer still showed up at the polls for Duncan.[24] Ominous, however, for the hopes of Miles Poindexter, was the fact that the combined tally of the progressive candidates amounted to well over 50 percent of the vote.[25]

Three candidates with vastly different philosophies now battled for Poindexter's Senate seat: James Duncan of the Farmer-Labor Party, a radical who lashed out at the "interests" and was fanatical over prohibition; Dill the dry progressive; Poindexter solidly conservative, as his support for the Harding administration attests. Surprisingly, Poindexter did not give up on either the labor or progressive vote. Secretary J.J. Davis of the Labor Department came to Washington to help Poindexter hold the labor vote, and William E. Borah, Idaho's nationally renowned progressive senator, also made a few speeches in an attempt to convince voters Poindexter still held progressive credentials. In addition, several newspapers came to Poindexter's aid in his endeavor to retain voters. The *Tacoma News Tribune* reminded the electorate of Dill's antiwar vote and Duncan's radicalism. Poindexter also charged that Dill was no Democrat, implying he was too radical for the state Democratic Party and would not fit in back in Washington.[26]

Poindexter's blast backfired as Judge Stephen Chadwick, the state Democratic Party's symbol of conservatism, came to Dill's aid late in the campaign. Chadwick strongly endorsed Dill and openly campaigned for him. The new support energizing his campaign, the would-be senator attacked Poindexter in the language of the Old West, "I'll hang Miles' hide on the Proscenium arch and shoot it full of holes."[27]

Dill's strategy included more than verbal gunplay. Even with Chadwick's support, he characterized the election as a contest between progressivism and conservatism. There was more to this strategy than Dill's antipathy toward facing Poindexter along party lines, a contest he would surely lose. In the Republican primary, though Poindexter had won, he had polled only 84,000 votes against his progressive challengers' 113,000 votes. Clearly progressivism was alive and well in Washington State and there for Dill to exploit.[28]

In his effort to convince voters to vote their politics and not their party, Dill gained the support of the Scripps newspapers, which included the *Seattle Star* and the *Seattle P.I.* The latter paper, which had become a part of the Hearst chain in December 1921, blasted Poindexter's votes on the Esch-Cummins bill. Esch-Cummins, the conservative response to the Plumb Plan for nationalization of the railroads, featured the return of the railroads to private operation. Labor feared a provision of the bill would make it difficult for labor organizations to effectively represent their membership. Even the conservative *New York Times* agreed. Critics of the bill predicted freight rates might rise as high as 40 percent above current prices. Not surprisingly, farmers, labor, and many progressives opposed Esch-Cummins. Nevertheless, Congress approved the bill; the railroads were returned to private control in 1920. The *P.I.* also castigated Poindexter for his vote on Newberry, for failing to secure a shingle tariff, and for allowing appropriations for Bremerton's naval yard to slip relative to the Mare Island, California, yard. On the other hand, the paper argued Dill kept his word, voted the wishes of his constituency, and would vote the progressive program if elected.[29]

Though a number of the state's labor papers such as the *Seattle Union Record*, the *Labor Journal*, and the *Tacoma Labor Advocate* supported Duncan, Dill also garnered support from labor groups.[30] In October, the Seattle Building Trades Council—representing twenty-five A.F.L. locals—overwhelmingly endorsed the Democrat. In addition, the railroad brotherhoods came on board the Dill campaign because he had favored the Plumb Plan.

Poindexter retained the support of the more influential papers in the state. The *Seattle Times* characterized Dill as a dangerous radical, while the *Spokesman-Review* reminded voters of the Democrat's war votes and described him as "shifty" and "untrustworthy."[31] The *Everett Daily Herald* attacked the Hearst-owned *P.I.*'s support of Dill appealing to the provincialism of Washington's voters. "First to last he [Poindexter] has worked with the Harding administration, seeking to further those things which the President has striven for, and this may account for some of the bitterness with which Hearstism, from its stronghold in New York City —3,000 miles removed from this state—has assailed him."[32]

In his campaign, Dill harped on Poindexter's Newberry vote and his move to the right. In fact, the two were linked. Poindexter was accused of voting to seat Newberry under the influence of Jules Bache, a New York banker, and William Todd, a New York shipbuilder with interests in the Puget Sound region. Bache was one of Poindexter's largest contributors and was cited as proof Poindexter had become a tool of Eastern interests. Allen argues the senator had not been unethical in his relationship with Bache; however, his prominence on the Senate Naval Affairs Committee and his support of a big Navy during the Washington Naval Disarmament Conference of 1922 combined with his acceptance of significant campaign contributions in 1920 (a failed bid for the presidency) and 1922 from Bache and Todd provided plenty of ammunition for Dill to blast the senator.[33]

Poindexter had changed his political philosophy. He came to believe government intervention in the economy was a dangerous thing. The senator also opposed federal development of Muscle Shoals, supported lower taxes on the rich, and argued against further legislation to help farmers. Poindexter held the latter position despite Washington farmers suffering from substantial income loss. His support of the higher Republican tariff (the Fordney-McCumber tariff of 1922) further angered farmers.[34] This move to conservative positions on key issues, combined with his relationship with his Eastern friends, clearly placed Poindexter outside the progressive tradition. Dill's deft handling of the prohibition issue further tipped the scales, casting doubt on Poindexter's return to the Senate.

Dill faced the difficult assignment of uniting rural drys with urban wets in the Democratic Party and securing enough Republican crossover votes to win the election. The trick was to define the election in terms of Poindexter's conservatism rather than prohibition. Should the election degenerate into a prohibition debate, Dill's Democratic Party would likely fracture into rural-urban segments, and the traditional Republican strength would ensure Poindexter's reelection. Fortunately for Dill, the Republican was wary about taking a stand on the divisive prohibition question. Poindexter was trying to attract the support of rich Easterners who cared little about the subject. The senator was more concerned with the opinions of his potential backers than with the hopes and fears of his constituents.[35] His reluctance to discuss prohibition suited Dill just fine.

If Poindexter had struck a staunch pose for prohibition, he would have forced Dill to respond. In such circumstances, it is highly likely Poindexter would have lost fewer votes than Dill, because the Republican Party was less divided over prohibition than the Democrats. Moreover, the Republican Party was much larger and more able to survive defections than the Democrats.[36] In the summer of 1922, a *Literary Digest* poll showed 87.2 percent of Washington's voters favored prohibition of some kind, 12.8

percent were opposed. Most of those opposed were city workers, registered as Democrats.[37] Dill kept prohibition in the background for good reason, preferring to run against Poindexter's record.

Compounding Poindexter's problems concerning prohibition was the fact that prohibition officials were appointed on the recommendations of senators and congressmen. Because those officials were largely seen as inept, much of the blame fell upon the allegedly wet Poindexter.[38] He was afraid to raise the issue, fearing a dry backlash. Dill, then, was successful in dictating the terms of the campaign, again demonstrating his political acumen and opportunism.

Moreover, Dill effectively argued that the election was about progressivism and not about parties, thus grabbing a significant number of Republican progressives and mitigating the damage from Duncan's Farmer-Labor candidacy on the left.[39] The twin pillars of Dill's campaign, Poindexter's vote on Esch-Cummins and Newberry, which together demonstrated Poindexter's reactionary record, cut across party lines.

Dill also needed to nullify the appeal of the Farmer-Labor candidate James Duncan, although Duncan in his idealism and naiveté was no match for the shrewd and seasoned politician from eastern Washington. The inept Duncan alienated the Whatcom County Farmer-Labor organization when he attacked the Democrats unmercifully, apparently unaware that the Whatcom County Farmer-Laborites had been trying to fuse with the local Democrats.[40]

Nor could Duncan hold the loyalty of Pierce County, which had given him about one-third of his primary votes. Early in October, the Pierce County Farmer-Labor Party joined forces with the local Democrats to elect local and legislative candidates. Homer Bone, an influential Pierce County Farmer-Labor Party member and candidate for the state legislature, threw his support behind Dill. Bone arranged for a meeting between Dill and the county's Farmer-Labor leadership, which resulted in the party supporting Dill instead of Duncan, an important coup.[41]

Dill had successfully determined the ground upon which Poindexter would be forced to campaign; he was not inclined to allow Duncan to do the same to him. Throughout the race Duncan wailed that Dill's campaign ignored the Democratic Party platform. Dill ignored Duncan and successfully sought the help of many farmers and laborers. In fact, Dill's effort to woo labor found such success that the vast majority of the state's AFL locals threw their support to him. Moreover, labor supplied a heavy share of Dill's financial support.[42]

As the campaign moved into its final week, Dill continued his assault on Poindexter's Esch-Cummins vote while Poindexter attempted to change the subject. The railroad issue fit Dill's strategy nicely because farmers now paid higher shipping rates on goods they both sold and bought, while workers paid higher prices for items bought in stores. Meanwhile, Poindexter continued to characterize Dill as a dangerous radical and reminded voters of his challenger's war record. It was not an argument likely to influence those who would decide the election: those progressives considered potential crossover votes. Meanwhile, Poindexter's supporters were frustrated that Dill had not made his position known on some issues—a standard complaint, but also indicative of Dill's setting the table.[43]

Late in the race, Dill responded to just about the only blow Poindexter had landed throughout the campaign: the former's alleged support for the repudiated League of Nations. Dill answered Poindexter's charge head-on. The *Seattle P.I.* and the few other papers favorable to the Democrat printed his response, which was as clever as the rest of his campaign. He argued that though he was opposed to the insanity of war, he had high hopes that nations would settle their differences peacefully. As to the United States joining the League, he believed such a momentous decision should be left to popular vote. Poindexter did not choose to argue with that position. The issue died.[44]

Still hopeful of retaining progressive support, or perhaps terrified of losing it, Poindexter persuaded Senator Charles McNary of Oregon, a progressive of unimpeachable credentials, to campaign for him in Seattle. McNary noted that, if reelected, Poindexter would become chairman of the Senate Committee on Naval Affairs, a committee that was of profound importance to Puget Sounders.[45]

On November 7 Washingtonians went to the polls. Early returns relieved Poindexter: he led in the cities. Spokane County showed him 5,000 votes ahead and the *Spokesman-Review* reported him leading on the west side of the Cascades as well. This was not good news for Dill. One might surmise that a politician from eastern Washington has to appeal to the people of the state's vast open spaces. This is simply not true in a statewide election. Granted, Dill could not afford large losses on those prairies; to win, he also had to capture the urban areas. There were just not enough votes in the eastern Washington grasslands to elect him.

Hours before the election, the mayors of Spokane, Bellingham, Tacoma, and Seattle predicted a Dill victory.[46] Though early returns favored Poindexter, the day after the election Dill had squeaked out a 2,000 vote lead.[47] But Poindexter's forces hoped later-reporting rural districts would push their man over the top. It was a forlorn hope; Dill clung to his lead and upset the two-term Republican senator. Election reports showed Dill had taken all three of Washington's most urban counties: King, Pierce, and Spokane, and had essentially split Washington's rural counties with Poindexter. Farmer discontent and the belief that Poindexter had abandoned progressivism, kept Poindexter from carrying rural districts.[48]

Poindexter focused his campaign on securing the progressive vote despite having changed his definition of progressivism. Poindexter argued that the essence of progressivism was protecting the people from their enemies. But for him, the enemies had changed. Before the war, the foes had been corporate America, monopoly, and greed. After the war, the enemy became Bolshevism and a frightening diversity. Unfortunately for Poindexter, Wilson's administration had taken much of the fire out of the radical movement in America, while World War I vastly increased the wealth and power of American business. By 1922 most Washingtonians were more concerned with their economic well-being than with foreign enemies. Progressivism still seemed to offer the hope of improving economic status. Thus Washingtonians threw Poindexter out and put Clarence Dill in the Senate. Nationally, progressives made a comeback as well; William E. Leuchtenburg has written that they scared "the daylights out of the Old Guard" in 1922. Not surprisingly, it was the farm states of the Midwest that exchanged conservative for progressive Republicans.[49]

More importantly, however, Poindexter stumbled over prohibition. If he had pressed the prohibition issue—made Dill campaign as the devout dry he was—much of Dill's Democratic support in the city would have slipped away. If Poindexter had emphasized his prohibitionist stance, some of those dry crossover Republican voters would have stayed by his side. But he allowed Dill to define the election in terms of Newberryism and Esch-Cummins, using those issues as proof of Poindexter's conservatism.

Dill's campaign strategy decided the Washington State Senate election of 1922. He skillfully welded the disparate elements of the Democratic Party together despite the prohibition issue. Moreover, the Democrat used Poindexter's conservatism to define the election in terms of ideology and integrity rather than party, and thus appealed to voters outside traditional Democratic Party ranks (i.e. rural progressive Republicans). At the same time, he garnered the support of the majority of urban laborers and rural farmers. Combining the rural element with the urban was an accomplishment worthy of the Squire of Hyde Park, who would do essentially the same thing ten years later on a national scale. Finally, Dill overcame the provincialism of western Washington in creating his rural-urban coalition.

Years later, while writing *Where Water Falls*, Dill observed that fate, or the vagaries of chance, often change life in ways impossible to foresee: "had I been reelected in 1918 I would probably have won in 1920 with little chance of future defeats. I would not have risked defeat by running against Senator Miles Poindexter in 1922."[50] Of course, if Dill had failed to gain Poindexter's Senate seat, that failure may have had significant consequences for Washington's long-term economic development. For that development was largely dependent on abundant and cheap hydroelectric power, and Clarence Dill would play an important role in the creation of that power.

Spokane, Washington, in the late 1920s. *#L83-238, Cheney Cowles Museum/Eastern Washington State Historical Society, Spokane, WA*

CHAPTER FIVE

"A Son of a Wild Jackass"

C LARENCE DILL, NO STRANGER to Washington, D.C., knew even before his election which Senate committees he desired. Premier among them was the Interstate Commerce Committee, which directly affected railroad legislation. Railroads were the lifeblood of Spokane. Dill had no trouble gaining a seat on the committee. He also secured positions on the Irrigation and Reclamation Committee, Public Lands and Surveys, and Indian Affairs, all of which impinged directly on Washington's interests and those of the West. But more than the provincial concerns of his state interested Dill. The nation's foreign policy concerned him greatly, as did the integrity of the Senate, and the recurring economic difficulties beset-ting American farmers.

In the first few months of the session, Dill developed a close associa-tion with George Norris of Nebraska. The two men found they agreed on nearly every issue. Indeed, Dill and Norris were among the western pro-gressive-insurgent politicians historian Ray Tucker described as "Sons of the Wild Jackass." Norris first noticed Dill when the latter refused to ap-prove the administration's nomination of Frank B. Kellogg as ambassador to Great Britain. Dill opposed Kellogg's nomination because he believed the appointment of former senators and congressmen to government posi-tions was not in the public's best interest (Kellogg had been defeated in his Senate race in 1922). As Dill left for his Senate office after the Kellogg vote, Norris took him by the arm and said, "Dill, I want to congratulate you on that vote against Kellogg. That vote was your Declaration of Inde-pendence. From now on, the Democratic machine leaders here know you will vote your convictions. They won't be shocked."[1]

Dill worried a great deal about how the United States used military force in the world. Thus, he kept an eye on American policy in Latin America. In the twenties, the United States was concerned that leftist revo-lutionary movements in Latin America neither harm American business and citizens, nor compromise American strategic interests. However, Dill believed American policy was inimical to the interests of the vast majority

of Latin Americans. In his opposition to American policy, he often followed the lead of Norris. Indicative of both men's feelings regarding the
Coolidge administration's Latin American policy was their response to the
president's decision to send U.S. Marines back to Nicaragua in 1926 to
protect American property and lives. In addition, Coolidge intended to
support the Nicaraguan government of Adolfo Diaz. However, rumors cir-
culated in Washington that the president's primary purpose was to impress
on Mexico the danger of nationalizing American property—especially
American oil interests.[2]

Dill, in fact, led the attack on the Coolidge administration along with
Senators Thomas Heflin (Alabama) and Robert La Follette (Wisconsin).
The senators feared the administration's policy would lead to war with
Mexico over issues that, should roles be reversed, the United States would
claim as issues of sovereignty. Failure to allow Mexico to decide for itself
the fate of foreign companies seemed hypocritical to insurgent Republicans and progressive Democrats.[3]

Norris chafed at the Coolidge administration's policy of sustaining
Diaz and supporting him with the American military even though he was
not the legally elected President of Nicaragua as essentially meaning, "the
United States was at war with Nicaragua."[4]

Norris did not stand alone in the Senate in denouncing American
policy toward Mexico and Nicaragua. Dill argued for another election in
Nicaragua, saying, "We cannot defend a policy of making the Nicaraguan
people have a government they don't want." Meanwhile, the administration had been working on just such an electoral solution. Unfortunately,
Coolidge's hoped-for elections did not resolve the Nicaraguan problem.

Dill remained irreconcilably opposed to the administration's policy
in Latin America. In January 1928 he said, "I am opposed to the armed
forces of America being used to protect investments of Americans abroad
and for the purpose of passing laws to impose more burdensome loans on
the Nicaraguan people." Dill would use the U.S. Marines only to "see that
Americans got safely away from Nicaragua."[5]

The question of representative government concerned Americans as
well as Nicaraguans. Dill was in part elected on the issue of whether or not
Miles Poindexter ought to have voted to seat Truman Newberry, and he
was not about to let a similar controversy cause him political trouble. The
1926 election brought a case similar to Newberry's to the attention of the
Senate. William S. Vare of Pennsylvania had received massive campaign
contributions from private power-holding companies in his successful bid
for the Senate.[6] The amount of money and its source irritated Dill and

prompted his antipathy to Vare. As with the Latin American imbroglio, Dill allied himself with Norris and other progressive senators, but it was the Democrat from Washington who openly led the fight against Vare while Norris called the shots from behind the scenes.[7]

On December 10, 1926, Dill presented a resolution to declare Vare disqualified to present his credentials of election. His purpose was to "close the door of the Senate against these men before they arrive here."[8] Dill claimed Vare had spent more than $800,000 in his campaign. His argument was that the expenditure of such enormous sums defeated the purpose of primary elections:

> When candidates for public office were chosen by political conventions big business and political bosses often managed to nominate the candidates of both leading parties, the result being that, regardless of who lost, big business and the political bosses always won.
>
> Those who led the movement for the adoption of the direct primary through the country some years ago believed the primary would end that practice...but during the past few months we have had some of the most flagrant examples of the violation of the spirit and purpose of the primary in the history of American politics. Candidates for the nomination for the United States Senate in Pennsylvania and Illinois have spent more money to secure nominations for the Senate than national campaign committees have ordinarily spent in the whole country to bring about the election of a President.[9]

Norris and Dill fought the seating of Vare for nearly two years. Finally, by a vote of 58 to 22, their long battle ended in triumph. The Senate denied William S. Vare a seat. It was a victory in principle, but practically speaking, meant little. The governor of Pennsylvania appointed high tariff lobbyist Joseph R. Grundy to the vacated seat.[10]

Such victories probably had little long-term significance for America's future, but the same cannot be said for the efforts to deal with the nation's farm problem in the 1920s. Men of good will and serious minds of both parties grappled with the leviathan of low crop prices in that decade; in the end they grappled to the death. The failure to solve the farm crisis has generally been laid at the feet of the successive Republican administrations of that decade. But both parties were guilty of advancing chimeras as viable solutions. Ultimately, both parties failed.

The farm problem of the twenties was a consequence of the coming of the industrial age and of the Great War. The industrial revolution allowed farmers to produce great crops and for a while, to distribute them effectively, resulting in what historians have called the "golden age" of

American agriculture. This golden age lasted from about 1900 to 1920. During this era, American cities, swollen with foreign immigrants and rural migrants, provided American farmers with a growing market despite dwindling important foreign markets. During the war, the American farmer supplied much of the food needs of the Europeans; prices rose, times were good.[11]

By 1919 wheat earned $2.19 a bushel, cotton $1.76 a bale. Farmers now put more acreage into production and often bought new equipment, sometimes borrowing money. Inevitably the war ended, as did the boom market; prices sagged. There was a sharp recession in 1920, and by the end of the decade, wheat returned only $1.04 per bushel and cotton 85 cents.[12] Farmers found making a living difficult, let alone repaying loans. They also deserted marginal land. Between 1919 and 1924, thirteen million acres were left fallow. In Dill's home state, farmers abandoned 750,000 acres.[13] On the other hand, the mechanization of the American farm proceeded; in 1918 there were 80,000 tractors plowing the nation's fields, by 1929, 850,000.[14] Moreover, more efficient farming practices and new fertilizers provided an increase in farm produce despite acreage reduction.[15] Increased supply resulting from these developments drove prices ever lower. The foregoing, combined with increasing costs of production, meant that the farmer's purchasing power, if measured on a scale in which 1913 represents 100, had dropped to 67 in 1921.[16]

Other factors magnified despair. Local taxes, with the expansion of state services such as roads, often rose. And competition for markets from government-subsidized European farmers increased as well.[17] The perspective of history allows us to see that the independent American farmer was not merely experiencing the usual boom and bust cycle of the American economy, but rather a fundamental shift in his relationship to the arising monopolistic and industrial world. Only a comprehensive government program could have softened this crushing blow, but government was not yet ready to perform that task.[18]

Farmers and farm groups advocated a number of plans to reverse their fortunes. In 1921 congressmen and senators from western and southern states organized the "farm bloc" in an effort to pass farm legislation. Their efforts met with legislative success, but did little to improve farmers' economic prospects. The Packers and Stockyards Act of 1921 was intended to preserve competition amongst middlemen; the Grain Futures Act of the same year placed grain exchanges under the control of the Secretary of Agriculture; the 1922 Capper-Volstead Act suspended the anti-trust laws for farmers; and the Agricultural Credits Act of 1923 established credit banks to provide farmers loans. These measures did not address the fundamental farm problems: over-production and the lack of markets.[19]

By the mid-twenties the program known as McNary-Haugen came to be the preferred solution of most farmers and their advocates. The plan took its name from Senator Charles McNary of Oregon and Representative Gilbert Haugen of Iowa, chairmen of the congressional committees concerned with agriculture. McNary-Haugen was a complex plan for raising the price of key agricultural commodities without restricting production. An Agricultural Export Corporation, headed by the Secretary of Agriculture, was to establish a fair price for a given commodity and then sell excess crops overseas. Farmers were to make up losses through an equalization fee to be levied on each unit of produce they sold. Supporters of the plan believed that the fee would be far less than the profits accrued by higher domestic prices.[20]

By 1924 other ideas for solving the farm problem—crop diversification, mechanization, easier credit, soil conservation, and better farm management , among others—had all actually contributed to the problem: too much food. Farmers now turned to McNary-Haugen with a zealotry usually reserved for camp meetings. Indeed, farm misery had long been a radicalizing element in America, causing many of the nation's farmers to abandon doctrines of individualism in the hope government would solve their problems. But the Republican administration of Calvin Coolidge had not solved the problem and did not appear likely to do so. Coolidge's own thoughts in 1924 had not progressed beyond the approval of using cooperatives for better marketing and easier credit for farmers.[21]

Support for McNary-Haugen came primarily from the West in 1924; Southerners were split over the plan largely because it did not protect cotton adequately. Consequently, the farm block simply did not have the votes in 1924 to pass the plan in the face of the administration's opposition. However, George Norris, one of the McNary-Haugen leaders in the Senate, knew he could count on Dill when it came time to help farmers. The Washingtonian voted for McNary-Haugen every time it came before the Senate.[22] Thus Norris came to regard Dill highly and included him prominently in what he called "our progressive bunch."[23]

By 1926 Coolidge faced increasing pressure to do something dramatic about the plight of farmers, who were now determined that government should address their lack of purchasing power and were more united behind yet another version of McNary-Haugen. But Coolidge too had bestirred himself and developed his own plan for agriculture, which included more cooperative marketing, better cooperation between business and agriculture, increased credit, and improved education; in other words, more of the same past and futile policies. But Coolidge's plan had strength enough to split the vote of those who favored farm legislation. McNary-Haugen died again.[24]

Still the advocates of farm relief would not go away. In 1927 a new McNary-Haugen bill, this time including features that bound the South to the fate of the West and garnered some support even from the nation's businessmen, came before Congress. The South now supported the bill because cotton and tobacco were included on favorable terms and because the region's farmers were perhaps the poorest in the country.[25] Businessmen concerned about agriculture supported the bill because it created a Federal Farm Board to administer the program. This board was to work through existing cooperatives rather than abolish them. However, the 1927 version of McNary-Haugen still envisioned artificial support of prices and overseas dumping.[26] It was this feature of the bill that most disturbed President Coolidge and Secretary of the Treasury Andrew Mellon. The latter argued in June 1926 that such a mechanism would

> increase the cost of living to every consumer of five basic agricultural commodities. We shall have the unusual spectacle of the American consuming public paying a bonus to the producers of five major agricultural commodities, with a resulting decrease in the purchasing power of wages, and at the same time contributing to a subsidy to the foreign consumers, who under the proposed plan will secure American commodities at prices below the American level.

Mellon went on to argue that such a state of affairs would allow foreign industry to operate more cheaply than American. American industry would then lose on the world market.[27]

No clearer pronouncement of the American government's Hamiltonian preference for aid to industry over agriculture was made in the 1920s. In short, the Republicans would protect American industry through the tariff, but would leave American agriculture to the vicissitudes of the world market and domestic overproduction. Ironically, both the farmer and his government were locked in the nineteenth century frame of mind that worshipped the industry and independence of the American agrarian.

Nevertheless, a number of business leaders such as Bernard Baruch and Owen D. Young now supported McNary-Haugen. However, Coolidge had to be most chagrined by the mutiny of a number of regular Republicans and his own vice president, Charles Dawes. When asked about Dawes' defection the taciturn Coolidge remarked, "I have noticed that the McNary-Haugen people have their headquarters in his [Dawes'] chambers."[28]

Coolidge grew defensive and recited Republican efforts through the decade on behalf of farmers. Then he advocated his program of 1926 as the answer to the farm problem in 1927.[29] But the president's proposal did not do nearly enough to satisfy desperate farmers. In the early months of 1927, the Senate began debate on the new McNary-Haugen farm relief bill.

Despite his interest in the farm problem and devotion to helping farmers, Clarence Dill did not take a substantive role in the Senate debate over farm relief in early 1927. He was wholly preoccupied with the problems of an American phenomenon: radio. But he was on the Senate floor to record his vote in favor of McNary-Haugen in February, and it was a good thing he was; the fight in the Senate was fierce and close. Vice President Dawes eventually interceded to pass the bill.[30]

Pressure now built on Coolidge to sign McNary-Haugen. Westerners talked about tariff retaliation against eastern business interests if Coolidge did not sign the bill. Moreover, there was open talk amongst western Republicans of dumping Coolidge in 1928 and supporting a candidate more sympathetic to farmers. George Norris had quite rightly come to believe that only new ideas in the White House could solve the farm crisis.[31]

To his credit, Coolidge did not cave in but remained true to his convictions and vetoed the 1927 farm bill. John Hicks summarized Coolidge's motives:

> However it might be phrased, the McNary-Haugen bill as Coolidge saw it, asked government to do what government had no right to do. It called for price fixing, for an improper delegation of the taxing power, and for the creation of a vast and cumbersome bureaucracy. It was economically unsound, for the higher prices it contemplated would lead to greater overproduction and larger surpluses, while the disposal of American goods abroad at cut-rate figures would arouse foreign resentment and promote retaliation.[32] Coolidge himself remarked that the bill "is not framed to aid farmers as a whole, and it is furthermore, calculated to injure rather than promote the general public welfare."[33]

Coolidge's detonation of farmers' hopes for relief brought quick and severe political fallout. The *New York Times*, though it approved the president's decision, argued that his action had opened the campaign for president; Republican farm block leaders announced that the McNary-Haugen bill would be a *casus belli* at the 1928 convention.[34]

Western senators, even more than others sympathetic to the farmers' plight, were livid over Coolidge's veto. They tried to pass McNary-Haugen one more time before the 1928 election. To that end McNary, a personal friend of Coolidge, went to great lengths to modify his bill so as to meet the chief executive's objections. But equally important to farm block Republicans was the effort to make farm relief the major issue at the 1928 convention. If Coolidge vetoed a modified McNary-Haugen bill, then surely substantial support would swing behind a candidate acceptable to farmers, or so it was thought.[35]

In 1928 Clarence Dill had more time to devote to the farm problem. He took an active interest in seeing McNary-Haugen pass the Congress one more time. Ironically, his greatest contribution to the measure lay in removing Washington's fruit growers from inclusion in the bill. In this effort Dill followed the lead of New York's Democratic Senator Royal Copeland.[36] In his remarks on the floor of the Senate, Dill cited the hundreds of letters and telegrams he had received from Washington's fruit growers in opposition to McNary-Haugen. He said:

> They [the growers] want the apple industry to have no connection whatever with this marketing system. They have built up their own marketing system [cooperating amongst themselves]. They have built their own plan of storing their fruits. The boxed apple industry is in a stable condition, and we do not want the apple business of the Northwest in any way handled by any board or under legislation of this kind."[37]

Copeland and Dill carried the day and the provision covering fruit was entirely dropped from the 1928 McNary-Haugen bill. The farm relief measure passed Congress again in May 1928, this time by substantial majorities. Dill, of course, voted for the bill.[38]

But the Westerners' efforts were in vain as President Coolidge wasted little time in vetoing McNary-Haugen once again. Despite McNary's efforts to modify his bill, the equalization fee that had so concerned the President in 1927 still formed the cornerstone of the legislation. The equalization fee was essentially a tax, paid by farmers, on various commodities produced in excess of demand. The tax was to offset the government's losses incurred by buying excess commodities at the new higher domestic price, then selling at whatever price could be obtained overseas. McNary-Haugenites hoped the higher domestic prices would be more than enough to cover the equalization fee. Coolidge vetoed the 1928 version of McNary-Haugenism with what historian Donald McCoy described as "unrestrained ridicule."[39] There was no hope of overriding the presidential veto.[40]

Coolidge was right. McNary-Haugen was ill-advised legislation that would have created more problems than it solved.[41] Farmers would be encouraged to grow more, not less, the very problem that gave rise to the farm crisis. The equalization fee was not adequate to the task of restricting supply.[42] Moreover, the bill blithely ignored the shrinking of foreign markets. This was pure folly; as Gilbert Fite has written, "To build a farm program on the idea of nearly unlimited agricultural export markets was to build on a delusion—unless the United States would have been willing to lower her tariffs so there could have been a freer flow of goods."[43] There was, of course, no chance of the latter. The president added disdain to defeat when he displayed a caustic attitude toward McNary-Haugen in his veto message. Many Americans now came to believe he was unconcerned about their problems. To these Americans, as Rexford Tugwell said, Coolidge demonstrated, "a stubborn determination to do nothing."[44]

In response, farm-bloc Republicans went to their 1928 convention determined to find a candidate who would represent their interests. But McNary-Haugenism had passed its heyday. Few of the rank and file Republicans required to make a meaningful demonstration at Kansas City showed up. In those circumstances, McNary-Haugen's leaders had little hope of success. In short the convention sustained Coolidge, who surprised everyone by choosing not to run for reelection. New ideas, espoused by new leaders, gradually replaced McNary-Haugenism.

In the 1920s Democrats and Republicans alike failed to come to grips with America's farm problem. Democrats like Dill, with their farm-bloc Republican allies like George Norris, advanced a plan that would not have worked in the long run. Republicans recognized that, but were themselves victims of their own ideology: the antipathy toward using government to help individuals, specifically farmers, while continuing to aid business. Split by East-West dissension and rural-urban antagonism, along with the traditional political parties, Americans were unable to adequately address the farm problem. Thus the American government fiddled while nearly half of its citizens burned with the despair of poverty. Ultimately all Americans paid the price.

Clarence Dill noticed the pain of America's farmers. He had grown up on a farm, knew poverty and hard work, and had eventually become disillusioned with that life. There is no record of his emotions concerning this subject, but the plight of farmers must have gnawed at him; his concern for reclamation, public power, and even radio must have in some way been a response to the pitiful sight of farm families attempting to draw a lonely, meager, and back-breaking living from the land.

The foregoing issues occupied significant portions of Dill's time, but in themselves they would have hardly constituted a record of achievement sure to return him to the Senate in 1928. Fortunately for the young senator circumstances combined to give him one issue that meant a great deal to the voters of Washington (a tariff on shingles and lumber), and another that provided an opportunity to substantially raise his prestige in the Senate (the necessity for regulation of radio). Toward the end of his first term, Dill fought hard for a shingle/lumber tariff. But before turning his attention to Washington's desire for such a tariff, Dill addressed himself to the noise coming from his constituents' radio sets, and thus defined his first term in office.

CHAPTER SIX

RADIO DAYS

I N 1895, A YOUNG AND TIRELESS Italian inventor, Guglielmo Marconi, succeeded in sending radio signals a few kilometers. For two and a half decades after Marconi's discovery, radio remained of limited use: merchant ships usually carried a radio set, navies made a wireless standard equipment, and a few curious tinkerers built receivers and transmitters for private use. However, with the passage of time, radio enthusiasts became so common in America that Congress felt constrained to bring some order to their world, thus passing the Radio Act of 1912. This act required anyone operating a radio transmitter to procure a license from the Department of Commerce.[1] The first commercial broadcasting stations cast their initial signals near the end of 1920. Others followed quickly. In July 1922, 382 stations vied for air space; by the end of the year there were 569 stations.[2]

Not only did Marconi profoundly change the twentieth century, he also affected the life of Clarence Dill. In the late 1920s, Washington's junior senator became the Senate's recognized expert on radio through his efforts in crafting and passing the legislation that became the basis for American broadcasting law. The catalyst for this legislation was broadcast interference resulting from too many stations on a wavelength. Stations often operated on the same wavelength at the same time resulting in unintelligible static. Secretary of Commerce Herbert Hoover began refusing new licenses to those who wished to broadcast in areas inundated with radio signals. As a response to Hoover's decision, Intercity Radio Company filed a successful lawsuit with a court of appeals. The court abrogated the secretary's power to withhold licenses, which he had assumed under the Radio Act of 1912. In its place, the Commerce Department developed a classification and zoning system to organize the burgeoning business of radio.

Radio station owners and other interested parties concerned that a plethora of new stations would diminish the value of their investments had met at the invitation of Secretary Hoover in the spring of 1922 to discuss radio's problems. The conferees decided that the only remedy to

A control room and studio at KWSC, Pullman, WA. The burgeoning communications industry of the 1920s and early 1930s necessitated federal legislation and control. *#78-628, Washington State University Libraries, Pullman, WA*

their predicament lay in the federal regulation of radio. Thus, radio entrepreneurs found themselves in the unusual position of imploring the federal government to regulate their industry. And Clarence Dill soon found himself leading the fight in the Senate for legislation that would regulate radio, though Dill's idea of appropriate legislation differed substantially from that of radio's leaders.[3]

Hoover's meeting with radio's business leaders in the spring of 1922 came to be known as the First National Radio Conference. The conference proposed legislation to Congress sponsored by Republican Congressman Wallace H. White of Maine.[4]

The radio bill went to the committee on The Merchant Marine and Fisheries, which held hearings and reported out on January 16, 1923. Because of rapid changes in radio technology, the committee recommended that any forthcoming legislation refrain from attempting to be highly specific, preferring instead to grant broad powers to the Secretary of Commerce, who presumably could respond to the changing needs of radio.

White's bill received little attention in 1923 but was reintroduced in early 1924. Meanwhile, a Senate bill addressing the growing fear of monopoly in radio was introduced. Many individuals were increasingly concerned that private radio corporations would lay claim to ownership of "the ether." Indeed, a long established principle of American law holds "that if a citizen openly and adversely possesses and uses property for a long period of time without opposition, or without contest, he acquires title by adverse possession."[5] Moreover, Secretary of Commerce Hoover preferred that the airwaves remain in the hands of private business. A sense of urgency thus arose regarding radio legislation. Congress was impelled to act before sufficient time had elapsed, which might allow the courts to find that rights of ownership of the airwaves had been established among private users. In fact, critics of White's 1923 bill argued it was too weak in regard to monopoly. The issue was a hot one. The hearings on H.R. 7357 were full of accusations and innuendo.[6]

In the spring of 1924, the Senate passed its bill regarding monopoly. The House combined it with its own and reported it out. Now Hoover unexpectedly withdrew his support from the combined bills, explaining rapid developments in technology (especially more powerful radio stations) and the arrival of the entirely new problem of radio advertising, with potentially enormous profits, caused him to recommend a delay of one year; in the meantime he advocated creation of legislation directly—rather than broadly—regulating radio.[7]

While the legislation was on hiatus, Hoover hoped technology would solve some of radio's problems, rather than create more. He believed new developments might eliminate interference between stations operating at the same frequency, and thus the concerns about monopoly would be mitigated.[8] By late 1925, however, Hoover's optimism had faded: the problems of interference persisted, and license applications continued to increase.[9] Hoover concluded that Congress must pass legislation that would deprive individuals of the freedom to erect radio transmitters. In a speech before the Fourth National Radio Conference, he argued that the rights of listeners preempted the rights of broadcasters:

> We hear a great deal about the freedom of the air; but there are two parties to freedom of the air, and to freedom of speech for that matter. There is the speech maker and the listener. Certainly in radio I believe in freedom for the listener....Freedom cannot mean a license to every person or corporation who wishes to broadcast his name or his wares, and thus monopolizes the listener's set.[10]

White's new legislation now encompassed the idea that the government would limit the number of stations and decline to issue licenses to some petitioners on the grounds that "the public interest" required that only a limited number of stations be in operation (the interference problem). The bill essentially followed the advice of the conferees (mostly business people) at the Fourth National Radio Conference. The new bill passed the House on March 15, 1926, and was forwarded to the Senate, where Dill's bill was still before the Commerce Committee.[11]

Dill had come to his leading role in radio legislation quite by accident. At the same time that agitation for radio regulation grew, trouble arose between broadcasters and composers. Composers were often not paid for the reproduction of their works over radio. Some non-profit broadcasters in the Pacific Northwest informed Dill that the American Society of Composers, Authors, and Publishers (ASCAP) was suing them for failure to pay royalties. Dill agreed to sponsor a bill that would exempt non-profit broadcasters from royalty payments. After announcing the bill, Dill found himself confronted by John Philip Sousa and a group of musicians who argued he was taking away their livelihood. The subsequent squabble over copyright law in radio made Dill the most knowledgeable radio man in the Senate in the mid-1920s. Consequently, he was the logical choice to handle radio legislation.[12]

In March 1926, the Dill legislation and the White bill called for wide powers to be placed in the hands of the Secretary of Commerce, but differed as to the composition of the radio advisory commission. If Dill's legislation had not undergone fairly rapid metamorphosis, radio legislation probably would have been passed in 1926. But shortly after Dill introduced his bill, Senator William Borah, Republican of Idaho, introduced a bill that sought to establish an independent commission to govern radio, thus taking control of radio away from the Commerce Department. Commerce Secretary Herbert Hoover had gone to great pains to expand his domain and was averse to seeing it shrink. But Borah convinced his fellow progressive Dill to support the independent commission idea. Indeed, from September 16, 1925, when Dill spoke at a radio banquet at the Hotel Commodore in New York City, to January 1926, his views concerning radio regulation underwent a transformation. In his New York speech, Dill lauded the freedom American inventors and entrepreneurs enjoyed and specifically warned against establishing a commission to regulate radio. The crisis in broadcasting—which was even then acute—combined with the opinions of men he respected, such as George Norris and William Borah, eventually brought him to support the independent commission idea. In May 1926, Dill resubmitted his bill, changing it in accord with Borah's original concept. The new bill addressed a number of concerns. Framers of the legislation believed it would prevent monopoly, control chain broadcasting (what came to be known as networks), regulate the selling prices of radio equipment, and provide a mechanism for denying licenses.[13]

Radio legislation became even more imperative when the United States lost its case against Zenith Radio Corporation in April 1926. In this case, the court ruled a licensee using an unauthorized wavelength at disallowed time could not be prosecuted under the Radio Act of 1912. This decision effectively meant there were no laws regarding radio broadcasting.[14]

On May 7, 1926, the Interstate Commerce Committee reported the Dill legislation with its creation of an independent commission. The Washingtonian was expected to call it to the floor forthwith. He elaborated on why the Senate preferred the commission system:

> After the consideration of the facts given your committee at the hearings, the committee decided that the importance of radio and particularly the probable influence it will develop to be in the social, political, and economic life of the American people, and the many new and complex problems its administration presents, demand that Congress establish an entirely independent body to take charge of the regulation of radio communication in all its forms.
>
> The exercise of this power is fraught with such great possibilities that it should not be entrusted to any one man nor to any administration department of the government. This regulatory power should be as free from political influence or arbitrary control as possible.[15]

But Dill's radio bill drew fire from conservatives. Herbert Houston, publisher and former president of the Advertising Clubs of the World, argued that under the Dill bill, control of radio would pass from private enterprise to the politician and propagandist. Though there were extreme conservatives who wanted no government regulation of radio, the majority on the right were perfectly willing to trust Secretary Hoover with the new medium. These people appeared to be moderate in their views and appealed to a significant number of Americans. Professor Michael Pupin of Columbia University was representative of this group. In a speech before the Radio Club of America, he attacked Dill's legislation and supported placing radio under the Secretary of Commerce.[16]

Dill had supporters from the left who argued his plan would provide a truly free medium, especially from government control, under an independent commission. Norman Thomas, executive director of the League for Industrial Democracy, wrote Dill a letter supporting the senator's efforts. Thomas argued a "radio trust" existed under the Secretary of Commerce and exercised a virtual censorship over political ideas:

> There isn't one of you who has ever heard a really uncensored program....I don't mean that a lot of foxed-faced men sit around the table blue penciling everybody's speech. I do mean that in the nature of the case you hear carefully controlled and censored presentation of public problems...labor organizations, particularly the AFL, somehow or other have a terrible time getting a license of their own.[17]

Thomas had intended to make his case over radio station WMCA, but the speech was suddenly cancelled. In explaining the refusal to let Thomas broadcast, Donald Flamm of WMCA said, "Why he slammed the daylights out of the companies on which we depend for supplies." Thomas's solution was to support Dill's independent commission and keep radio as far away from government control (meaning Hoover and other conservatives) as possible.[18] Dill and Thomas believed that an independent commission whose members would be appointed by the president and approved by the Senate would be less politically motivated than a commission under the control of the Secretary of Commerce.

Pressure on the Senate to pass radio legislation increased in the summer of 1926. Several senators spoke with Dill before his legislation came to the floor and urged him to yield and support White. Americans from all over the country sent telegrams pleading for action on radio. Interference had become such a problem many radios were useless. By late 1926, there were more than 600 stations in operation with seventy more under construction. Applications for radio licenses skyrocketed, and Hoover had no authority to deny them. Everyone wanted to get in on the radio bonanza, for commercially, in spite of its problems, radio had arrived. Radios, and everything associated with them—tubes, how-to books, and components—became the rage for the Christmas season of 1926.[19] Radio entrepreneurs anticipated the Christmas season in that year. In September they held a Radio World's Fair at Madison Square Garden designed to excite the public over radio innovations and possibilities.[20]

Even before the events of the fall of 1926, substantial pressure on the Senate to pass legislation existed. To that end, senators resumed deliberation on Dill's radio bill on June 30, 1926. Dill explained the purpose of his bill:

> First, and most important of all, radio in the United States is free. It is so free to the listener-in that anybody anywhere may listen in to any broadcasting whatsoever, whether it be by amateurs who are experimenting

or by telegraphers who are sending wireless messages in code or by broadcasters who are giving programs to amuse, entertain, and instruct, without any restraint or hindrance whatsoever by the Government.

This freedom of radio reception by the American people is the feature of radio that distinguishes and differentiates radio conditions in the United States from radio conditions in every other country in the world. In practically every other country the government levies a tax on receiving sets. In some countries the government has prevented listeners-in from having sets that will receive broadcasting on more than two or three wave lengths.

The other condition regarding radio in the United States that is different from conditions in foreign countries relates to broadcasting. In practically all other countries the government either owns or directly controls all broadcasting stations. In this country there has been practically no control exercised by the Government, except as to the assignment of wave lengths and regulations as to the amount of power to be used.

What has been the result of this policy of freedom for radio broadcasting and radio reception? The result is that American initiative and American business ingenuity have developed radio broadcasting in the United States far beyond anything known in other parts of the world. With only 6 per cent of the world's population living in the United States, we have more than 80 per cent of all the receiving sets on earth and five times as many broadcasting stations as all the rest of the world combined.

Let me add that not only are radio reception and radio broadcasting free from Government restraint in the United States, but it is our desire and purpose to keep them free so far as it is possible to do so in conformity with the general public interest and the social welfare of the great masses of our people. It is this combination of conditions and purpose that complicates the problem of legislation on this subject and compels Congress to pioneer the way in the passage of a radio bill. We must steer the legislative ship between the Scylla of too much regulation and the Charybdis of the grasping selfishness of private monopoly.[21]

The Charybdis of the right, however, was formidable. Senator Hiram Bingham of Connecticut spoke against Dill's bill as calling for too many rules and regulations and highly paid commissions. He had added to his remarks in the *Congressional Record*, an editorial from the *Torrington Register* of May 24, 1926. The editorial writer preferred the White bill as the "least objectionable plan." Such were the sentiments of many in an era in which the American economic system seemed to be on the threshold of providing undreamed-of luxuries to the common people.[22]

Dill reported to the Senate on July 3, 1926, the conferees' failure to reach a compromise.[23] In lieu of comprehensive legislation, the conferees recommended S.J. 125, which would preserve the status quo (so threatened in the Zenith case of April), especially as it pertained to monopoly and ownership of the airwaves. Unfortunately, though S.J. 125 passed both branches of Congress, it was too late in the session to present the bill to the president. It was not signed until December 1926.

When Congress took up radio again in December, Dill's insistence on an independent commission and White's insistence on an advisory commission, blocked compromise.[24] Dill's support among the conferees came in part from Senator James Watson of Indiana (R) and Representative Ewin L. Davis of Tennessee (D). Davis believed the White concept of an advisory commission was "spineless." He further argued radio was significant enough to warrant full-time attention from a professional commission. Meanwhile, Dill fought stop-gap measures, because they would take pressure off the main legislation and possibly result in delay.[25]

On January 8, 1927, Dill reported to the Senate his belief a compromise with the House was near. Over the next few days, senators asked him as to the status of the accord. Dill was forced to admit the intensity of the struggle over the independent commission in negotiations with the Republicans–especially those from the House. He also had to correct inaccurate leaks as to the nature of the compromise, leaks that implied the Republicans had been victorious.[26]

Many senators and representatives grew restless waiting for the conferees to conclude business. Their mailboxes were inundated with petitions demanding Congress fix radio before adjourning on March 4, 1927. Dill calmly responded that the agreed-on legislation would certainly beat that deadline. He released to the *New York Times* information that indicated that more than 1,200 stations would be on the air by July 1927. In this news release, Dill provided ammunition for petitioners should they choose to write their congressman, thus placing a little pressure on his colleagues.[27]

To this point, Congress had felt a great deal of pressure to not only legislate in regard to radio, but to legislate in a manner acceptable to radio's business leaders. These people had generally supported returning radio to the Secretary of Commerce's control.[28] Though some members of the business community opposed any legislation, most realized the necessity of it. They were also aware of the political realities in the Senate that made some form of compromise necessary if legislation were to be passed. Once the conference committee reached a compromise, conservatives generally supported the conference report.

Those who feared that radio's major operators might monopolize radio, however, were yet to be heard. This opposition to the conference report in the Senate now came generally from the progressive element of the upper house. Successfully maneuvering between the demands of radio's business interests and the opposition of those concerned for public ownership of the ether would require all the estimable conciliatory talents of Clarence Dill and more. Fortunately, he possessed other talents as well. The *New York Times* described him as a "distinguished speaker who avoided extravagant gestures and had a brightly intelligent if not deeply intellectual mind."[29] One can safely add to that description the virtue of patience. For Dill, over the next few weeks, demonstrated the requisite patience to endure the load the controversy over radio placed upon him.

On February 3, 1927, Dill finally presented the conference report to the Senate. He did not waste much time getting to the heart of the controversy: the nature of the proposed commission. In conference, Dill had won in his effort to make the commission independent and the supreme authority—other than the courts—over radio. But the Republicans had forced him to compromise. He agreed to limit the life of the independent commission to one year, during which it was believed most of radio's problems would be solved. At the end of that year, the commission would become an advisory body to the Secretary of Commerce (White's plan). In agreeing to this compromise, Dill was shrewd. Calvin Coolidge recognized, as did Dill, that once a commission is established in Washington, D.C., it almost never dies. Coolidge remarked to Dill in regard to radio legislation, "I think you bested him [White]."[30] Coolidge was correct; regulation of radio remained in the hands of the Federal Radio Commission (FRC) until the Federal Communications Commission (FCC) replaced it in 1934.[31]

But the radio bill was a long way from arriving on Coolidge's desk. Opposition to the Dill bill, especially from those fearing a private enterprise monopoly of radio, formed under the leadership of Senator Key Pittman of Nevada. Dill knew the Nevada Democrat was concerned with vested rights to the air accruing to private enterprise and with the possible rise of monopolies. In explaining his bill before the Senate, Dill addressed that issue before Pittman even had a chance to bring it up:

> No station license shall be granted by the commission or the Secretary of Commerce until the applicant thereof shall have signed a waiver of any claim to the use of any particular frequency or wavelength or of the

ether as against the regulatory power of the United States because of the previous use of the same, whether by license or otherwise.[32]

Now others opposed to the radio bill entered the fray. Senator Howell argued the language of the bill provided for private ownership of the ether with government regulation thereof—in short, the establishment of vested rights. Dill's response challenged Howell's interpretation, but left questions in the minds of many senators as to who owned the air. It is easy to see why:

> The government does not own the frequencies, as we call them, or the use of frequencies. It only possesses the right to regulate the apparatus, and that right is obtained from the provision of the Constitution which gives Congress the right to regulate interstate commerce.
>
> The conferees thought that it was better to have a waiver that was sufficiently clear in its terms to shut off any claim as against the power of the United States to control stations and have that waiver constitutional, than to hold to a waiver of doubtful constitutionality, which would probably be overturned by the courts, and we would have no waiver whatever in existence.[33]

Senator Norris, unafraid to admit confusion, asked Dill, "Does the senator concede the accuracy of the statement made by my colleague that under this conference bill vested rights could be acquired?" Dill replied emphatically, "I do not." To which Norris quite reasonably replied, "I wish the senator would make that plain." Dill proceeded to do so:

> We have three provisions, if I may summarize for the senior senator from Nebraska. We have the provision first that no license shall be construed to give the licensees any rights not given in the license. We have the provision that makes them sign a waiver that they do not claim any right to use the ether or any wavelength as against the regulatory power. We have a provision that the license must state on its face that the licensee secures no rights beyond the time for which the license is granted.[34]

Dill was attempting to explain that rights to the airwaves remained generally in private hands, but no specific individual or corporation owned those rights. The government bestowed them for a limited time on those who applied for a license according to law.

Senator Borah then pressed Dill as to the intent of the conferees. He asked whether or not it was the purpose of this bill to "deny the right to acquire a vested right in the ether." Dill responded, "That was the intent."[35]

Still, senators were not satisfied, and the discussion that ensued devoted the better part of the day to the issue of vested rights and related matters. Essentially, senators Robert Howell, Republican of Nebraska, Pittman, Norris, and several others wanted the language of the original Senate version of the bill restored. That language had clearly placed ownership of the airwaves in the United States government. However, it also appeared, at least to the conferees, to give the government confiscatory rights outside of due process should the licensee be found in violation of the agreement.[36] Howell and Thomas Heflin, Democrat of Alabama, now pressed Dill as to why restoration of the Senate's language was not possible. Dill responded that the conferees had dropped the Senate's original language "because we could not get it back in conference and we accepted language that means the same thing."[37] Dill argued that the right of ownership was essentially irrelevant as long as the government had the power to regulate and ownership did not fall to specific individuals or corporations. Other language in the bill guarded against the latter. It is also important to note the obstinance this issue engendered among the conservatives on the conference committee.

On the left, Senators Howell and Heflin, unsatisfied with Dill's defense of the bill, attempted to derail it by raising a point of order. They argued the clause of the conference report repealing the radio bill passed in December was not in the original House or Senate bill. Therefore, including that clause in the conference report exceeded the authority of the conferees. The same point of order arose in the House. Intense opposition to Dill's bill came from those fearing the creation of vested interests. But their numbers did not constitute a majority. The chairman of the Senate overruled the point of order. Howell protested on another similar point of order and was again overruled.[38]

The Senate then moved on to another aspect of possible radio monopoly: chain broadcasting. Dill believed his bill provided sufficient power, under the public interest clause, to prevent monopoly. In addition, section 4(h) of the radio bill instructed the commission to "make special regulations applicable to radio stations engaged in chain broadcasting."[39] However, it was not intended to eradicate chain broadcasters.[40] Senator Pittman now voiced his concerns, citing Representative Davis's chagrin with the form of the radio bill as it had come out of conference. Davis had been a supporter of Dill's original Senate version. Pittman resumed the attack on the legislation's weakness regarding ownership of the air. Moreover, he pleaded for more time to study the bill. Dill responded that the situation in radio did not allow for more time.[41]

Having attacked Dill's legislation on the monopoly issue, Pittman now assailed the bill on a sensitive point for Dill: the one-year limitation on the independent commission. Pittman forced Dill to admit that he preferred a permanent independent commission. But Dill responded that he could not get the White conferees to accept one, describing the opposition to a permanent independent commission as "strenuous."[42] Dill was a shrewd judge of political realities. He held out the hope that perhaps the Senate could get more of what it wanted in the future. Yet Pittman persisted. He argued there was no way the bill could be amended in the future, it had to be done right the first time, especially concerning the permanence of the commission. Senator Kenneth McKellar, a Tennessee Democrat, then asked a question that allowed Dill to explain his motivation in agreeing to the compromise: "I will put it in a different way. Is the Radio Corporation of America (RCA) satisfied with the bill?" Dill responded:

> The Radio Corporation, through its president, said it does not want any legislation on radio. I want to say, further, that if those who oppose the conference report have their way, the Radio Corporation of America will win because there would be no legislation.[43]

The discussion then rambled over lesser matters such as distribution of stations and new technology that might be used to force listeners to pay for broadcasts. Dill responded that the commissioners' instruction to regulate in the "public interest" would cover these problems.[44]

Pittman now raised the issue of equal access to radio by those campaigning for public office. He argued the Dill legislation would allow for one candidate to gain a distinct advantage over another. Dill did not agree: "Because under this bill, if they permit one candidate to use the facilities, they immediately become liable to give equal opportunity to the other candidate, and the commission would immediately protect the candidate who was discriminated against."[45]

Pittman's objection to the protection afforded political candidates in the conferees' radio bill no doubt stemmed from the fact that the original Senate bill would have made radio stations subject to common carrier status. The objection, however, to the common carrier provisions—which would have required radio stations to accept any political message as long as it was paid for—was so great the wording was withdrawn. Among those complaining about the common carrier provision were W.G. Cowles, vice president of broadcasting with Traveler's Insurance Company. Cowles argued the common carrier doctrine would create a situation in which there would be "no end to such broadcasts." He further argued that such a clause would require stations to broadcast the opinions of cranks and even Bolshevists. Cowles agreed airing opposing viewpoints was necessary, but asked that stations retain the right to refuse access to individuals. Senator Howell was not happy about Dill's capitulation to the right. He argued the new language raised the possibility radio might not adequately provide air time for public issues. Dill responded that Howell's solution would recreate the common carrier problem, and argued the Senate ought to pass the legislation and give it time to work.[46] Unimpressed, Pittman continued his harangue over potential discrimination between political candidates.

The discussion had been raging and wallowing for a week. The House had already passed the conference report. On February 7 the Senate again considered Dill's radio legislation. Pittman now tried to defeat the conference report by sending it back to the conferees with instructions to strengthen the language regarding vested rights.[47] He castigated the Dill bill as being a tool of RCA. Apparently Pittman was not listening when Dill explained the differences between the desires of RCA and the legislation before the Senate.

Democratic Senator Joseph Robinson of Arkansas now asked Dill what position he would be in among the conferees should the Senate vote to recommit the radio legislation. Dill responded, "It would put me in the position of going back and fighting for what I fought for before and failed to get." Pittman's motion to recommit the conferees' report lost, 48 to 29. Dill pressed for a vote adopting the conference report, but Senator Howell objected, and by prior arrangement, the Senate moved on to farm relief.[48]

The upper house resumed discussion of radio legislation the next day. Senator David Walsh, Democrat of Massachusetts, argued for passage of the bill as the lesser of two evils.[49] The day's further discussion of the bill did give Dill the opportunity to clarify the role of the commission after the first year expired:

> I cannot allow to pass unnoticed his [Walsh's] statement that after one year the commission becomes merely an appellate body. I do not believe that the terms of the bill justify that view. In the first place, the commission retains at all times the power of revocation of licenses. That is never transferred to the Secretary of Commerce. In many ways that is the most important power aside from the power of granting the licenses. The Secretary of Commerce has no power under the legislation, even after the first year, except as there is no objection on the part of anyone.[50]

Senators Pittman and Walsh then lamented the fact Dill had been unable to gain from the House conferees a permanent commission. Dill responded, revealing his strategy all along, with the hope the work of the commission would be so intricate as to require meeting indefinitely.[51]

Pittman and his associates would not give up. The Nevada senator raised a point of order similar to the one previously defeated, but the chair rebuked him. Undaunted, he appealed the decision and lost again. He now considered organizing a filibuster but ultimately thought better of it.[52]

On February 18, 1927, the radio bill came before the Senate one more time. Nothing Dill said in the preceding weeks had changed Pittman's mind, and the Nevadan had been successful in drawing away some of Dill's supporters. Nearly all of the progressive senators now opposed the conferees' report. Aware a vote was imminent, Pittman took one last opportunity to attack the bill, reeling off a long list of objections. Finally, Dill broke in, seeking to correct misstatements and stating the whole purpose of the bill was to provide a public service. Pittman briefly lost his composure, responding, "Mr. President, that statement from the senator of Washington would be as absurd as this bill if the bill were not tragic."[53] Then, as if sorry for his outburst, he complimented Dill for his honesty and seriousness in championing his bill.[54]

Dill listened patiently to the various senators repeat their arguments as to why they opposed his legislation; he even had to listen to a few supporters deride the bill. Senator Royal Copeland of New York (D), who intended to vote for the conferees report, lamented its shortcomings and had wanted to delay it to improve it. Finally, Dill rose in his own defense and argued that the bill, though not perfect, was good legislation.[55]

Senator Coleman Blease, a Democrat from South Carolina, was the last to speak and in so doing suggested a concern that no doubt occupied the minds of a number of his colleagues:

> Personally, I do not want it. I do not want to talk to anybody I cannot see. If I talk to an audience, I want to look at them and I want them to see me....I do not want a machine fixed here [broadcasting the proceedings of the Senate was under consideration as well] for the purposes of a select few, and that is all that this bill means.[56]

Senator Blease's comments aptly demonstrate the conflict between past and present very much involved in this legislation. There were, of course, the old issues of private property versus public interest and they were dominant. However, many senators' concerns with the old familiar issues were exacerbated by their unfamiliarity with radio and their apprehension for what radio meant to the future. Regardless of the emotions prevalent within the chamber, it was clearly time to vote. The bill passed.[57]

Dill believed the Senate had passed "reasonably safe legislation" that would provide the nation a "basic law to meet the present situation." He emphasized that the law withheld ownership of the ether from private interests and placed control of radio in a bipartisan commission. Dill admitted the legislation was not perfect and would require amending as developments in broadcasting warranted. And he well knew the crucial role the commission would play in developing broadcasting: "In case the commission finds an applicant for a license or for the renewal of a license is guilty of practicing against the public interests the license may be refused. In other words, the success of the bill depends upon the devotion of the members of the commission to the public interest."[58]

The 1927 Radio Act created the Federal Radio Commission with the purpose of establishing regulations to prevent interference (static), assigning frequencies and wattage, determining the class of stations (national, regional, local), establishing, in a broad manner, the nature of programming that stations provided to the public, and creating regulations for chain broadcasters if needed.[59]

Dill's warning about the composition and philosophy of the commission was prophetic. President Coolidge appointed three Republicans, Rear Admiral William Bullard, Orestes H. Caldwell, and John F. Dillon, and two Democrats, Henry A. Bellows and Eugene O. Sykes. Dill opposed the nominations of Caldwell, Dillon, and Bellows, believing they were devoted to the interests of business. His opposition was fruitless. Coolidge had his way and created a commission that favored the interests of private enterprise, much as the Interstate Commerce Commission did after the Coolidge appointees altered the nature of that board in 1925.[60] On this issue Coolidge bested Dill.

Conservatives in the House denied the commission adequate funding.[61] It was not long before Dill and his allies in the House sought suitable legislation to address some of the decisions of the commissioners, especially geographical distribution of stations.[62] Clarence Dill was not through with radio; it would occupy a considerable amount of his time well into the future.[63]

As a result of his work on radio, Dill rose substantially in the eyes of his colleagues. Radio's technical aspects caused many senators to defer to his acknowledged expertise. Moreover, he received notoriety in the press. Radio interested nearly everyone, as did radio legislation. Dill's name appeared in the headlines often. For a first-term senator, he had made significant contributions to the country. He had also contributed to his state in a very unique manner for "the radio as much as anything drew Washington into the heart of national life."[64] Clarence Dill's work on radio legislation contributed to the unifying of the country, the linking of the East with the growing West, in a very meaningful way. The work he had done was also symbolic of the man: he had chosen "middle ground," a path between the two extremes of free enterprise or government ownership; and he had contributed to the building of a lasting institution.

CHAPTER SEVEN

TARIFFS AND TROUBLE

WITH THE BATTLE for the Radio Bill of 1927 behind him, Clarence Dill turned his attention to another possibility, the affections of Rosalie Jones, and a problem, how to secure reelection in 1928. As it turned out Rosalie substantially aided Clarence with the challenge of reelection, but the campaign forced the senator to make a promise he could not keep.

In March of 1927, shortly after his radio legislation became law, Dill married Rosalie Gardner Jones of Long Island, New York. The senator first met his future wife in 1924 when she came to Washington, D.C., for a Jane Addams peace conference. In recalling this first meeting Rosalie said, "The women wanted to ask him some important questions....He answered evasively and I raked him over the coals." Dill's obfuscations made her increasingly angry until she finally left his office in a huff, before they had even been introduced. Apparently, however, he was as smitten with the New York fireball as she was with him. They both later described their emotions as "love at first sight." For two weeks, Dill prodded his secretary to discover the identity of the "lady in pink." The secretary's quest met with success, and Dill received encouragement when Rosalie wrote him a note congratulating him on his role in the fight to save Muscle Shoals from private development. In the note, she identified herself as a fellow progressive. It was not long before friends arranged to have the two formally introduced.[1]

Rosalie Jones was a formidable woman. A native of Cold Spring Harbor, New York, she earned the nickname General Rosalie in 1913 when she led a group of women suffragists, known as the Army of the Hudson, on a march to Albany, New York. In Albany the marchers presented a petition to Governor-elect William Sulzer to remind him of his pledge to support their cause.[2]

Not content with campaigning for woman suffrage in its home state, the army determined to march on Washington, D.C., to confront Woodrow Wilson. The president had made himself odious to the suffragists through his refusal to pursue suffrage at the national level. As a true son of Virginia, he believed the states should decide the issue. General Rosalie and her troops hoped to persuade Wilson. It took years, but the president eventually supported national woman suffrage in 1916 and pushed for the Nineteenth Amendment, which eventually became law in 1920.[3]

Rosalie's feminism went beyond marches and upbraiding presidents. After the march on Washington, D.C., she worked one summer as an apprentice auto mechanic in a Chevrolet dealership. She spent her spare time touring New York in a yellow Chevrolet, provided by the dealership, drumming up support for woman's suffrage.[4]

In addition to being forceful and determined, she was intelligent and highly educated. She studied at New York and Columbia universities and eventually earned five degrees. Among them were a law degree—she was a member of the New York bar—and a Ph.D., which she received at George Washington University. In 1922 she published a book on the legal status of women.[5]

Rosalie's strength of mind and accomplishments probably sent most men running; however, she had one other quality, besides her vivacious good looks, which brought them to her door: money. Her father, Dr. Oliver Jones, had invested heavily in real estate in New York and in other states. When he died, he left his wife Mary most of the money. When Mary died in 1918, the estate amounted to more than $5 million. Rosalie Jones managed the estate herself, including the real estate holdings, even after her marriage to Clarence Dill.[6]

Politically, Rosalie found herself attracted to socialism and had voted the socialist ticket on two occasions, but in the 1920s, her politics moved toward progressivism and the Democratic Party.[7]

Clarence Dill and Rosalie Jones were married in Cold Spring Harbor, New York, on March 15, 1927, in the St. John's Episcopal Church, which her family had built about 1830. There were no invitations extended, but workers on the estates in the vicinity, friends in the area, even the postman, combined with a number of New York's high society—including a former Secretary of the Navy and a former governor of New York—overflowed the church. Rosalie refused to be "given away," and her vows reflected both her feminism and her temperament—the word *obey* was dropped. After the wedding, the guests took a special train to the Gotham Hotel in New York where the new couple received congratulations.[8]

The wedding received extensive coverage from the *New York Times* primarily because of the social status of the bride. But Clarence Dill was no longer an obscure politician from somewhere out west.[9] His work on radio legislation had placed his name in the newspapers often. His marriage to Rosalie did nothing but help his public image. Still, it would not be fair to Dill to suggest he didn't love his new wife; by all accounts he did. But neither should it come as a surprise that the woman he chose to love was capable of helping his career in a number of ways.

The Dills had been married but three days when Rosalie decided to help her husband financially. She proposed to give him one thousand dollars per month to help cover their household expenses. He agreed but asked that she deposit the money directly into their bank so that his name would never appear on the checks. Clarence was self-conscious about taking money from his wife. As it turned out Rosalie contributed much more than the thousand dollars per month; she often paid bills stemming from her husband's political activities.[10]

With his new wife at his side, Clarence Dill turned his attention in 1928 to securing reelection in what turned out to be one of the closest and most interesting contests in Washington's political history. Ironically, but not surprisingly, his relationship with his own party would prove to be one of the obstacles to victory, while his ability to appeal to progressive Republicans would prove to be a source of strength. In addition, he took advantage of a traditionally Republican issue: the tariff.

The first major political event of 1928 was the state convention held in Spokane in April. Washington's Democratic Party had coalesced behind Al Smith for the presidential nomination before the convention even met, making Dill an outsider. The senator supported Smith's economic program but differed with the New Yorker over prohibition. Dill believed prohibition would play a major role in the 1928 campaign, if for no other reason than that Smith's anti-prohibition stand would make it an issue. In spite of its commitment to Smith, the state convention—in deference to his stature as a United States senator—made Dill a delegate to the Democratic National Convention in Houston with a half vote.[11]

But two developments now distanced Dill from both the national and state Democratic Party. First, the Democrats at the Houston convention chose Al Smith as the party's champion; second, Washington State's Democrats nominated Scott Bullitt, a well-known wet, as candidate for governor. Dill knew his state well; Washingtonians liked prohibition. To campaign as a wet Democrat was to commit political suicide. Dill decided to let the Smith-Bullitt forces have the state Democratic Party; he regarded it as of little consequence anyway.[12]

Dill kicked off his reelection campaign in the Spokane-area town of Hillyard. Even in the primary, Dill designed his campaign more to defeat a

Republican challenger rather than to defeat any Democrat foolish enough to run against him.[13]

Early in the race he made clear his stance on prohibition and progressive issues:

> As to Governor Smith, I desire to say that I am opposed to his stand on the Volstead law, and if re-elected shall do everything in my power as a senator to prevent modification of that law, except to make it more stringent....What this country needs most is honest and lawful enforcement of the Prohibition law....
>
> I was a progressive before I was elected to the senate. I have been a progressive on every fight and on every roll call since I went to the senate, and I shall be a progressive if I am reelected. In every contest between the rights of property and the rights of humanity, I am on the side of humanity.[14]

Dill was well aware that Smith's wet views would define the presidential campaign in Washington State, which had grown more dry as the decade passed. Thus Dill could not afford to repeat his 1922 prohibition strategy. He had to separate himself from Al Smith's wet stance and hope his Republican opponent was as dry as he was, thus relegating prohibition to the back burner. Consequently, Dill made unequivocally clear his opposition to any weakening of prohibition.

Other issues also required a carefully chosen position. Dill wanted to identify himself solidly with farm relief and did so more successfully than the provincialist from New York. He also sought to make an issue out of public power and supported Smith in that debate. Though these were the primary issues on which he campaigned, the Democrat had not forgotten labor; he supported a bill, as did Smith, "to prevent the arbitrary use of court injunctions on labor disputes."[15]

Dill easily won renomination in the primary, and Judge Kenneth McKintosh defeated Miles Poindexter in the Republican primary.[16] This time the race was a straight-forward battle between two candidates; Dill's record had eliminated the need for third parties to run a more liberal or progressive candidate.

Washington's lumber industry became a political issue in the 1928 campaign. The decade had not been as kind to lumber entrepreneurs as it had been to business in general. Entering the 1920s, Pacific Northwest lumbermen hoped good times would continue, and were optimistic that shipments to the East would increase. New technology for pulp made paper production a cornerstone of the Pacific Northwest economy in the twenties. Plywood also supported several mills, and exports to Japan helped

offset losses in other markets. But there were so many new mills in operation that even with the foregoing development, times were tough in the
lumber business. The revival of southern pine producers, combined with
slumping post-war demand, squeezed the market. [17]

Overproduction hurt most. In spite of lower demand through the
twenties, Washington's mills poured out seven billion board feet per year.
Prices fell accordingly. Douglas fir plummeted from $27.26 per thousand
feet in 1923 to $19.39 in 1928. Prominent lumberman George Long "com-
pared the industry to 'a large army in disorganized retreat.'"[18] Indeed the
retreat had begun as early as 1925. In an effort to control prices, some mill
and logging companies attempted mergers and many discussed allocating
production among various producers. But unified action was blocked by
long-standing disagreements between independent-minded lumbermen,
combined with the fear of anti-trust problems from such price-fixing.
Consequently, lumbermen—who as a group were extremely powerful in
Washington politics—demanded a protective tariff on lumber and
shingles.[19]

Dill had established a solid record in the Senate on issues that were of
concern to lumbermen. He favored Washington's timber interests on everything from control of pine blister rust to revising the tariff on shingles.[20]
Dill explained his position on tariffs in general and the shingle tariff in
particular on the floor of the Senate:

> I do not believe in absolute free trade. Nor am I one of those who
> believe that simply because some industry wants tariff protection it
> should be granted such protection. I believe that if the tariff commis-
> sion does its work as it was intended it should do, and Congress would
> follow its recommendations, we would then evolve a tariff which would
> equal the difference between the cost of production at home and the
> cost of production abroad. That should be our policy....
> We formerly had a great shingle industry in the state of Wash-
> ington....Previous to the enactment of the last tariff law there was no
> tariff on either logs or shingles. Since the adoption of the discrimina-
> tory tariff on logs and the failure to place a tariff on shingles, 131 shingle
> mills in the state of Washington have been forced out of business, and
> approximately one-half of the shingle business has been destroyed, due
> to the discriminatory tariff against our own business.[21]

During the debate on the shingle tariff, Dill cast three votes in support of tariff increases and argued strongly for Washington's interests. In so
doing, he advocated a 25 percent *ad valorem* tariff on shingles. His progressive friend, George Norris, opposed Dill on the tariff issue; both men
were watching over the interests of their states.[22]

Despite their differences over the shingle tariff, Norris visited Washington in early October to campaign for his friend. The *Seattle Times* had a laugh at the expense of the two progressives, calling them "mavericks," which was certainly true, but adding they were "useless to their states, the nation, or any party."[23]

In the campaign, Dill claimed he could deliver sixteen Democratic Senate votes on the tariff issue. The claim did not go unnoticed. Mark Reed, perhaps the most powerful of Washington's lumbermen, knew he had Senator Wesley Jones to deliver the Republican votes so he decided to gamble: he crossed party lines and openly supported Dill for the Senate, much to McKintosh's consternation.[24]

Dill emphasized the relative lack of importance of political party designation in the Senate race of 1928. He knew his only hope of winning lay in convincing voters that the tariff issue crossed party lines in Washington State. He urged voters to cast their ballots based on other issues, especially public power and farm relief. Always, he expressed his strong support for prohibition. In addition, Dill attacked McKintosh for his campaign expenditures in the primary, thus cleverly associating McKintosh with Newberryism. The judge faced an accomplished opponent.[25]

In Tacoma, a Dill stronghold, Dill opened his campaign for Pierce County by having Judge Blanche Miller introduce him. The senator had not forgotten the important role women had played in all of his campaigns. If he were to win again, he would need every woman's vote he could muster; with Rosalie at his side, he made a concerted effort to gain the female vote.

The first statewide poll of the campaign showed him trailing McKintosh by a two-to-one margin, about the same margin pollsters gave Hoover over Smith.[26] Conservative southwest Washington particularly concerned Dill. The timber industry dominated the region, and Dill had not done well there in 1922. Rosalie observed the strain the campaign placed on her normally cheerful husband and asked what more she could do to help. Dill suggested she go to southwest Washington and campaign for him there. In later years, Dill gave Rosalie credit for helping him substantially in the 1928 campaign.[27]

Dill trailed early perhaps because he had taken some scoring punches from Floyd Danskin, former speaker of the Washington House of Representatives. Campaigning for McKintosh, Danskin argued that Dill's claim of being able to deliver Democratic votes on the tariff issue was spurious. How could Dill, a man who had gone out of his way to alienate himself from the Democratic Party, deliver that party's votes, Danskin asked.

Moreover, he described—not always accurately—Dill's defection from the Democrats. Danskin especially harped on Dill's lukewarm support of Al Smith. The *Seattle Times* also repeatedly brought up the irony in Dill's promise to deliver Democrats on the tariff issue.[28]

But Dill refused to alter his campaign to please Danskin or the editors of the *Times*. In Tacoma, Dill returned to his theme, "This is the day of the independent in politics so far as the state of Washington is concerned."[29] McKintosh set himself apart from Dill in terms of party loyalty and said he was "for the party, down the line," and lashed out at his opponent as a "nondescript senator, running as an independent."[30]

Dill did run as an independent; the split with Bullitt and Smith was deep and nearly irreconcilable. But he was running as the more progressive candidate in a state with a history of progressivism and beset with economic troubles in its two major industries: farming and lumber. Nevertheless, the *Times* and *Everett Daily Herald* boldly predicted, based on a survey of the state, Dill's imminent return to private life.[31]

Dill never let the voters forget his bone-dry position on prohibition. He expounded on the subject at length, identifying himself with the strict Washington state law—as opposed to the more lax Volstead Act. Moreover, he advocated greater prohibition enforcement efforts as the correct response to the liquor law's critics who argued it was a failure. By mid-October Dill had been touring the state by automobile speaking in the small and large towns along the way, yet still trailed in the polls two-to-one.[32]

The editors at the *Seattle Times*, however, still feared him. They believed Dill's strident harping on prohibition necessitated a reminder to the public of McKintosh's efforts, as prosecuting attorney of King County, to close down road-houses twenty years earlier.[33] Prohibition was definitely at the fore of the campaign, but it could not be the deciding issue. Both candidates were dry. In banging the drum for prohibition, Dill ran not against Kenneth McKintosh, but against Al Smith, hoping to sway dry voters prone to vote a straight ticket.

Fortunately, Dill did not have to worry about his staunch position on prohibition siphoning off labor support. Indeed, the Democrat hoped to obtain 90 percent of Duncan's 1922 farmer-labor vote. There was no third party candidate to turn to and labor despised McKintosh. The Railway Clerks endorsed Dill in mid-October, arguing, "Our organization wants men in Congress who are known to be favorable to labor. When we get them, we do not intend to take a chance at losing them." Other railway brotherhoods and the Washington State AFL also endorsed Dill. *The Labor Journal* urged all union members to spare no effort in electing Dill.[34]

McKintosh sought to define the election in terms of the tariff on lumber and shingles. The *Spokesman-Review* caught the tenor of McKintosh's campaign:

> Judge McKintosh, whose speech was applauded, said that the most important issue for the whole country and for this state is the protective tariff. The destructive effect of the Democratic protective tariff, for which his opponent stands, would allow foreign eggs and dairy products to undersell the products of the Colville Valley.[35]

The *Seattle P.I.* came to Dill's aid, as it had in 1922, with an editorial headlined "The Straight Voter Doesn't Use His Head." The Republicans were well aware of Dill's ability to steal the progressive wing of their party. Consequently, they spent a great deal of time advocating a straight party vote. With Hoover, an extremely attractive candidate with at least modest progressive credentials at the head of the ticket, it was a compelling argument. The *P.I.* countered with the claim that the nation, and the state, needed the best of both parties.[36]

By late October everyone knew the state was solidly in the Hoover camp; the question was whether Dill could rip McKintosh from the presidential coattails.[37] The fact that Hoover and McKintosh were friends, having attended Stanford together, made Dill's task more difficult. McKintosh did not fail to let his friendship with Hoover slip to the press. In mid-October Hoover sent McKintosh a telegram of support; the tariff was the first issue Hoover mentioned.[38]

Dill preferred to speak on the issue of public power, but McKintosh kept attacking his opponent on the tariff issue, forcing him to respond. In Spokane, Dill hit on his favorite theme and reminded voters how his work on radio had kept private individuals from establishing a vested interest in the airwaves.[39] But as he wrapped up his campaign in King County, McKintosh's home, Dill felt constrained to respond to the judge's tariff-centered campaign. McKintosh appeared to be winning the contest over who would define the Senate election. Moreover, he was scoring points whenever Dill did respond. Days before the election, Dill felt he had possibly overdone his independent theme, and he agreed to speak at a Smith rally at the Metropolitan Theater. In his speech, he returned to attacking the private power trust and stressed the importance of having a Democratic senator to line up Senate Democrats on issues of concern to Washington. The *Seattle Times* did not buy Dill's argument for a minute: "the people of this state will realize that one who can't line himself up is hardly to be trusted with the task of lining up others."[40]

As the election neared, Dill shifted into an exhausting last days' sprint. Combining public appearances with radio addresses, he fought from behind, as he had the entire campaign, but now with renewed energy. Polls showed him closing in on McKintosh but still substantially behind.[41] On the Saturday before the election, Dill lambasted McKintosh for attempting to ride the coattails of an old college pal into the Senate and insisted McKintosh's only success as a senator would be in supplying a few patronage jobs to friends. The senator then addressed the needs of the people of the state: "I am not interested in jobs for a few friends, but I want to see the half million workers of the state employed at good wages and if we can get a tariff on shingles, cement, farm products, and foreign goods that compete with us there will be more jobs, more prosperity for everyone."[42]

McKintosh was certainly not resting, but in the last week of the campaign Dill outworked him.[43] The senator also received some much needed help and encouraging news just before the election. The *Seattle P.I.* once again came to Dill's aid, urging the voters to split their tickets. In addition, Senator Thomas Walsh of Montana (D) came to the state to remind voters of the Republican's Teapot Dome fiasco, and appeal for Republican crossover votes. On the eve of the election, bettors considered Dill to be closer to McKintosh than he had been at any time in the campaign. Indeed, a sampling of the state's voters recorded a late surge for the incumbent, putting him ahead of McKintosh for the first time.[44]

As the climax of the campaign approached, Dill took the time to mend fences with Bullitt, endorsing him strongly and campaigning for him on the night before the election. It was not enough to save Bullitt; incumbent governor Roland H. Hartley defeated him soundly, while Hoover routed Al Smith. Dill, however, clung to life, trailing McKintosh by only 1,020 votes late on election day.[45] Overnight, however, Dill surged into the lead and stayed there. The *Seattle Times* bitterly reported, "On the face of the returns the voters of the state of Washington in yesterday's election gave Herbert Hoover a stupendous majority of 120,000 or more. But they perversely withheld the support he asked by not sending a solid Republican delegation to Congress."[46]

Dill's victory came in the midst of the largest "perverse" voter turnout Washington had ever seen. Moreover, the *Everett Daily Herald*, which had enthusiastically supported McKintosh, called the Dill-McKintosh race "one of the [most] thrilling political races in Washington in years."[47] Indeed it was.

Clarence credited his win to labor and women:

> I can never fully repay the people of the state for the confidence they
> have shown in me by the large independent vote they cast for me on

Tuesday. I am especially indebted to the organizations of laboring men throughout the state and to the Capital Conference for Progressive Political Action in Spokane County for the work they did in my behalf. Mrs. Dill and the women who cooperated throughout the state did invaluable services.[48]

Dill was no doubt correct in thanking both labor and women. But the 1928 Senate election was replete with issues that affected the outcome. Many Washingtonians saw Dill as a sincere dry candidate and as someone determined to improve the lot of farmers, hence his strength in rural agricultural counties. He virtually swept rural eastern Washington. Of course, hailing from that side of the state did not hurt him there. In fact, it was probably the biggest reason he pulled a 16,000 vote majority in Spokane County.[49]

As the labor candidate, Dill did well in the urban areas on the west side of the mountains. His home base in the west, Tacoma, gave him a 10,000 vote majority. King County, McKintosh's home, though it went for its favorite son, provided him only a 5,000 vote cushion. King County, then, was a key to the election since it did not offset Dill's Tacoma majority.

A look at a few rural western Washington counties will clarify what happened in King County. Lewis County has historically been one of the most conservative counties in the state. The lumber industry formed the heart of its economy. In the 1928 Senate election, Lewis County went for Dill 7,011 to 5,729. In 1922 Lewis County went for Miles Poindexter over Dill 3,641 to 2,786. Nor was such a switch unusual in conservative rural western Washington lumber counties. In Kitsap County, Dill lost by more than 400 votes in 1922; in 1928 he won by nearly 1,500. In Gray's Harbor County, Poindexter smashed Dill by 1,800 votes; in 1928 Dill upset McKintosh by 700 votes. In Mark Reed's Mason County, Dill narrowly lost in 1922; in 1928 he pulled a majority of more than 440 votes.[50] Other counties were similar. Clearly Dill had persuaded the voters in these lumber counties that he was the candidate who could do the most to deliver a protective tariff and thus ease their economic burdens.

The tariff issue determined the outcome of the 1928 Senate race in Washington. Of course there were other factors: the emotional presidential race combined with a gubernatorial race and a Senate race that featured startlingly different candidates brought out a record vote. Large voter turnout almost always favors the candidate identified with the concerns of the common man, in this case Dill. But there had to be a reason that many Republicans crossed over to vote for Clarence Dill.

McKintosh had forced Dill to respond to the tariff issue, but the Democrat had handled it to the satisfaction of most of Washington's voters, as the returns from Washington's lumber counties so clearly show. The issue that cost McKintosh the election, the issue that affected the vote in the urban counties of Pierce and King (still heavily dependent on timber industries), was the lumber-shingle-log tariff, and the anemic condition of the timber industry in Washington.[51] Dill successfully captured McKintosh's issue of choice and campaigned as a man who could help the state on the tariff issue while appealing to farmers.

The publishers of the Republican newspapers of the day realized the importance of the tariff issue to the Senate race. Hence their non-stop efforts to portray Dill as a man without a party—unable to deliver Democrats on the tariff issue as promised. Rank and file Republicans, however, paid little attention to the *Seattle Times* and *Spokesman-Review*. They dutifully cast their ballots for Hoover then betrayed their party by the thousands for Dill.

Other factors influenced the election. Dill lost only twelve counties, all of which were notable for their coolness toward reform. Some of them were also conspicuous for a lack of interest in timber, such as Yakima and Walla Walla counties.[52]

Prohibition had only a marginal impact on the campaign as both candidates were dry. Allowing that some voters cast their ballots for Dill because they were more secure with his record on prohibition than McKintosh's, it remains unlikely such a factor would explain a swing in diehard Republican counties. Nor would it seem to be a plausible explanation for Dill's astounding strength in urban counties. Prohibition, along with religion (Smith was the first Catholic ever nominated for president by a major party), helped to turn out the vote in the presidential race, but it had only a minimal effect on the Senate race. Hoover defeated Smith by more than two-to-one in Washington State, validating Dill's strategy of divorcing himself from the New Yorker. Approximately 100,000 people who voted for Hoover did not vote for McKintosh. Given McKintosh's record as a prohibitionist, it is not conceivable that prohibition caused such a great number of people to cross over.

The poor economy of Washington State was the fundamental issue that made the lumber tariff and farm relief such compelling factors in the 1928 Senate election. Washington's lumbermen were so desperate for a good sign in the late 1920s that when the stock market crashed in October 1929, newspapers speculated that the disillusion with stocks that was sure to follow might cause people to put their money in more solid investments such as buildings and homes, thus helping the lumber business. Farmers were just as desperate. The price of wheat was on a downward slide in the twenties. It fell from $1.83 a bushel in 1920 to sixty-seven cents by the end of 1929. As Robert Ficken and Charles LeWarne note in their history of Washington, "Farmers, pressed to the wall before the stock market crash, were pulverized in its aftermath."[53]

The lumber tariff was of prime importance in the western portion of the state; farm relief appealed to the largely agricultural east side. Dill's remarkable accomplishment was that he managed to appeal to both, thus uniting the eastern and western portions of a state noted for its division along such lines. He successfully convinced many voters, as he had Mark Reed, that the Republican Party needed help passing a tariff that would truly benefit Washington State. The argument was plausible: Republicans had failed to deliver an adequate lumber tariff for eight years. Washingtonians were tired of waiting.

Clarence Dill went back to the Senate determined to do something to help the nation's farmers. President Hoover, too, had made this promise in his campaign and to that end called a special session of Congress in April 1929. The president proposed that farmers form marketing organizations and that government create a farm board to supervise the distribution of public funds advanced to those organizations. Dill proposed that the president approve the export debenture plan, which would have, in effect, required the U.S. government to pick up the difference between the world market price of a commodity and the protected price paid in the United States. Senator Norris, no enemy of farm legislation, remarked that no one's plan addressed the root of the country's farm problem: over-production.[54] Unfortunately the plan signed into law in June 1929 did not address the farm surplus either. Just before the vote, Dill rose to assess the work of the Senate on farm relief:

> After nine years controversy the Congress of the United States is about to pass a farm bill that will probably become a law. It is not a bill such as the majority of the Congress believe will really bring the results the farmers are entitled to have. It does not meet the desires of a majority of the Congress. The bill is in its present form because it is the only kind of a bill the majority of the Congress believe the President of the United States will sign.
>
> The Senate has abandoned the provisions that were designed to control the surplus at the expense of those who create the surplus [McNary-Haugen]. I believe that a majority of the Senate are still of the same opinion they entertained when they voted for bills containing such provisions in past sessions of the Congress. That matter having

been eliminated, the Senate proposed the Debenture plan to assist in giving the farmer a part of the tariff that is provided on farm products. That has been dropped, not because a majority of the Senate believe it is not desirable, but because the House and the Senate members believe the President would not sign a bill with such a provision in it.[55]

The debenture plan Dill proposed would not have addressed the farm surplus except to require the American people as a whole to pick up the tab. Under the debenture plan there would have been no motivation for the farmer to curtail production, but significant incentive for him to grow as much as possible, thus exacerbating the problem. The only solution lay in either allowing the market to force a significant number of farmers out of business, thus reducing supply and practically ensuring recession, or legislating that government restrict production with draconian thoroughness. The latter was not an option, given the cherished beliefs of most Americans in 1929. In the end, Dill voted for the president's plan, as did Norris, in the belief some form of farm legislation was better than nothing.[56]

Hoover's farm relief program did not solve the nation's agricultural problems, and Clarence Dill continued to advocate the debenture plan as the nation descended ever deeper into the abyss of the Depression. Neither man's solution would have altered that unhappy event.

Farm relief was irrevocably tied to the tariff question. Senators like Dill argued it was essentially unfair to protect one portion of the country at the expense of another.[57] The farm belt labored under the tariff of 1922; having lost the fight to pass strong farm legislation, senators from agricultural states tried to reduce tariff duties on other products to benefit their people on that end of the equation. Dill now faced a dilemma: he had promised his constituents in Washington to support increased tariffs on shingles, but his political allies and ideological brothers in the Senate were determined to lower the tariff. Senator Norris, one of those so determined, recognized Dill's quandary. The Nebraskan realized several of his friends "would have to go along the selfish route in order to maintain themselves in Congress."[58]

In the tariff fight, Dill argued persuasively in support of Wesley Jones, Washington's Republican senior senator, that the Wilson tariff of 1913 had devastated Washington's shingle industry. He also argued for the tariff on conservation grounds. Since the normal logging method of the era was to clear-cut, cedar, if not used for shingles, remained on the ground—wasted. In addition, Dill skillfully met New York Democratic Senator Royal Copeland's argument about shingle quality. Copeland argued the reason Canadian shingles sold better than American shingles was because of their superior quality. Dill's rejoinder emphasized the economic advantage Canadian manufacturers possessed because of their use of cheap Asian labor—an option not open to American mills. Consequently, American mills produced lower-grade shingles because the expense of producing high-grade shingles simply made them noncompetitive, hence the need for a tariff.[59]

Dill also took on Senator Gerald Nye, a North Dakota Republican. Nye argued that Pacific Northwest shingle mills were the victims of their own log suppliers and when not the victim of suppliers, were partners of the same. Dill demonstrated that though other aspects of the lumber business were still profitable in Washington, the shingle mills were being run out of business. His effort on the part of the shingle tariff demonstrated a thorough knowledge of the issue and its importance to Washington State.[60]

Differing economic interests split the timber, lumber, and shingle businessmen of Washington State and had an impact on the tariff fight in the Senate. Dill was not interested in securing a tariff on logs, a tariff that could only harm the shingle manufacturer who depended upon imported Canadian logs. Nor was he in favor of a tariff on lumber, realizing this would drive a wedge between him and his progressive colleagues in the Senate who desired cheap lumber for their constituents. Thus, he was opposed to the Reed strategy, so ably explained in Robert Ficken's *Lumber and Politics: The Career of Mark E. Reed*.

Reed, fearing the weakness of his position in the Senate, opposed a record vote on any aspect of the timber tariff. He preferred the senators go to the conference committee free to compromise. This strategy meant the sacrificing of any tariff on softwood but placed the remaining timber tariff issues largely in the friendlier hands of the House. However, Dill, who was against all timber tariffs except for that on shingles, and perhaps somewhat anxious to defeat the tariff on logs and lumber to appease his progressive friends, called for a record vote in the Senate on the shingle tariff, gambling he could win on that issue and that a negative vote on the other timber items might ensue as well.[61] In this strategy, he had the support of the lumbermen's chief lobbyist, a man by the name of Condon. Unfortunately, the Condon-Dill strategy failed miserably and the shingle tariff lost 49 to 29.[62] As the *Seattle Times* had warned, Dill could not deliver on his campaign promise. The vote on the log tariff Reed feared now ensued. It was defeated. There was, however, some small consolation for Washington's lumber industry. The final tariff bill included a duty on lumber of one dollar per thousand feet. Dill, leery of his political position in the Senate and at home, agreed to vote for the tariff if his vote was necessary to pass the bill. It was not. The tariff passed the Senate 44 to 42, Dill voting in the negative with many of his progressive friends. Unable to secure the promised rate on shingles, Dill did not want to return home having voted for a tariff that raised the price of a wide assortment of goods necessary to the well-being of most of his constituents.

Dill's marriage to Rosalie Jones was a happy one in the late twenties; and her wealth greatly alleviated the financial burdens that a senator, especially one in the midst of a campaign, faces. Still, he had barely won against the conservative McKintosh and in the effort, had made a promise regarding a shingle tariff that he had not been able to keep. But Dill moved beyond his failures and misfortunes to look for new challenges, new ways to serve the people of Washington, and in the process, demonstrate the indispensability of C.C. Dill. He did not have to look far to find that challenge; it had been flowing through his adopted state for unknown millennia and had watered the imaginations of dusty farmers for two generations.

Riding along Fourth Ave., Seattle, during the 1932 presidential campaign. Left to right, Governor Roosevelt, Mayor Dore, and Senator Dill. *#L93-66.98, Cheney Cowles Museum/ Eastern Washington State Historical Society, Spokane, WA*

CHAPTER EIGHT

ELECTION OF A GRAND COULEE MAN

HAVING FAILED TO BRING a protective tariff to the shingle industry of Washington, Clarence Dill sought to demonstrate his worth to Washingtonians. He soon found a project that met that need and fit his political and social philosophy. Dill decided to support the Grand Coulee Dam project on the Columbia River. The people of central Washington hoped to build Grand Coulee as an electrical power and irrigation project that would bring increased prosperity to the eastern portion of the state. Dill also knew it would be a monument to those who built it and to their western builder mentality. As it turned out, Grand Coulee Dam became the capstone of Dill's Senate career.

The vast majority of lands in central and eastern Washington are extremely arid. The idea of using the waters of the Columbia to irrigate those lands probably originated in the mind of the first farmer to look upon the region. But the great river's bed lies well below the parched and windswept plateau. Just south of the Columbia, in the north central end of the potential agricultural lands, lies the Grand Coulee, a huge dry river bed. Thousands of years ago a glacier blocked the flow of the Columbia forcing it to find a different path. When the glacier withdrew, the turbulent waters escaped into the original lower channel leaving the Coulee dry.

The idea of building two dams, one at the southern end of the Coulee to form a reservoir, the other on the Columbia near the Coulee's mouth to raise the level of the river as the glacier had done long ago, then filling the Coulee with the Columbia's treasured water, had been around for some time.[1]

In 1918 William Clapp, an Ephrata attorney, suggested to Rufus Woods, the publisher of the *Wenatchee Daily World*, that the Columbia be dammed. Woods published Clapp's idea and became a key supporter of the project until it became reality.[2] In the 1920s, two rival plans—the gravity plan and the pumping plan—competed for the support of both governments and people. Spokane in general, and private power interests in particular, supported the gravity plan because it would have brought water from Idaho past Spokane's front door without creating new, and potentially public, hydroelectric power.[3] Central Washingtonians boosted the pumping plan, which featured a 500-foot dam on the Columbia and a powerful pumping system with which to fill the Coulee. This group was not averse to the public power potential of the dam; neither were they concerned with the barbs of the Spokane interests who accused them of being "a little band of land speculators."[4]

The gravity plan soon found favor with many people in the state including Governor Ernest Lister. Preliminary studies encouraged the supporters of the project. The governor then urged the formation of the Columbia Basin Survey Commission (CBSC) in 1919. The CBSC cooperated with the United States Reclamation Service in studying the gravity plan. Meanwhile, the pumpers asked an engineer, James O'Sullivan, to study the entire project. O'Sullivan became convinced of the pumping plan's superiority. Thus began a decade-long fight between the supporters of the rival plans, the story of which is replete with public versus private power intrigue, typical Washington provincialism, and more than a little greed and glory seeking.

In late 1927, Senators Jones and Dill introduced a bill that would have made the Columbia Basin Development a federal project, but the bill went nowhere. Senator Jones then sought funds that would have made possible a complete federal study of the project. With the approval of Secretary of Commerce Herbert Hoover, Major John S. Butler of the Army Corps of Engineers undertook a thorough study of the Columbia Basin Project. Unbeknownst to the supporters of the gravity plan, Senators Jones and Dill quietly asked Butler to direct the bulk of his investigation toward the pumping plan. Butler's study began in 1929; it showed the gravity plan to be economically unfeasible while supporting the pumping plan.[5]

Meanwhile, the pumpers organized into a group known as the Columbia River Development League (CRDL) and hired James O'Sullivan as executive secretary. O'Sullivan's job was to push for the development of the Columbia Basin through the pumping plan and to oppose projects that would compromise the objectives of the CRDL.[6]

Support for the pumping plan now coalesced in the state primarily because of the rising public power issue. The Grange, an avid public power booster, supported the pumping plan because of the power to be generated at Grand Coulee Dam, though it had reservations concerning the reclamation aspects of the project (the Grange, a farmers' organization, was concerned that reclamation would exacerbate the farm surplus problem). Public power supporters pushed the project as well, whereas private power interests argued that sufficient power would soon be available from other sources. Though new power generating facilities were under construction, the fact that the aircraft carrier U.S.S. *Lexington* had been dispatched to Tacoma to provide electrical power for that city tended to cast doubt on the argument of private power proponents. Dill had been responsible for securing the services of the Lexington in providing Tacoma with electrical power. He took good care of his coastal center of support.[7]

Bolstered by Butler's report and various groups in the state, the pumpers next worked to gain the cooperation of the federal government. Meanwhile, public power advocates in Washington State secured the passage of the District Power Bill through the initiative process in November 1930, which Albert Goss, a leading figure in the grange movement, believed would help lower rates and improve service.[8] The bill empowered those living in unincorporated areas to create public utility districts just as city residents could, and Goss saw it as a step toward a statewide public power system. Dill supported the District Power Bill, placing a copy of the initiative in the *Congressional Record*, and taking time out from his Senate duties to campaign for it back home.[9] Dill also asked one of the more influential advocates of public power—Franklin D. Roosevelt, the governor of New York—to support the District Power Bill. Roosevelt often dodged controversial issues that did not directly impact New York; but this time he unequivocally endorsed the Washington State bill. In fact, he informed Dill that "he was infuriated by the 'loose talk that municipal, county, or district supplying of electricity is socialistic!'"[10] Though firmly committed to public power, Dill was aware that his campaign for the District Power Bill was a no-lose situation. In a letter to Rosalie he wrote, "If we win I'll get much of the credit, and if we lose I'll have renewed the farmers' faith in me."[11] Dill genuinely cared about farmers, but he was also a pragmatic politician.

In the fall of 1931, the United States Bureau of Reclamation reviewed the Army Corps of Engineers' report and concluded the Army had it right: the Bureau supported the pumping plan and the further development of the Columbia Basin. Rufus Woods, a longtime Republican, now went to see President Hoover in hope of persuading him to support Columbia Basin development. Senator Jones also saw the president in an effort to elicit his support. They failed. Moreover, the Rivers and Harbors Board rejected the Columbia Basin Project on the grounds it was too expensive, there was no market for its power, and the nation already had a surplus of farm acreage.[12]

On the legislative front, Senators Jones and Dill, along with Representative Sam Hill, a Democrat from Dill's old Fifth District, introduced a bill in Congress in January of 1932 providing for developing the Columbia Basin and constructing Grand Coulee Dam. Jones was not sanguine concerning the bill's chances, citing the empty coffers in the treasury and the Depression in general.[13] James O'Sullivan, whose volatile emotions sometimes clouded his judgment, now lashed out at the Rivers and Harbors Board, before whom hearings on the Columbia Basin bill were being held. O'Sullivan pilloried the Board, Dill, and Jones in a letter to Rufus Woods, writing that the board was "a slaughterhouse of proposed projects to kill them off before they can embarrass members of Congress and the administration. By appearing before this board and championing projects advocated by their constituents, members of Congress appear to have done their duty."[14]

Thus did O'Sullivan begin to give evidence that after spending much of the twenties battling for Grand Coulee Dam, he was slipping into paranoia concerning the Columbia River Basin Project. Though Jones and Dill supported the project, none of their efforts would convince the suspicious and self-righteous O'Sullivan.

Unfortunately for all of the supporters of the Columbia Basin plan, in 1931 the Hoover administration had committed itself to building what became Hoover Dam on the Colorado River and was clearly opposed to further power and reclamation projects.[15] Clarence Dill saw the eventual outcome of the Columbia Basin Development bill long before it actually happened. Indeed, Hoover's opposition was evident even before Jones and Dill introduced the bill. President Hoover and the junior senator from Washington clashed repeatedly over issues relative to their differing governmental and economic philosophies. Nevertheless, they were both very much typical western builders. Unfortunately, the Depression, which damaged both the resources of government and the spirits of the people, also kept these two Westerners from cooperating and building Grand Coulee Dam.

Thoroughly infected with the "incurable western disease" (the desire to build a country made still more intense by the fascination for reclaiming arid lands through irrigation), Dill was determined to see Grand Coulee built. The question for the Westerner, in light of Hoover's opposition, was how to go about it.[16]

With the Depression gripping the country, Democrats knew the party had a unique opportunity in 1932. Dill, an astute politician, saw evidence Grand Coulee might benefit from having the right man in the White House. Franklin Delano Roosevelt, the newly reelected governor of New York, came immediately to mind. Dill had written Roosevelt a letter in December 1928 congratulating him on his first election to the governor's chair in

New York. In the letter, Dill urged a progressive stance on the nation's problems and avoidance of prohibition as a national issue. Roosevelt's smashing 725,000 vote victory in November 1930 had vaulted him into the presidential spotlight. In December 1930, the Dills attended a social occasion at the governor's mansion in Albany. Senator Dill explained to Rosalie that their host was the Democratic Party's best hope for 1932.[17]

A few weeks later, Dill had the opportunity to visit Roosevelt again in Albany. FDR had invited him to dinner and an evening of political discussion.[18] The two men hit it off, the conversation centering on the Depression and FDR's possible candidacy for the presidency in 1932. Eventually, Dill brought up Grand Coulee Dam. Roosevelt had been made aware of the Columbia Basin development scheme when he campaigned as the 1920 vice presidential nominee in the Pacific Northwest. Dill explained how the plan had changed over the years and elaborated on the opposition private power interests posed. The idea of a Democratic president developing a portion of the country first explored at the order of the original Democratic president, Thomas Jefferson, intrigued FDR. The two men discussed the dam for some time; the governor impressed Dill with his knowledge of geography. Dill briefly laid out the Army Corp of Engineers' comprehensive plan for development of the Columbia River for FDR. He emphasized the public power aspect of the proposal, knowing the governor was keenly interested in that subject. FDR expressed dismay at Hoover's attitude concerning the project, saying to Dill, "I don't suppose I'll ever be President, but if I am, I'll build that dam." Dill responded, "That's what I came here to get you to say."[19]

Some historians have been skeptical of Dill's relation of this conversation. But Roosevelt's proclivity for making seemingly spur of the moment promises has been well documented. Moreover, FDR had a habit of attempting to appear to be all things to all people and would often say what a visitor wanted to hear. Furthermore, public power development was one of the mainstays of FDR's philosophy; it would have been surprising if FDR had not been interested in the project. Finally, Dill wrote down the details of his encounter with FDR shortly after his meeting, and his relation of various parts of the story changes little throughout his long life, as various examples show. Thus there is little reason to suppose the evening did not transpire much as Dill describes.[20]

Certainly a new closeness between the two men commenced shortly after their evening together, for Dill now demonstrated a clear determination to advance FDR's candidacy. He inserted one of the governor's speeches on water power into the *Congressional Record* shortly after their visit. He also mentioned Roosevelt's "fine example of constructive statesmanship" in proposing solutions to the problem of high power rates.[21] FDR sent him a letter, "Thank you so much for putting my message on water power into the record and also for what you said."[22] The two men also exchanged views on legislation pending before Congress, and the senator congratulated Roosevelt on his birthday.[23]

Not content to merely build his relationship with FDR, Dill went to work creating esteem for the governor wherever he went and was especially careful to extol FDR's virtues to his Senate colleagues.[24] In 1936 when the Dills were estranged and had few complimentary things to say to one another, Rosalie said, "I feel that due credit should be given Clarence for being the first man of prominence who backed Roosevelt's nomination."[25] Dill trumpeted the New Yorker's praises upon his return to Washington State in March: "Governor Roosevelt has two outstanding qualifications…he is a winner and he would make a good President."[26] The senator did not confine himself to advancing Roosevelt. He also lashed out at Hoover, placing the blame for unemployment and high power rates on the President's policies.[27]

In June Dill and his wife took a trip to Europe. Reporters there often asked what the United States intended to do about the Depression. Dill responded that the only solution was a new president, and FDR was the man for the job. When he returned to the United States, Dill lauded Roosevelt for his work as governor and informed the eastern media of FDR's strong support in the West.[28]

Dill optimistically hoped to energize Washington's Democratic Party and lead it in supporting Roosevelt. He believed the Depression provided an opportunity to rebuild Washington State's Democratic Party. In November 1931, the senator led Washington's FDR Democrats in the nation's first attempt to have a state delegation instructed by its state convention to support FDR at the national convention.[29]

Dill attacked whoever challenged Roosevelt. He was one of the first Democrats to criticize John Raskob, chairman of the Democratic National Committee, but an opponent of FDR, for sending out prohibition questionnaires apparently designed to harm FDR's chances.[30] Late in the year there was talk in Washington, D.C., of running a progressive Republican, possibly George Norris, as a third party candidate. In spite of his admiration for the Nebraskan, Dill jumped on that possibility in an effort to stamp it out before it got started. He said Roosevelt was the "best way to meet the threat and even the creation of a third party in 1932."[31] As the election year dawned, Dill intensified his efforts on FDR's behalf. He pushed the governor's candidacy in the Senate, inserting his speeches into the *Congressional Record* and speaking out on his behalf from the Senate floor.[32]

At the Spokane County Democratic Convention in February, Dill's FDR forces suffered a setback, failing to secure an instructed delegation to the state convention. Opposition to an instructed delegation from the county came from the Edith Dolan Riley faction of the party. Riley, a prominent leader of local Democrats, had feuded with Dill for some time.[33] After the campaign of 1928, Dill had sent Riley a ten dollar donation to the Spokane County Democratic Party with his apologies for being tardy. Riley responded, "Had I received this contribution two years ago it would indeed have been appreciated but I am glad to say that the Spokane County Democratic Organization, despite the efforts of your friends, is in such shape that your contribution is neither needed or desired."[34] The letter declined in its admiration for Dill from that point. In 1932 Riley felt compelled to warn FDR that Washington State's progressives would try to steal the party from regular Democrats.[35] There is no record of FDR's response, but it must have involved a chuckle.

Dill was no more successful at the state level in securing a firmly instructed delegation for Roosevelt. Instead, Washington's delegates were to "labor earnestly, faithfully, and loyally" for the governor's nomination.[36] Fortunately for Dill and FDR, Judson Shorett, head of the Washington delegation, took these instructions seriously and refused to entertain any thoughts concerning another candidate until, as he put it, "the New York Governor's fate was settled."[37] Should the governor stumble, however, the delegation favored the candidacy of John N. Garner of Texas. Nevertheless, Washington's delegation was the first to receive orders to work for FDR's nomination and, as such, was a tribute to Dill's efforts.[38]

In February 1932, after Roosevelt had made clear his intention to seek the presidency, Dill, Senator Cordell Hull of Tennessee, and Homer Cummings conferred with dozens of undecided Democratic senators. These three men persuaded a number of their colleagues to announce themselves for Roosevelt.[39] Dill wrote FDR concerning the progress being made in his behalf in Washington, D.C.: "Things are going very fine here and I think you are getting stronger every day."[40] In the spring of 1932, the Washingtonian's reputation as an FDR booster had grown to the point that he, along with Senators Burton Wheeler of Montana and Hull, became known as FDR's "three musketeers."[41]

The Roosevelt campaign considered the battle for Maine to be a crucial test for their candidate. In March, James Farley, one of FDR's top campaign strategists, asked Dill to go to Maine in an effort to assist in gaining an instructed delegation for Roosevelt. The senator protested, he did not know anyone in Maine, but he agreed to go at Roosevelt's request. Upon arriving in Portland, Maine, Dill downplayed his role at the state convention. Newspapermen asked him if he thought he could gain an instructed delegation for Roosevelt. The savvy Westerner demurred, saying that he could not "hope to influence" the convention to that extent. Another reporter asked, "If you were a delegate to this convention, what would you try to have the convention do?" Dill thought for a moment and responded slowly, "I would try to have this convention do what would help most to win the state election here in September."[42]

Dill retired for the evening but awoke after midnight when Roosevelt supporters knocked on his hotel room door. They informed the senator that his advice had helped immensely and asked him if he would speak at the end of the convention instead of at the beginning, thereby allowing them to arrange for an instructed delegation. Dill happily obliged. When FDR heard Maine had voted for an instructed delegation, he was elated and repeated to Dill his promise to build Grand Coulee. Of course, Maine had gone for Roosevelt primarily because of the work of Bob Jackson of New Hampshire, one of FDR's top campaign aides, and his co-workers. But perhaps Dill's presence had helped clarify the thinking of a few Maine delegates.[43]

While the prospects for the Roosevelt campaign were bright, conditions in the country were bleak. In April Dill inserted into the *Congressional Record* one of FDR's speeches that suggested that the danger the country faced was as serious as war but solutions were at hand.[44]

Dill's optimism for FDR's candidacy grew despite the large number of candidates who hoped to capitalize on Hoover's unpopularity. In a letter to J.D. Ross, Seattle superintendent of lighting, Dill predicted FDR would win the Democratic nomination on the first or second ballot. But the Roosevelt campaign feared a plethora of "favorite son" candidates that could keep their man from quick nomination. Senator Alben Barkley of Kentucky was reputed to be entertaining "favorite son" aspirations. Dill conceived the idea of offering the temporary chairmanship of the convention to Barkley in return for his effort to instruct the Kentucky delegation for Roosevelt. After conferring with Farley and Roosevelt, who agreed to the deal, Dill spoke with Barkley and persuaded him to accept the offer.[45]

On June 5, 1932, Dill attended a strategy meeting at Hyde Park along with fifteen other Democratic Party leaders. The meeting resulted in several important decisions. First, Dill was chosen to represent the Roosevelt forces in the fight over prohibition at the national convention.

The senator himself favored submitting the prohibition issue to the voters in some form of a referendum, thus neatly sidestepping the issue. However, FDR's forces preferred to play the liquor question by ear. Following orders, Dill successfully placed the cautious Roosevelt position on prohibition on the party platform. But when the convention met, Senator David Walsh argued forcefully for complete repeal and offered an amendment to the platform along those lines. Sensing the convention's mood for repeal, Dill called Roosevelt and informed him of the development. The platform committee voted 35 to 17 for repeal.[46] Three days after Dill's call, Roosevelt made his appearance in Chicago proclaiming, "The American people are for repeal."[47]

The strategists at the June 5 meeting also decided to advance Senator Thomas J. Walsh of Montana as permanent chairman of the National Convention in opposition to Jouett Shouse, a Raskob ally unfriendly to FDR's candidacy.[48] Indeed, Shouse had made several speeches calling for uninstructed delegations. When the Roosevelt camp announced its intent to install Walsh as permanent chairman, the fight commenced openly. At the convention, John Davis, the party's nominee in 1924, led the campaign for Shouse; Dill and Senator James F. Byrnes of South Carolina argued for Walsh. The Washington delegation and the folks back home were proud of the leading role their senator was playing at the convention. The *Seattle Times*, never one of Dill's allies, remarked that allowing Dill to lead the fight for Walsh was a reward for his "pioneering work for the Roosevelt movement."[49] The senator's gift for public speaking came in handy and Walsh won the chairmanship, though Dill thought he had blown his assignment on behalf of Walsh because when he had characterized the chairmanship fight as one between conservatives and progressives, Shouse's forces booed him roundly.[50]

The convention moved on to nominate a presidential candidate. Roosevelt led after three ballots, but there had been no major movement in his favor. Farley and the other strategists believed Texas held the key. On the morning of July 1, Dill met with Sam Rayburn, John Garner's campaign manager. Garner, no mere favorite son for the presidential nomination, had the support of William Randolph Hearst's newspaper chain. The Washington delegation was prepared to move to Garner should FDR stumble, as were several other states. Dill and Rayburn discussed Garner's chances and the probability that Newton D. Baker would end up with the nomination should Garner and Roosevelt fail to compromise.[51] Other Democratic leaders also spoke with Rayburn, who eventually met with Farley. Farley virtually assured Rayburn the vice presidency would be

Garner's should FDR be nominated which, of course, he was.[52] The vice presidency went to Garner.

Clarence Dill was prominently mentioned as a possible running mate for FDR. Indeed, he may well have been the front-runner at one time, but he dropped out of the picture before second place on the Democratic ticket went to Garner. Dill later maintained he did not want the vice presidency. It may well be that he made his position known during the convention, which is why the *Seattle P.I.* would then report he had dropped out of the running. On the other hand, James Farley argues Dill was upset over being denied the vice presidency. Whichever account is true, Dill's support of FDR was long-term and invaluable.[53] The Washingtonian had been instrumental in the two most important fights at the convention: the prohibition plank and the election of Thomas Walsh to the permanent chairmanship.

Whether Dill had wanted the vice presidency or not, he retained no bitterness over Garner's selection and eagerly offered advice to the nominee. In a letter to Farley, Dill congratulated him on his convention strategy and predicted Garner would offset the eastern press's tendency to portray FDR as a radical. Dill believed, as did other Roosevelt confidants, that the nominee would be wise to refrain from "making jaunts about the country." The Westerner hoped that FDR would conduct a more "presidential" campaign. Perhaps he had in mind Harding's front porch campaign of 1920. Finally Clarence suggested the possibility of a rapprochement with Al Smith. Farley responded that Smith had already made a statement and then agreed with Dill's advice about the campaign, without much sincerity.[54]

In early August, after matching wits for ten days with rainbow trout, Dill received a letter from Farley asking him to come east in a few weeks to help with the campaign. Dill again advised Roosevelt against "barnstorming" trips, claiming his support in the West was as good as gold. Dill's advice stemmed from his belief that candidates who engaged in such trips seldom won. He cited as evidence William Jennings Bryan, Charles Evans Hughes, and James Cox. FDR politely received the advice and wisely disregarded it. Roosevelt would campaign in the West. Had he not done so, he would have appeared to be unconcerned, perhaps even arrogant, about a region sensitive to its status. FDR was not about to be perceived as an eastern provincialist.[55] Roosevelt himself responded to Dill's concerns about a western trip, explaining he was no Hughes or Cox (he might well have added Al Smith); the people knew him and expected him to come west to hear their concerns.[56] FDR was right; the times were different, people wanted to believe the man who would be president cared about their problems and was determined to help them.

Later, Dill gave Roosevelt some good advice. Apparently it had originally been Roosevelt's plan to speak in only one Pacific Northwest city. Dill explained the folly of such a course to Louis Howe, a longtime Roosevelt aide and advisor: "For him to come here and make only one speech would be doubly bad. If he speaks only at Portland, the people of Seattle and this state will feel slighted, and if he speaks at Seattle only, the people of Oregon would feel the same way."[57]

A letter from Farley, combined with a phone call, reiterated FDR's desire to have Dill in the East when the campaign picked up steam in September. Dill replied Senate business would detain him until later in the month but hoped to be of help in the campaign.[58]

A chance to be of service came quickly. In August, Stephen Chadwick, a prominent Washington Democrat, wrote Governor Roosevelt informing him of a situation that had been developing in Washington State:

> Seattle has three daily newspapers, *Times, Post Intelligencer, Star*. Since the day of your nomination all three have supported you. On August 10 I conferred with Colonel C.B. Blethen, Editor of the *Times*, who told me that the continued support of his paper would depend upon your pronouncement as to whether or not you would be the President when elected, or whether the presidency would be a triumvirate composed of yourself, Mr. McAdoo and Mr. Hearst.
>
> Mr. Hearst owns the *P.I.*, which is a competitor of Mr. Blethen's paper the *Times*....
>
> The Republican National Committee is doing its utmost to regain the *Times* support, and Mr. Blethen told me that whether or not he returns to the advocacy of Mr. Hoover will depend entirely upon the strength of your expression of your entire independence of any domination [from Hearst].

The Roosevelt campaign informed Dill of the newspaper situation, asking for his advice. The senator responded that a non-committal reply seemed best.[59]

Dill went on to advise Howe in regard to campaign support for FDR: "Let me add one suggestion. I think it is extremely important that some notable man who has an excellent radio presence and radio voice make some speeches on the nation wide hook-up during the closing month of the campaign. I have always believed that the speeches of Senator Borah...were of tremendous aid to Mr. Hoover in 1928."[60]

Roosevelt's campaign strategists thought his suggestion regarding the newspaper situation sound and were equally impressed with his advice on using radio in the campaign.[61] FDR fully intended to make use of radio, but he also knew there could be no substitute for personal appearances across the stricken nation. Determined to campaign in the West, FDR made plans for just such a trip.

FDR's train rolled west through the country in the late summer of 1932. The changing landscape symbolized a nation also in the midst of transition. Passing trees filled with decaying auburn and gold leaves represented a people closer to death than life. Should Roosevelt be elected president in November, he would face the greatest challenge an American president had encountered since Lincoln had confronted a defiant South in 1861. Franklin Delano Roosevelt was perhaps the most accomplished politician the American nation had ever produced. Yet he was also fully human; he cared deeply about people, about their future, and about the country. As the rolling wheat fields gave way to the stubborn peaks of the Rockies, he must have wondered if the Depression would prove equally obstinate and if he could really help the people.

Dill boarded FDR's train in Missoula, Montana, to have time to help him with his Spokane speech, which would feature comments on Grand Coulee. But the train was delayed and did not reach Spokane until after midnight. FDR did not give his speech, but he decided to include his comments on Grand Coulee in his Portland, Oregon, speech; after all, he reasoned, Portland was on the great river.[62]

In Seattle, FDR began his remarks with "heartfelt respects" to Senator Dill, and mentioned Clarence Martin (candidate for governor) and Homer Bone (candidate for Wesley Jones's Senate seat). FDR went on to affirm his support for the Navy; as a former assistant secretary of the Navy his words held great meaning to the people of Puget Sound. Finally, he assured the people of Washington of his own awareness of their tribulation: "I have seen enough, however, and heard enough to know how heavily the hand of the great depression has fallen upon this Western country; to see what has happened in this great seaport brings back with keen irony some of the things that Republican leaders used to tell us about stimulation of foreign trade."[63]

In Portland FDR hammered at the power trust, advocating strict government regulation, and championed four great river projects, including developing the Columbia. But he did not specifically use the words Grand Coulee. The omission hit Dill hard. Roosevelt had, in the midst of his speech, fashioned it to fit his audience. Portlanders were interested in Columbia River development, but not Grand Coulee. Dill related in his memoirs that Roosevelt's original speech mentioned Grand Coulee specifically. There is no question, however, as to whether or not FDR made clear his promise to build Grand Coulee. Homer Bone campaigned on that promise in Washington, describing the election of himself and FDR as victories for public power and Grand Coulee Dam. [64]

After FDR's western sojourn, Dill continued to campaign on his behalf, spending much of his time barnstorming in the Midwest. He returned to the Pacific Northwest in time to headline a Seattle rally for all of the Democratic Party candidates. He took the opportunity to blast the power trust one more time. The Democrats virtually swept the state in November. Roosevelt, Martin, and Bone triumphed, and the Democratic Party of Washington transformed itself into the dominant political power in the state. [65]

The Depression would have probably propelled whichever party was out of office into power in 1932. However, the Democratic Party's move to the left helped enormously, finally supplying an ideological alternative to Republican conservatism. Dill had urged this course throughout the 1920s with little success. The Depression brought about circumstances that helped prove the validity of his philosophy. In 1914 Dill had demonstrated the wisdom of his politics, and had begun, in a very small way, to move the party to liberalism. For that effort he was often outcast from his own party and often chose not to associate with party members. In a very real sense, the election of 1932 was a personal vindication for Clarence Dill.

The election of FDR provided a glimmer of hope to a country that, perhaps for the first time, had begun to question the essential worth of its cherished beliefs and institutions. Agonizingly, the nation hoped for the transition period between Hoover and Roosevelt to expire, before the banking system could do likewise. Finally the reins of government passed to a man intent on bold new solutions. Clarence Dill, now the state's senior senator, anxiously awaited the opportunity to take part in the great experiment FDR planned to launch. Dill also envisioned a huge new dam, a Westerner's monument, which would turn arid wastelands into rich croplands.

Senator Dill breaking ground in a ceremony at the Grand Coulee Dam site, July 17, 1933. *Cheney Cowles Museum/Eastern Washington State Historical Society, Spokane, WA*

CHAPTER NINE

THE WATER RISES

A FTER THE INAUGURATION of Franklin Delano Roosevelt, the nation's capital entered a period of frenzy known as the Hundred Days. Dill's primary role in the New Deal came in regard to the Communications Act of 1934 and in the battle for Grand Coulee in 1933. In his battle for the great dam, Dill had to contend with those who were opposed to the dam, both in his own state and in Washington, D.C., with those who were zealous for the dam but knew little of how things were accomplished in the nation's capital, and with a president who had far greater concerns than Grand Coulee. In 1933 Clarence Dill helped out-flank the dam's opponents, guided its supporters toward what was possible, and was the leading member of Washington's congressional delegation in gaining FDR's approval of the great dam.

Dill's initial plan to secure the dam in March 1933 included incorporating it in an unemployment bill, but there were a number of possible ways to proceed.[1] However, he recognized the banking crisis paralyzed the nation and thus he exercised the virtue of patience in relation to Grand Coulee. This prudence and sense of priorities has been inaccurately cited as evidence the dam meant little to Dill.[2] He wanted the dam for many reasons: jobs, future development, long-term reclamation projects, and perhaps most importantly, as a lasting monument to his own political career. Dill was vain and proud; the dam would be a fitting monument to any western politician. It is also likely that he hoped to gain financially from the project; and there is some evidence he used unethical means to profit from Grand Coulee.[3]

On April 1 Dill wrote to James O'Sullivan congratulating him on his appointment as executive secretary of the Columbia Basin Commission (CBC). The CBC, a creation of the Washington state legislature, purposed to guide development of the Columbia Basin and negotiate with the federal government toward that end.[4] Dill cautioned the energetic and headstrong O'Sullivan that the nation's agricultural surplus meant that Grand Coulee could never win approval as a land reclamation program.

Only pursuing Grand Coulee as a public power project offered any chance of success.[5]

In April Washington's congressional delegation remained uncertain as to how to gain approval for the dam. Dill and Representative Sam B. Hill favored procuring Reconstruction Finance Corporation funds, thus avoiding the need for congressional endorsement. Both Dill and Hill told Albert Goss, master of the Washington State Grange and CBC member, that pressing Columbia Basin development as a reclamation project was sheer folly. Goss agreed, having come to that conclusion himself sometime earlier.[6] Dill and Hill also informed Goss the project would not become reality without the president's support. Goss stood amazed at the degree to which everything in the nation's capital awaited the president's personal approval:

> I can confirm what they say with reference to the President's approval. He holds this Congress in the hollow of his hand and they will take no action whatsoever except upon his request. I never saw anything quite like it. Therefore, I feel that our whole effort must be made on concentrating upon the President.
>
> The President is under the greatest pressure I have ever seen, and it is very difficult to get an appointment. There are so many very grievous problems pressing that all but the most important are being deferred until after Congress adjourns. Senator Dill feels confident however that he will be able to get an appointment soon, and I know of nothing to do except press for this appointment as soon as possible.[7]

So FDR's support for the dam was crucial, and Clarence Dill had the closest relationship with the president of anyone from Washington State.

Fortunately for the dam's supporters, FDR had long been interested in hydroelectric power development, rural electrification, and developing efficient agriculture.[8] Indeed, as governor of New York, FDR had led that state's fight for public power. In the course of the battle, he had come to believe that a well developed public power system must become a reality to be a "yardstick" by which private power companies might be regulated.[9] Moreover, the president saw much of the West as a vast wasteland that, given cheap electrical power, irrigation, and transportation, might be used as an experiment in social and economic planning. It was with these things in mind that FDR, as the Democratic Party's nominee for president in 1932, gave a speech in Portland in which he said "that the next great hydroelectric development to be undertaken by the Federal government must be that on the Columbia River."[10] The president favored Columbia Basin development in some form; it was now up to Washington's congressional delegation and the CBC to move that interest from the abstract to the concrete.

Probably about April 14 Dill saw the president briefly to provide some information on the Grand Coulee project. The material Dill gave FDR estimated the cost of the project at $450 million. Roosevelt said to Dill, "I didn't realize this dam was so big." The two men discussed the project for a while. Then the president said, "I've got to go to bed with this."[11]

On April 17 Roosevelt's secretary called Dill and asked him to come to the White House to discuss the dam with the president. Albert Goss accompanied Dill; Sam Hill would have been there but traffic delayed him. Upon entering the president's office, Dill shook hands with Roosevelt and noticed his unusually friendly manner. The senator sensed bad news. The president began to extol the virtues of the project but then slipped into reiterating all the arguments against the dam. Dill decided to risk reminding the president of his many promises to build Grand Coulee. In his memoirs, this reminder becomes a verbal beating. Dill wrote, "I was like Joe Louis raining punch after punch on his opponent."[12] In reading Dill's memoirs, one cannot help but gain the impression that he embellished his argument with FDR. In a letter to Rufus Woods, Dill mentions his disagreement with FDR but makes much less of it than he did in his memoirs. Dill's account to Woods is probably fairly accurate; there was a brief disagreement, Dill probably worried he had gone too far, then, to Dill's relief, the president proposed a low dam that might cost only $40 million.[13]

Albert Goss argued that a low dam would not control floods and would make the eventual cost of electricity too high.[14] The president stated he knew very little about the project, but had the impression it was too large to finance under the present circumstances.[15] Congress would never authorize the money. Goss suggested pursuing the RFC alternative, and FDR responded such a course might be wise. He agreed to assist in securing RFC funds in increments if the project could be approached in that way. The president's help was very much conditional. While Dill and Goss explored the RFC alternative, FDR wanted to see cost estimates of building the project in two phases—first a low dam, then a high. The president then mentioned his desire to do something for unemployment relief in the Pacific Northwest, remarking Grand Coulee might help in that regard. The meeting ended on that note. Dill left some information on Grand Coulee with the president. However, both men recognized FDR would commit to nothing until he had hard figures to study.[16]

Goss described Dill's response to the meeting as elation, but was himself a bit nonplussed at the president's reticence. Goss and Dill reacted differently to their meeting with the president because Dill had little problem beginning Grand Coulee as a low dam. Thus, the meeting encouraged him because it demonstrated Roosevelt's sincerity about the low dam. Goss discovered Roosevelt's antipathy to the high dam only during the meeting. Dill apparently had not informed Goss of his previous conversation with Roosevelt, perhaps because he considered Goss's presence in Washington, D.C., as unnecessary and bothersome. The two men had little use for one another.

Dill later suspected FDR had wanted to begin Grand Coulee as a low dam all along and thus had sought a working compromise at the April 17 meeting. This was probably true. Though FDR felt great pressure to cut government expenses in 1933, several factors compelled him to build the dam. First, he had repeated his promise to build Grand Coulee Dam on numerous occasions, and not just to Dill. Ceremonies at Muscle Shoals in February were just the most recent occasion upon which he had mentioned damming the Columbia at Grand Coulee. Second, the public power issue was directly tied to Grand Coulee and the president had campaigned as a public power man. Roosevelt's detailed vision for regional development of the United States was largely based on a systematic use of the nation's great waterways; public power formed the cornerstone of that usage.[17] Third, the Pacific Northwest badly needed jobs; Grand Coulee would help a great deal. Finally, Dill's relationship with Roosevelt gave the senator access to the president and made FDR amenable to helping him.

After the meeting, Goss advised Governor Clarence Martin that telegrams supporting the project were a waste of time; he needed hard figures. In response to Goss's request, O'Sullivan wrote on April 20, "I have made tentative figures based on the knowledge of the cost, and believe we can put in the foundations of the dam and go as high as probably sixty feet above low water, for about sixty million…it is my opinion that we could put in the power plant also for this cost, and that we could utilize the turbines that would be required for the high dam."[18] O'Sullivan further assured Goss that the CBC was not asking for federal government funds for power construction without having a market for the new power. The power would be sold, he asserted.[19]

O'Sullivan now made plans to travel to Washington, D.C., to present the Grand Coulee project to the president in detail. O'Sullivan, who possessed an encyclopedic knowledge of Grand Coulee, was the best man for this job. Moreover, everything seemed to hinge on the president's personal approval.[20]

After a meeting with the president on May 2, Dill announced the government's tentative plan to develop the Columbia Basin. He explained the plan as it stood would not require congressional action and would cost only about $60 million, exactly O'Sullivan's figure on the cost of the low dam. The RFC and Washington State's unemployment relief fund were to supply the necessary financing. In addition, a power district would be formed in Washington to sell the power. The resulting contracts would then be used as a basis for the loan from the RFC.[21]

Most Washingtonians were euphoric at the news, but then Oregon punctured the mood. The Oregon congressional delegation, led by Senator Charles McNary, saw the president on May 4 in an effort to stop Grand Coulee and secure a Columbia River dam of their own. The Oregonians preferred developing the lower river rather than the upper. They reported to the media FDR's apparent support of their position. The Oregonians were under the impression there would only be one dam on the Columbia in the foreseeable future.[22] Though McNary may have believed FDR agreed with him, the president had told him to see Dill.

Meanwhile, Dill, Goss, and O'Sullivan worked on the details of the Columbia Basin plan. It is important to note that at this time the project did not have the approval of the president. FDR had merely encouraged Dill and the CBC to work on the project, assuming it would be financed largely through the RFC. The Washingtonians were to bring him a proposal in line with a multistage development of Grand Coulee at substantially lower cost than originally projected. The key to developing Grand Coulee as an RFC project centered on the formation of a power district in Washington State that would contract for the sale of power and thus establish the necessary collateral for an RFC loan.[23]

Hope for the president's approval of Grand Coulee Dam now rested on the financial attractiveness of the project and, some believed, Clarence Dill's influence with the president. O'Sullivan expressed the latter in a letter to his secretary: "Dill can get us the dam if he really wants to, because of his influence with the President....Dill can overthrow influence of McNary and Steiwer, Republicans, if he will strive hard enough. It is up to Dill, and if he feels that the people out there want this proposition bad enough, he will get us the dam."[24]

O'Sullivan's estimate of Dill's power was too strong, just as his expectations of Wesley Jones had been too high. If FDR decided against the dam, as Hoover had, there was nothing Dill could do. However, the letter does accurately indicate that Dill was the lead man in the effort to gain the president's approval.

Interestingly, O'Sullivan did not at that time care who got the credit for the dam, as long as it was built: "I am not giving out any publicity letting Senator Dill do it. We cannot forewarn opposition of our moves and the more Senator Dill 'fathers' the dam, the more certain we will get it. He is powerful with Roosevelt. I would give him the whole state if he puts it over, as I think he will and soon at that."[25] Dill believed he would as well, not so much because he was "powerful with Roosevelt," but because he knew the president wanted to build Grand Coulee. For his part, O'Sullivan continued to urge his colleagues in Washington State to create the power district that would handle Grand Coulee's electricity.[26] Though O'Sullivan was willing to give Dill credit for gaining Roosevelt's approval of the dam, at least in 1933, he did not particularly like Dill.

Dill now discovered that if the project were to use RFC funds, Washington would have to come up with one-third of the total, or $20 million. He informed the president that Washington State simply could not raise that much money. Apparently undisturbed, FDR promptly responded it might be possible to finance the project through the $3.3 billion Public Works Administration package then working its way through Congress. After discussing the possibility of using PWA funds, Dill and FDR decided the senator had better make sure that PWA funds could be used for power projects. To this end, Dill went to see Democratic Senator Robert Wagner of New York, chairman of the Senate committee responsible for the National Industrial Recovery Act, which included the PWA. Wagner referred Dill to Senator Carl Hayden, Democrat of Arizona, chairman of the Senate portion of the conference committee handling the bill. Hayden objected to including a vague reference authorizing dams; he feared opposition from those who did not want any more reclamation dams. But when Dill explained that all he wanted was a power dam, Hayden agreed to insert the words "development of water power" into the paragraph describing acceptable projects for PWA funds. These four words would eventually provide FDR the legal basis for beginning Grand Coulee.[27]

In mid-May, work on Grand Coulee proceeded on several fronts. Dill filed an application with the Federal Power Commission to build Grand Coulee Dam.[28] More importantly the Public Works bill passed Congress. The Columbia Basin Commission and the rest of the state of Washington, even many former Coulee opponents from Spokane, now waited to see what Dill and FDR could come up with. James E. Ford, managing secretary of the Spokane Chamber of Commerce, who was in Washington, D.C., advancing the cause of the dam, told the *Seattle P.I.*, "The fight for the Columbia Basin Project virtually has simmered down to a one man proposition. Senator C.C. Dill has undertaken the task of putting the project across they say and is doing excellent work."[29] Ford's pursuit of the dam in the nation's capital is indicative of how the project had won over many in

Spokane who had preferred the gravity plan.[30] Even Dill's longtime enemy William Cowles, publisher of the Spokane *Spokesman-Review*, now supported the dam.[31]

In late May, it appeared Grand Coulee had the president's confidential approval and would be built through Public Works Administration funds. But concern remained that FDR might change his mind. The CBC relied on Dill to avoid that pitfall.[32] It was not long before O'Sullivan and the other dam supporters could relax a little, at least privately. In the last days of May, Roosevelt sent a confidential letter to Dill endorsing the project. Although the president had not provided public support, nevertheless, O'Sullivan was ecstatic and even had warm thoughts for Dill. O'Sullivan predicted that upon their return to Washington State, he and Dill would "show those guys up who are trying to block this project."[33]

Those opposed to Grand Coulee were a strange mixture of Washington's private power interests and public power supporters from west of the Cascades. Ralph D. Nichols, a Seattle city councilman, and James D. Ross, head of Seattle City Light (a publicly owned utility), were both advocates of public power but opposed to Grand Coulee. Times were tough for both the city and the utility. The Depression had reached its nadir and budgets shrank with each passing month. They were both afraid the massive Grand Coulee project would either provide cheap power to private utilities or allow the federal government to directly compete with public utilities to sell electricity. Moreover, Seattle had its own plans for more power production on the Skagit River. To Ross and Nichols, Grand Coulee seemed ill timed at best and perhaps completely unnecessary.[34]

Of course, private power interests opposed Grand Coulee in an effort to protect their investments and profit margins. Roosevelt and Dill had specifically in mind the idea that public power projects would provide a "yardstick" by which private power rates could be judged and possibly controlled. Private power advocates, often led by Spokane's Washington Water Power Company, argued that the Pacific Northwest already had an abundance of power, that Grand Coulee's power would be enormously expensive, and that the project's reclamation aspects would seriously undermine the administration's effort to take excess farm land out of production.[35] In the summer of 1933, several newspapers advanced the private power argument, and Pacific Power and Light Company President Paul McKee declared that Grand Coulee would only add to an existing power surplus.[36]

In June the lower Columbia flooded in combination with a record high tide. River watchers feared the worst as warm weather threatened to melt snow, further swelling the turbulent river. The Willamette, too, overflowed its banks and added to the Columbia's torrent. Still the dikes along the river appeared to be holding, though farmers patrolled them as if by doing so they could hold the river back. They could not. On June 14, dikes on the lower river's islands and banks crumbled away; the raging water swept crops and livestock into the sea. The weather bureau offered little hope for relief. The rampaging river did not peak until June 21, a full week later. It was not one of the Columbia's great floods, but it reminded Pacific Northwesterners of the awesome power of the great river.[37]

Dill now faced a crisis of his own. Ralph Nichols, in a Spokane speech, accused the senator of pushing Grand Coulee for personal gain. Nichols said Dill owned large amounts of land in the Columbia Basin. Dill responded to the accusation:

> Whether you said it, I do not know, and if you did say it, I have no knowledge of where you secured your information. I am sure you do not want to do me an injustice or tell anything that isn't true about me. For that reason I am writing you to say I do not own a foot of land in the Columbia Basin Project, that I haven't any real property in the world with the exception of my home in Spokane, some lots in Spokane and an interest in some property just south of Seattle. I never owned any Columbia Basin land but with one exception. A number of years ago someone induced me to buy a half interest in a 640 acre tract there with a view to raising wheat on it. We didn't raise wheat, we sold it, and I think I made a few hundred dollars out of the transaction.[38]

Nichols wrote back to Dill apologizing for inaccurately claiming Dill had anything to do with land speculation in the Columbia Basin. He did not, however, correct his erroneous belief that the entire Grand Coulee project was the dream of avaricious land speculators. Later in July, Nichols also wrote a letter to former Governor Marion E. Hay, which was passed on to the CBC and read before that group. In the letter, Nichols apologized for inaccurately associating Dill's name with land speculation. However, shortly after his apology to Dill, Nichols wrote a letter to the widow of A. Scott Bullitt (Bullitt had died suddenly while serving as FDR's campaign manager in the Northwest) in which he again associated Dill with land speculators. J.D. Ross also repeated this charge and ordered aides to look into the land records of the Columbia Basin to find proof of a scandal. Dill had no part in land speculation. Of course charges that Grand Coulee's supporters were a pack of land speculators were added to the arsenal of weapons private power interests brought against the dam.[39]

In mid-June, FDR informed Dill that Washington would have to come up with $377,000 for preliminary engineering work if the project were to go forward. If the state raised the engineering money—which Dill believed could be taken from the state's $10 million relief fund—he felt certain FDR would "put his stamp of approval" on the project publicly. Grand Coulee plans at the time anticipated 30 percent of the project would be paid for with PWA funds, the rest would be borrowed from the PWA on a bond issued by the proposed Grand Coulee Power District. Contracts between Washington and the United States Bureau of Reclamation for the necessary engineering work were in preparation.[40]

Opposition quickly arose to spending $377,000 in state funds on Grand Coulee, as did opposition to placing "the entire burden" of the project on Washingtonians. But that opposition again came from private power interests and the uninformed: even under the plan outlined above, the state did not carry the "entire burden."[41]

On June 16, Dill conferred with the president concerning Grand Coulee and informed him of the progress being made in the state's effort to raise the engineering money and create a power district. Dill also announced the FPC had decided to waive the sixty-day waiting period on the state's request to build the dam.[42]

There were certain members of the CBC and other dam supporters who wanted the state to retain control of the project while borrowing federal money to pay for it. Albert Goss was one of those who preferred state control—even to the point of abandoning the project should the federal government take it over. However, Goss left the CBC in the middle of the battle and became federal Land Bank Commissioner. Though leaving the fight, Goss advised Rufus Woods to resist letting the federal government run the project.[43] O'Sullivan and Dill thought this attitude foolish and short-sighted. Woods, however, agreed with Goss.[44]

Dill returned home in late June to conciliate the project's friends and face its critics:

> I was amazed to learn that there are those who are trying to delay and prevent the building of this dam through insidious propaganda. They say we cannot sell the power. We need sell only 250,000 kilowatts.
>
> Some say there is more power being produced now than we can sell. Of course there is, and why? Because of the profiteering prices charged by the power trust subsidiaries that are paying dividends on watered stocks. Bring down the prices of power to what Tacoma pays with municipal ownership and we will increase power used in Washington by one hundred percent.[45]

The senator also explained the details of the Columbia Basin project as it then stood. He emphasized there was no plan to make Washingtonians responsible for a huge bonded debt. Rather, the federal government would provide the state's share of the money, using future power revenues as collateral, while providing 30 percent of the necessary funds itself.[46]

The editors of the *Spokesman-Review*, having taken the time to study the plan, liked it much better. But W.E. Southard and Rufus Woods still wanted Grand Coulee to be a state-controlled project and pressured O'Sullivan accordingly. The *Spokesman-Review* editorialists, however, would have no part of any plan, such as that of Southard and Woods, which placed the state's taxpayers on the line. The paper much preferred the plan Dill had explained to the press or outright federal building of the project such as was occurring in the Tennessee Valley.[47]

After touring the flooded regions of the lower Columbia, Dill sat down with Governor Clarence Martin to map a strategy for procuring the $377,000 needed for preliminary engineering work. Dill told the people of Washington that the president's final approval rested on securing the $377,000 in engineering funds. After a meeting of the CBC, the governor, Senator Dill, and the State Emergency Unemployment Relief Commission, Dill announced that the necessary money would be forthcoming, taken from a $10 million state bond issue. That accomplished, the CBC signed a contract with the United States Bureau of Reclamation to do the necessary engineering work. Dill now proceeded to secure a contract between the federal government and an as yet unnamed state agency to build the entire project. He informed Washingtonians that the president had given his verbal assurance and would make his formal approval soon.[48]

Nevertheless, influential people in the state remained opposed to Grand Coulee. Ralph Nichols wrote a lengthy letter to Dill detailing his opposition to any Grand Coulee project that meant the state's taxpayers had to carry part of the financial burden. Dill must have laughed to himself, as Nichols's objections bore no relation to reality—the sale of Grand Coulee's power was the only collateral being offered the federal government.[49] J.D. Ross also remained firmly opposed to the dam.[50]

Supporters of the project were ecstatic that work on Grand Coulee was actually going to begin. They decided to hold a groundbreaking ceremony at the site featuring all of the state's dignitaries. Dill turned the first shovel full of dirt to the applause of more than five thousand people and spoke briefly saying the credit for building Grand Coulee belonged to the people of Washington who elected him to the Senate and to those who had worked so long on the project. But Governor Martin, O'Sullivan, and Judge Charles Levy said of Dill, "He has been the force that has put it over when the time came for it to be put over."[51] Even Rufus Woods, who had opposed Dill in every election and called him a "near traitor" in 1918, said, "And now here I find myself following and supporting Senator Dill today, and ready to be a good bird-dog when he wants anything done. You've got to hand it to Dill, our Democratic senator."[52] Again, the accolades for Dill were a bit too strong. He was not a "force" that put anything over on the president. He was a team player, a compromiser, as he had been his entire career. His access to the White House allowed him to keep Grand Coulee in front of a president already disposed to work with westerners and build the dam.

Governor Martin also correctly cited the cooperative spirit, the spirit that had built the West, as the key ingredient that had gotten the project under way: "…without a doubt the dam would now be built, because the President of the United States, Washington's Congressional delegation, the Columbia Basin Commission, and the Governor of Washington were all working together, harmoniously and determinedly to put it over. He praised the work of Senator Dill as indispensable to the success of the project."[53] Publicly, Dill was a hero, though privately, Nichols continued his campaign against the dam and Washington's senior senator.

Though groundbreaking ceremonies had taken place, the preliminary engineering contracts had been signed, and a good amount of back-slapping had gone on, the project had not received the essential final approval from the president. Dill himself was "confident President Roosevelt will provide funds to entirely complete the Columbia Basin Project as rapidly as possible," and he was personally so dedicated to the project he would "resign from the Senate or do anything else possible to further this great project."[54] Dill returned to Washington, D.C., in late July to meet with federal officials concerning Grand Coulee. He met with Harold Ickes, secretary of the interior and head of the PWA, Colonel A.W. Waite of the PWA, Dr. Elwood Mead, head of the Bureau of Reclamation, and Daniel C. Roper, secretary of commerce. Later he met with Budget Director Lewis Douglas. Dill expected to meet with the president after all of the preliminary conferences were completed to seek final approval.[55]

While Dill was in Washington, Congressman Charles Martin of Oregon caused a wave of concern to sweep Washington State when he claimed Bonneville Dam had been approved and thus Grand Coulee was "off the books." Martin asserted Bonneville would supply the region's power needs, leaving Grand Coulee as a reclamation project with no need of reclamation in sight. Moreover, consternation among Grand Coulee dam supporters increased when Harold Ickes appointed Marshall Dana, editor of the *Oregon Journal*, to be one of the regional advisors to the PWA with authority over the Pacific Northwest. Martin's proclamation, combined with Dana's appointment, made it appear Oregon was besting Washington for federal projects.[56]

News from Washington, D.C., made spirits sag even more. The PWA board, assigned to pass judgment on Grand Coulee, became concerned there would be no market for the dam's power. Dill suspected private power interests had prejudiced the board; he wired O'Sullivan in Spokane requesting rebuttal information as soon as possible.[57]

Though Grand Coulee's enemies were legion, Dill had a few friends himself. The senator beseeched the president to encourage the Public Works board to give Grand Coulee immediate attention. The president agreed. In addition, O'Sullivan came through for Dill with data on the prospective market for the dam's power; then, as Roosevelt requested, Dill met with the PWA board on July 26.[58] The next day, Dill advised O'Sullivan the meetings had gone well and not to worry about Congressman Martin's "propaganda...the President is behind us now."[59]

Though Dill did not have time to be concerned with Martin and McNary, the *Spokesman-Review* used its sharpest pen on them: "In future dealings with these Portland interests and their bragging Congressman, Senators Dill and Bone and Governor Martin will be justified in taking off gloves and speaking bluntly...the people must get behind Senator Dill and Governor Martin in their insistence that the Grand Coulee Dam be started as soon as plans are completed."[60]

The *Spokesman-Review* need not have worried. Dill had managed things in Washington, D.C., nicely, in spite of the fact Harold Ickes had been opposed to the project, as had Secretary of Agriculture Henry Wallace.[61] Wallace objected to Grand Coulee because of its long-term reclamation aspects. Nevertheless, after Dill met with the president on July 26, FDR instructed Ickes and the PWA Board to approve the project.[62]

The *Spokesman-Review*'s headline on July 28 ran, "Money Ordered Advanced After Dill Confers With President." The story went on to say in part: "This action was taken under specific instructions given by President Roosevelt after his conference yesterday with Senator Dill, which left the Board [headed by Ickes] no discretion but to follow orders."[63] After his meeting with the president, reporters asked Dill for a comment. He remarked he was "delighted," but "never had any doubt the project would be approved." He went on to say Grand Coulee was just the beginning of a vast development of the Pacific Northwest, the "President has big plans for this development." Meanwhile, newspapers that had claimed "Dill couldn't deliver" were being ridiculed by papers with more faith (a Rufus Woods editorial in the *Wenatchee Daily World* blasted the *Yakima Republic*).[64]

Though Dill worked hard to see Grand Coulee built, and the newspapers were flattering, it is too much to say that he "delivered" or in some way convinced a reluctant FDR to approve Grand Coulee for the simple reason that FDR wanted to build Grand Coulee all along. Dill's role was to present information, provided by O'Sullivan, to the various agencies, jump through the bureaucratic hoops, and keep an already supportive FDR informed. Convinced of FDR's support, Dill was generally sanguine about the dam in the spring and summer of 1933. As he said, he never really doubted the dam's approval. He would be equally confident, while others were frantic, about the high dam. In 1933 if the president wanted something done, it was usually done.[65]

With the dam approved, Dill encouraged the Northern Pacific Railroad to build a spur line to the dam site so as to expedite construction.[66] Then a few days later, Dill headed west to Ohio to spend some time with his mother and then moved on to his home in Spokane. Upon returning to Washington State, Dill toured the countryside, explaining what Grand Coulee would mean to the Pacific Northwest and listening to pleas for help with smaller dam and reclamation projects. Some of these (i.e., the Roza project in Yakima and the Skagit project for Seattle) he had been working on for some time and would continue to pursue.[67]

In mid-September, Dill returned to Washington, D.C., and met with the president to discuss Grand Coulee. The senator informed FDR that the state had taken steps to halt land speculation in the Columbia Basin. Roosevelt was very pleased, perhaps remembering such speculation deeply concerned Ickes. After the meeting, Dill assured reporters that funds for a town and a bridge at the dam site would soon be released. Two days later Ickes authorized the funds.[68]

Back in Washington State, members of the CBC worried that "flank attacks" might derail Grand Coulee. Indeed, the Washington Water Power Company argued in October 1933 that Grand Coulee should not be the cause of its losing the Kettle Falls site, and that federal construction amounted to an unfair subsidy. Frank Post, president of WWP, called for the power sold from Grand Coulee to be priced at the true cost of production and requested that the agency selling the power be required to return equitable taxes to the state. If WWP retained its rights to Kettle Falls, the high dam at Grand Coulee could not be built because a high dam would flood the falls. Thus Grand Coulee's power production would be held in check.[69] In light of such attacks, Ellsworth French urged Dill to push for authorization of five or six million dollars before Congress reconvened so as to put the dam on solid ground. This kind of concern plagued Grand Coulee until Congress formally approved the high dam in 1935.[70]

Dill announced late in October that PWA hoped to make Grand Coulee an entirely federal project. The federal government possessed powers the CBC and Washington lacked. For example, it had superior powers of eminent domain. These powers enabled it to begin condemnation proceedings against lands to be used for dams and then begin construction without waiting for final adjudication of the suit.[71] Yet there was serious opposition to making Grand Coulee a federal project. A.S. Goss and Rufus Woods remained staunchly opposed. They saw federal control as a disaster that would make Washington State subservient to the federal government. However, members of the CBC, including Woods, and Governor Martin eventually concluded that Grand Coulee could be built in no other way.[72]

In early November, the Columbia Basin Commission met with Senator Dill and Governor Martin and signed contracts with the federal government that made Grand Coulee Dam a completely federal project. The entire project would be financed through PWA with the United States Bureau of Reclamation in charge of construction. Moreover, the federal government intended to maintain ownership of the dam. Dill immediately called for a comprehensive authority along the lines of TVA to administer the Columbia River Basin. However, Ickes persuaded FDR that a regional authority for the Columbia River Valley was not necessary.[73]

Though Dill lost that fight with Ickes, he won another one about the same time. A number of Washington's cities had proposed projects that depended on funding from Ickes's Public Works Administration. But Ickes hesitated to approve such projects for fear Washington was getting more than its share of the federal purse because of massive outlays for Grand Coulee. On November 16, 1933, Dill protested such treatment to FDR. The president directed Ickes to transfer the municipal projects in question to Harry Hopkins' Civil Works Administration. Dill's efforts meant that those smaller projects would be built and that 10,000 more men would get jobs in Washington State.[74]

Clarence Dill kept his eye on Grand Coulee as the last year of his second term came to a close—as did some of the members of the CBC. James O'Sullivan and others pestered Dill with letters claiming the plans for the low dam were not adequate to allow the later superimposing of the high dam, even though the plans for the dam had just been changed to ensure that a high dam could be erected on the low dam at some future date. What O'Sullivan was really after, however, was initial construction of the high dam, or at least its foundation, rather than the low dam.[75] In January Dill responded to O'Sullivan's entreaties:

I do wish you would try to put a stop to this agitation about the foundation of the low dam not being satisfactory for superimposing the high dam. Dr. Mead stated when he was in Spokane that the plans are being changed to make the low dam entirely satisfactory. I have just talked with him and he tells me the entire plans are being revised on that basis. Neither he nor I can understand why this agitation should have been started again. It causes a lot of mail for me to answer and only tends to arouse dissatisfaction out there regarding the work we are doing.[76]

O'Sullivan answered Dill with a letter in which he asked the senator if it were not possible to get more money for the dam to make the low dam more compatible with the high dam. O'Sullivan was no politician and Dill attempted to explain the realities of Washington, D.C., to him:

My reasons for being so insistent that we avoid too much public discussion about the high dam now is that another public works appropriation is coming up in Congress and I am anxious to avoid any possibility of a limitation against the Grand Coulee. If those who are opposed to it, could make it appear that this dam is to irrigate more land [the low dam was only a power dam] now or in the immediate future, they might use that as an excuse to prevent expenditure of even the $63 million.

I am sure we can get satisfactory plans for the foundations of the low dam but we must build the power plant and the dam for $60 million. It is unthinkable to reopen this question for more money at this time. Once we get the low dam actually started and have the foundation actually worked upon, you will find me just as aggressive for the high dam as you have ever been. I am simply trying to avoid pitfalls by keeping away from that discussion now and I must depend upon you and other friends of the project to help me. It is extremely important that we get the contract let early this summer so we can have a big force of men working when the President visits the dam site.[77]

O'Sullivan paid no attention. His love for the high dam combined with his concern for the details of the project blinded him to the realities of politics. He responded to Dill's letter with assurances that he was not "striking for the high dam now," then proceeded to do just that. He had the support of another engineer who claimed the low dam, as planned, would not be adequate to serve as a base for the high dam. O'Sullivan advocated using the $60 million to construct a firm base for the high dam, effectively abandoning Roosevelt's low dam idea.[78]

Dill probably telephoned S.O. Harper, acting chief engineer of the project, because O'Sullivan soon received a letter from Harper explaining that the low dam was entirely adequate to serve as a base for the high dam.

Harper explained to O'Sullivan: "practically all the investment made at this time can be utilized to full advantage in the construction of the high dam."[79]

In addition to Harper's letter, Dill wrote to O'Sullivan in another attempt to make him understand the political dynamics of the project. However, this time his frayed patience showed.

> I have read the letters of Mr. Morse and Mr. Darland [associates of O'Sullivan], and all I can say is that we simply must not attempt to change the $63 million allocation and we must build the dam to whatever height it is possible to build it with a power plant also for the $63 million. If there isn't enough money to build it to a height of 1,085 feet [elevation], then build it to 1,060 feet; if not enough for that, then make it 1,040 feet, if not enough for that, make it 1,000 feet. In other words, we must have a dam and power plant for this money, and then get additional money for a higher dam at a later date.
>
> We want to get just as much foundation for the high dam in as possible, but once the specifications are made up for this low dam, we must go through with it and then if there is some loss when the high dam is built, that must be absorbed in the future.[80]

Dill had problems in the nation's capital as well. There were some minor hold-ups in calling for bids on the project, which required his time, but Mead and Ickes cooperated in solving the problems. However, O'Sullivan had become very agitated about the delays and sent a telegram to Dill advising he request the CBC to send a "resolution" to Ickes. Dill's calm response no doubt caused an increase in O'Sullivan's suspicions that Dill was "not on board for the high dam."[81]

O'Sullivan's long-term mistrust and dislike for Dill, exacerbated by their disagreement over the low dam specifications, now developed into hatred. In a letter to Ray Clark on July 5, 1934, O'Sullivan asserted there was a graft-laden effort to throw the main contract for construction of the dam to the Six Companies, one of the main contenders for the job of building Grand Coulee. Moreover, O'Sullivan associated his stand for the high dam with honesty, implying those favoring the project as approved by the government were grafters. O'Sullivan was also concerned the Spokane crowd would be "running the show" when the president visited later in the summer. O'Sullivan's letter to Clark reveals his state of mind:

> My job here is a hot spot. Lots of gravy mixed up in the Six Company's bid. Politicians, grafters, etc., are trying to horn in on Mason [a company competing with Six Companies for the main contract]. The issue between the high dam and the low dam is acute. My stand for the high dam and for honest bids has made things pretty warm for me lately.

W.R. Jarrell, Secret Service Agent, Pacific Northwest, Seattle, Washington, seems to be the one who can tell the most about the President's trip. I wrote you about getting the different communities down there organized, and keeping Spokane from running the show. The same old game which was played for years is intended.[82]

Two days later, O'Sullivan wrote to Rufus Woods, making more explicit his accusations. O'Sullivan claimed that Dill arranged for his long-time associate and Spokane attorney Frank Funkhouser to meet with Sam Mason, head of the Mason Company. Funkhouser suggested to Mason that he could act as Mason's attorney in securing the dam contract. Funkhouser wanted $100,000 for this service. Mason wanted nothing to do with Funkhouser's scheme. O'Sullivan went on to claim that Dr. Elwood Mead, head of the Bureau of Reclamation, was trying to "throw the job" to the Six Companies. O'Sullivan also asserted that James E. McGovern, a member of the CBC from Spokane, was also attempting to unethically profit from Grand Coulee.[83]

Most of the charges O'Sullivan made were untrue or completely unsubstantiated. However, Harold Ickes, whose reputation for honesty was well earned, ordered an investigation of the Grand Coulee project in the summer of 1934. Agents Oscar Brinkman, C.E. Grier, and Roy Young submitted reports. Mead, Mason, McGovern, and the Six Companies were cleared of any wrongdoing; but Frank Funkhouser, a longtime Dill associate and Spokane attorney was certainly guilty of unethical conduct in regard to Grand Coulee. Moreover, it would seem Dill was a party to Funkhouser's schemes.[84]

According to the investigations, Funkhouser signed a contract with W.E. Southard, an Ephrata, Washington, attorney and the representative of a number of landowners in the Columbia Basin who hoped to sell their land to the federal government as part of the Grand Coulee development. The contract stated that Funkhouser was to receive 25 percent of Southard's 20 percent of the money obtained for the landowners. Why would Southard sign such a contract? Funkhouser had led him to believe that Dill could influence how much the government paid for Grand Coulee land. When it became apparent that government appraisers were not going to allow bloated land appraisals to stand, Southard wanted out of his contract with Funkhouser. However, Funkhouser had another scheme to profit from Grand Coulee.[85] O'Sullivan appears to have been right that Funkhouser approached Mason with the proposition that the attorney would use his influence with Dill to guide the contract for the dam to Mason for a fee of $100,000. Mason would have nothing to do with Funkhouser. O'Sullivan's assertion regarding Funkhouser's schemes comes from an architect named Hargrove who worked for Mason. Hargrove, however, refused to make his testimony public.[86]

Nevertheless, the investigators concluded that Frank Funkhouser was engaged in unethical and probably illegal conduct, but gaining a conviction was unlikely. There was no evidence Dill was a party to Funkhouser's activities. Thus when Elwood Mead wrote a summary of the investigation to Ickes he could write that Dill was innocent of any wrongdoing.[87] However, historians are not limited to what can be proven in a court of law; what may be insufficient to send a man to prison, may well point to probabilities. Such is the case in regard to Clarence Dill and Grand Coulee.

It seems probable that the financial possibilities inherent in Grand Coulee development were too great a temptation for Dill to overcome. He and Funkhouser had been friends for years. Funkhouser used Dill's name repeatedly over a long period of time. Word of such activity could have easily returned to Dill. Therefore, it does not seem likely that Funkhouser could use Dill's name in his Grand Coulee schemes without the latter's permission. What does seem likely is that Dill and Funkhouser had an unwritten understanding that Dill would receive some of the money Funkhouser managed to make off the senator's name. Ironically, Dill had

Opening bids for Grand Coulee Dam construction at the Davenport Hotel, Spokane.
Cheney Cowles Museum/Eastern Washington State Historical Society, Spokane, WA

little power to affect contracts or land sales. If the deals Funkhouser had tried to create had gone through, his clients would have been paying him for nothing.[88]

So Dill probably engaged in unethical conduct in a failed attempt to make money. It would be easy, and simplistic, to cast the senator in a villain's role and make his accuser, O'Sullivan, something of hero. But history is not so simple. Though O'Sullivan had many positive qualities—perseverance, single-mindedness, and a willingness to sacrifice himself for the sake of the project—he was also overly suspicious of anyone who did not agree with him. For this reason Mead wrote Ickes: "Reading these reports shows the wisdom of the department in divorcing Mr. James O'Sullivan from all the operations at Grand Coulee. It is not that he is dishonest, but he is unbalanced and apparently thinks he is the only righteous man connected with this development."[89] O'Sullivan's motives were pure and his goal was the high dam, but his judgment concerning men and motives was weak. Dill occasionally allowed self-interest to overrule his better judgment, but he was a shrewd judge of political realities and men. O'Sullivan and Dill continued to clash over Grand Coulee.

In the summer of 1934, O'Sullivan turned to selling "the president for the high dam on his visit."[90] O'Sullivan's enemies, as he perceived them, were clearly Dill and McGovern, Spokane men who favored FDR's plan for the low dam to serve as a basis for the high dam:

> There are an amazing number of rumors regarding what the president will do concerning the high dam. Some of these indicate that he is on the verge of authorizing the high dam. However, the activity of Senator Dill and J. E. McGovern in securing control of all invitations would indicate an effort to keep the President from learning of the need of the high dam. It is particularly important that President Roosevelt should understand that the power trust is still working hard to defeat the high dam and that he should personally direct the Federal Power Commission and the Bureau of Reclamation to protect the power and water rights necessary for the completed structure.[91]

O'Sullivan's errors and concerns in this letter reveal a startlingly misinformed and suspicious mind. He assumed the president was uninformed about the high dam when in fact both Dill and Goss had explained it to him, Dill on more than one occasion. He apparently had no understanding of how cost dictated a low dam, not private power interests. Moreover, he associated Dill with those interests and believed the senator had no desire to build the high dam. Finally, he saw malevolence in the state's senior senator organizing a presidential visit to his state.

In early August 1934, FDR visited Grand Coulee. The ceremony featured all of the standard trimmings and speeches. Clarence Dill and FDR were the men of the hour. In his speech, Dill mentioned how he had brought the dam to FDR's attention, how the president favored a low dam, and how the project came to life. Then Dill graciously, and appropriately, gave FDR the credit for building the dam.[92] Indeed, throughout his long life, in both public and private, Clarence Dill would often give FDR the lion's share of the credit for Grand Coulee. In Dill's mind existed two versions of how Grand Coulee came about. In one, Dill was the man who won the dam from a reluctant president who owed him a favor. In the other, FDR's leadership and vision made Grand Coulee a reality.[93] Which story one got from Dill probably depended upon how the question was asked. That Dill could hold seemingly contradictory ideas about the origin of Grand Coulee Dam is not surprising, for he held a number of apparently conflicting ideas, values, and dreams.

Shortly after the celebration, O'Sullivan wrote this letter to Ray Clark:

I think you are right in saying that a showdown is very near at hand. The gang here have been framing me. McGovern, assisted by Funkhouser and Dill, grabbed control of the President's reception. This gang here secured the publicity from Washington D.C. stating that the commission was through and that I was offensive. They tried to keep any information about the high dam or reclamation from getting to the President. They have suppressed all publicity about the Soap Lake meeting, which was the biggest event of all. I showed the President all of the exhibits of Columbia Basin products and then introduced myself. He said, "You do not have to introduce yourself, O'Sullivan, I know all about you. You have done wonderful work for this project and you will have my support in carrying on your work." He said that loudly in the presence of Senators Bone and Dill and a number in the audience. Senator Ronald writes me that he has learned disquieting things in Olympia. The plan was to oust me at the next meeting of the commission.

The real issue is whether we are going to get the high dam or the low dam. I am in close touch with the secret service, and believe me, they have got McGovern, Dill, Funkhouser, and that gang tabbed....

McGovern, Dill and Funkhouser plan to shut me out entirely. I forced them to have the President's car stop at the exhibit at Soap Lake. All the boys cooperated fine in getting out banners, ribbons, etc. on the high dam. We actually sold Roosevelt on the high dam and on reclamation in spite of them....

The administration knows of the efforts of the gang to keep any information regarding reclamation and the high dam from him [Roosevelt]. I can say that I stand ace high with Ickes and the President.[94]

It is ironic that O'Sullivan would claim to stand "ace high" with Ickes, who would have never built the dam had it been up to him.[95] This letter also mentions the complete fiction, so often repeated, that banners on the roadside combined with O'Sullivan's efforts on the day of the celebration, convinced FDR to build the high dam.[96] The truth is Clarence Dill and FDR always intended to build the high dam; only O'Sullivan's imagination concocted a different scenario. Moreover, if FDR had not been inclined to build the high dam, roadside banners would not have convinced him to build it. However, Ickes, who accompanied FDR on this trip, and had long held reservations about the whole project, admitted that the sheer grandeur of the landscape and potential of the project caused him to become a supporter of the high dam.[97]

In the 1930s, there was no doubt as to who had led the Washington congressional delegation in gaining federal approval of the dam. Clarence Dill was a hero in the eyes of most people and easily the most popular political figure in the state. Even W.H. Cowles sought to make his peace with the senator. Hearing he was considering retirement in 1934, Cowles visited Dill in Washington, D.C., and expressed his intention to publicly support the Democrat's return to the Senate so that he could watch over the dam. Dill rejected Cowles's offer.[98]

Though Dill was a hero in the thirties, history has not been kind to him in regard to his role in building Grand Coulee Dam. George Sundborg's *Hail Columbia* gives most of the credit to James O'Sullivan, from whose papers Sundborg's book is almost exclusively drawn. Sundborg's disparaging view of Dill is essentially O'Sullivan's.[99] Rumors of Dill's attempts to make money on Grand Coulee would not go away and they hurt him when writers like Sundborg assessed his work for the dam. Later accounts of how the dam gained approval unfortunately followed Sundborg's lead and de-emphasized Dill's role. The primary problem with works that focus on the lengthy local battle for Grand Coulee is that they do not explain adequately how this local campaign turned into a federal project. The obvious link between the local interests and the federal government—Washington's senior senator—was ethically distasteful both to the principles of the time and later historians. Correspondence between the dam's major backers contain references to Dill's unethical activities and also make clear political animosities. I suspect historians could not reconcile the rumors of Dill's avarice and his unpopularity amongst Grand Coulee supporters, with an important role in securing the dam. Unfortunately, the United States has had no shortage of politicians who have performed vital public service while attempting to enrich themselves. History is seldom clean and neat.[100]

Clarence Dill was Washington State's key figure in the effort for Grand Coulee Dam in 1933 and 1934.[101] Dill's access to the president allowed him to present FDR with information that helped maintain FDR's commitment to the project. But Dill would have had little with which to impress the president had it not been for the countless hours of work devoted to the project over the previous fifteen years. Even the fight between the pumpers and gravity plan supporters had not been entirely in vain, as it allowed a consensus to form for Grand Coulee, even in Spokane.

There were several men without whom the project would have been difficult to achieve; four were essential: James O'Sullivan—who sacrificed himself for years to see the dam built and who provided Dill with the facts he needed to convince FDR that the dam could be built at a reasonable cost; Rufus Woods—who consistently publicized and supported the great project to keep the dream alive; Clarence Dill—who possessed the political office and personal relationship necessary to bring the project to FDR's attention; and most importantly, Franklin Roosevelt, who had the vision and authority to order the dam built.[102] The efforts of these men, and those of their supporting cast, contrast the myth of the West's individualist base to reality: despite their differences, these men cooperated to help build the West. Moreover, the building of Grand Coulee Dam is one of the key developments in the region's history: Grand Coulee and the dams that followed provide the power for the modern Pacific Northwest.

Grand Coulee Dam construction in the 1930s. *Cheney Cowles Museum/Eastern Washington State Historical Society, Spokane, WA*

CHAPTER TEN

A Man in the Middle

THE GREAT DEPRESSION: seldom has the name of an era more accurately reflected the minds of the people who lived through it. The fourth winter of hard times punished Americans as they waited for Franklin Roosevelt to take office in March 1933. Thirteen million people could not find work, farmers organized for revolt, hundreds of banks had collapsed, and a vocal minority espoused the panacea of communism. The president-elect negotiated the troubled seas of transition with uncommon grace, refusing to compromise the politics of experimentation that had brought him to the hour of trial. He remarked to Dan Roper, secretary of commerce, "Let's concentrate upon one thing, save the people and the nation, and if we have to change our minds twice every day to accomplish that end, we should do it."[1]

In the first year of his administration, FDR confronted the banking crisis, the farm problem, business regulation, and a host of assorted ills. Still, the unemployed and hungry faced another winter of worry and want. Harry Hopkins advised the president that some effort had to be made to meet the basic needs of the helpless. FDR, on humanitarian grounds, agreed, though he worried about the deleterious effect deficit spending would have on the economy. Hopkins organized the Civil Works Administration in nearly miraculous time as winter fell upon the country, and in so doing, he eased the suffering of millions. As a by-product, the economy was somewhat improved in the spring of 1934.

Americans responded to the Depression as if they had lost at love: they tried to forget their misfortune. In so doing they sought to drown their sorrows in weak beer and distract their minds in cheap movie houses. Clark Gable strode across the silver screen making women weak and men jealous, while Claudette Colbert held up traffic with a single leg. Nor had the nation forgotten the national pastime; Americans went to baseball parks in droves to watch the greats of the game: Dizzy Dean dazzled batters with his fast ball and charmed the nation with his country humor, and Lou Gehrig appeared in 2,130 straight games for the New York Yankees, symbolizing the toughness of Americans, and endlessly irritating the hapless Boston Red Sox. While the nation enjoyed a rousing chorus of "Take Me Out to the Ball Game," other forms of music came into favor. The thirties saw the birth of the big band sound of Tommy Dorsey, Glenn Miller, and many others. People flocked to dances, and dance marathons helped the weary to forget troubles.

If going to a dance were not possible, there was always the radio. Less than two decades old, the radio was the center of entertainment in the homes of most Americans. Sports, popular music, educational programs, gardening programs, agricultural reports, classical music, drama, and comedy came over the air into American homes. Most stations of the thirties tried to provide a little bit of everything.[2] The idea of playing a single kind of music endlessly was one misery spared Americans in the 1930s. To paraphrase a line from a 1939 movie, they also had one thing we do not have: Will Rogers. Rogers' common sense humor kept Americans laughing at themselves, at their government, and most importantly, at the Depression. His words of wisdom and humor came to Americans through newspapers and over radio. Indeed, it was over radio that the nation heard the voice of calm assurance and hope. Franklin Roosevelt used radio to reach the people in a manner never before tried or since equaled. He provided a mental image to listeners of a caring, fatherly figure sitting fireside, books on the wall, while explaining the intricacies of government in terms factory workers, farmers, and housewives could all understand. Radio was the key to Roosevelt's bond with the American people. Through radio Roosevelt led public opinion, explained policies, directed energies, and calmed fears.

The regulation of radio, which faced the constant threat of monopoly, became a goal of the Roosevelt administration in 1934. One of FDR's staunchest supporters, Clarence Dill, had risen to chairman of the Senate Interstate Commerce Committee, the body that would guide the Senate version of FDR's communication act. Dill was the primary figure in the Roosevelt administration's fight for communications reform. To fully appreciate his role, it is necessary to understand the developments in radio between 1927 and 1934.

After the Radio Act of 1927 went into operation and the Federal Radio Commission (FRC) began to function, radio entered a phase of growth that pleased many and alarmed some. From 1927 to 1934 commercial broadcasting came into its own and dominated the medium. It did so with much help from the FRC. Taken together, the networks accounted for nearly 30 percent of American radio stations by 1933.[3] In addition, the purpose of broadcasting was undergoing fundamental change. This phenomenon was brought on by the discovery that advertising could bring radio stations immense profits. Consequently, already scarce frequency space became even more valuable, putting economic pressure on nonprofit broadcasters to sell their interests to commercial broadcasters.

Nonprofit broadcasters faced other pressures as well. The FRC interpreted the 1927 Radio Act's phrase "public convenience and necessity" to mean that it was to consider a station's programming in determining whether to renew a license.[4] The commission further ruled the phrase meant that it was to ensure programming that served the interests of the broadest number of people. These interpretations of the "public convenience and necessity" would have a dramatic effect on the shape of American broadcasting. Both Congress and the commission have received no little criticism for the clause. Congress deliberately created a vague statute to give the commission enough leeway to effectively regulate a rapidly growing and innovative industry.[5] The commission, then, gradually defined the clause to make it an effective tool. Unfortunately, its definition, seemingly democratic in its decision to serve the majority, also served the interests of the larger broadcasters, who accurately claimed to be reaching the greater numbers. The commission's definition also favored the more densely populated Northeast. Consequently, the commission began denying license renewals to stations with limited audiences such as religious organizations and educational institutions, especially when such stations were the only broadcasters in their area. In metropolitan regions, limited interest nonprofit stations generally survived because stations serving the broader public interest existed there as well.[6]

In 1929 the FRC committed the above policy to writing and expanded on its meaning for religious and educational stations: "There is not room in the broadcast band for every school of thought, religious, political, social, and economic, each to have its separate broadcasting frequency, its mouthpiece in the ether. If franchises are extended to some, it gives them an unfair advantage over others and results in a corresponding cutting down of general public service stations."[7]

It did not take long for those denied licenses under the FRC's ruling to claim their right of free speech had been violated, but the courts ruled in favor of the FRC. The FRC's decision regarding channel allocation resulted in a fairly rapid drop in nonprofit radio stations. In 1925 there were 171 educational stations and a substantial number of religious broadcasters. In 1934 there were only thirty-five educational stations and nineteen religious broadcasters. Clearly, the economics of radio, combined with the FRC's policies, were resulting in the demise of nonprofit radio.[8]

A vocal group of diverse people was concerned that either nonprofit radio survive or that educational and religious programming be presented on general interest stations. Their hopes lay in legislation that would direct the FRC to consider the interests of these broadcasters and their listeners in allocating licenses. Naturally, the concerns of these people and the growing debate over the direction American broadcasting was taking reached the senior senator from Washington. The interests of nonprofit broadcasters also coincided with the desires of the president to reform communication law in 1934—which is not to say that Dill and FDR had the same reforms in mind.

Of course, there were other pressures on the senator as he attempted to guide the president's communication bill through the Senate. Those pressures had been building for some time. As early as February 1928, Dill had grown concerned over the encroachment of network broadcasters on smaller stations. In hearings on the confirmation of O.H. Caldwell to the FRC, Dill complained that chain broadcasters were often controlling the best channels at the optimum hours of the day. The senator added he was prepared to ask for additional legislation concerning this issue if the FRC did not address the problem. He did not follow through on his threat to chain broadcasters, but he did secure the extension of the FRC for one more year—considering it preferable to Hoover's management of radio—as Coolidge predicted he would.[9]

Rather than take on chain broadcasters, Dill was determined to do battle with his own creation, the FRC. He was angry the FRC had sanctioned an unequal distribution of radio stations, clearly violating what Dill believed Congress had intended. The Northeast had too many stations while the rest of the nation, especially the West, had few. He argued that the FRC must be controlled by "the great organizations of capital,...or else they have no desire to carry out the law." The standard commission response to critics was that they were bound by the Radio Act of 1927; Dill argued the commissioners were flouting it. Indeed the relationship between the members of the FRC and radio's leaders could be very close. Henry Bellows, one of the first commissioners of the regulatory agency, became a vice president of CBS shortly after leaving the FRC. [10]

The fight over redistribution of radio stations took an ironic turn when the House proposed legislation—which Dill believed was too drastic—to rectify the problem. The House bill would have directed the FRC to "allocate wavelengths to the various states according to population."[11] Dill's objection centered around the fact that the House's language would have meant some stations in the Northeast would have been closed. He believed this unnecessary because the problem had more to do with power allocation than number of stations. In other words, the problem could be more easily rectified by reducing the power of some northeastern stations, thus creating clear frequencies in areas of the country sufficiently removed from those stations. It was not necessary to close the northeastern stations to do this. The conference report eventually followed Dill's thinking and became law in April of 1928 (Davis amendment).[12] However, the FRC, to Dill's great consternation, paid little attention to the law.

But what does equal distribution of radio stations on a regional basis have to do with nonprofit radio? Simply this: the more frequencies or watts available in a region, the more likely it was for a nonprofit station to survive.[13] Dill made this point clear in January 1929 when he used as an example the diminishing of Chicago labor station WCFL's wattage in 1928.

Dill also took shots at the FRC's limited definition of public interest and necessity:

> What is the "public interest necessity and convenience" which the law fixes as the sole test for granting radio licenses? Certainly it is the same as the "public welfare." That which contributes to the health, comfort, and happiness of the people is in the public interest. That which provides wholesome entertainment, increases knowledge, arouses individual thinking, inspires noble impulses, strengthens human ties, breaks down hatreds, encourages respect for law is in the public interest. That which aids employment, improves the standard of living, and adds to the peace and content of mankind is in the public interest.
>
> Is it in the public interest, necessity, and convenience that this marvelous means of communication should be placed within the control of a few great corporations?[14]

He further pointed out that the FRC's definition of public interest was so warped it took WCFL off the air in the evening, the only time laboring people normally had access to radio. If Dill had become a tool of radio's money changers, as some students of radio contend, he must have been a disappointing purchase. Not content to mouth words, Dill initiated legislation that would place a cap on the wattage (10,000) of any one station. However, it was common knowledge that Dill's wattage restriction amendment did not have the necessary support in either house to pass, and even if it did "perform the miracle" and get to Coolidge's desk, the president was determined to veto it. Thus Dill's wattage restriction was not part of the Radio Bill of March 1929, which extended the life of the commission for one more year. Opposition from conservatives was just too strong, and their self-serving arguments had no trouble getting into print.

Despite this opposition, editors at the *Washington Post* believed radio's Senate expert was determined to pursue wattage restrictions and would run directly into "the so called radio trust" in the effort.[15]

In March 1929, Senator Dill addressed radio's problems on several fronts. He indicated his desire to bring comprehensive communications legislation before Congress in 1930. He was also contemplating radio legislation that would fix advertising rate schedules. Nor did Dill let up on the FRC. He attacked the commission for allowing "monopolization" of the air at the expense of smaller broadcasters. Specifically, he lambasted the FRC for creating "cleared" channels (a cleared channel was one that only a single station in the entire country could use). Thirty-eight out of forty existing cleared channels went to network stations at the expense of small and nonprofit broadcasters. In his fight against cleared channels and for equal distribution of stations, Dill specifically had the interests of nonprofit broadcasters in mind. He was also advancing the interests of the West, which would have benefited from the reduction in the number of cleared channels through an increase in the number of radio stations in the region.[16]

In this fight for the West and nonprofit broadcasters, Dill criticized the Court of Appeals of the District of Columbia in February 1929 when it ruled that General Electric's radio station WGY of Schenectady, New York, should not be required to share time with station KGO of Oakland, California. This decision recreated a cleared channel on the frequency the two stations had shared since the previous November when the FRC, following the dictates of the Davis amendment, had tried to spread stations more equitably around the country. In commenting on the WGY decision, the senator argued that the court had been unduly impressed with General Electric's counsel, Charles Evans Hughes. Dill also made the point that Hughes was representative of the quality of counsel the "radio trust" could afford; therefore the FRC must be continued and funded to the extent required in its battle with radio's big business.[17]

Radio's business leaders were not content with court victories over the Davis amendment; they also attacked the law in the press. A private investigation of the cleared channel issue sponsored by the National Electrical Manufacturers Association argued that merely reducing wattage, eliminating some cleared channels, and spreading stations around the country would not provide the best radio service to Americans; it would be far better to repeal the Davis amendment and create more cleared channels.[18]

In supporting extension of the FRC, Dill was not suggesting he was satisfied with the commission's work; though he found some of its members more philosophically acceptable than others, he saw it as the best of the alternatives. For he now argued that if the FRC did not begin to regulate radio as Congress envisioned, the public would demand a government-run system such as Canada's. Dill cautioned against such a development however, then he reminded the nation of the proposal, which the friends of the Radio Corporation of America (RCA) and International Telephone and Telegraph (ITT) had advanced, to combine RCA's overseas stations with ITT. Dill argued such companies were threatening to monopolize radio. The senator was attempting to create a position between those who would allow radio's business interests to run the medium and those who wanted government ownership of radio. Because he advocated private ownership with substantial government regulation, neither extreme viewed him with much warmth; each thought him a tool of the other side.[19]

As the 1920s gave way to the 1930s, Dill continued to fight for an FRC that would truly regulate radio and against radio's tendency toward monopoly. In December 1929, in spite of unhappiness with the FRC, he and Congressman Wallace White introduced legislation extending the life of the radio commission indefinitely. This legislation passed because it had become clear that the intricacies of radio mandated a full-time and highly knowledgeable commission to deal with the new medium's problems.[20] However, Dill and White wanted more; they also hoped to pass legislation that would force the commission to deal with the problem of monopoly in radio. This was not to be; conservative forces were so powerful that the primary fight over the Radio Bill of 1930 was whether or not the antimonopoly features of the 1927 law should be discarded, not strengthened. In that fight, Dill was the leader of those who argued for retaining the 1927 radio act's strictures against communications monopoly and for including the forfeiture of a license should a monopoly be proven. Opposition to such legislation came from radio's business interests such as RCA. Colonel Manton Davis, vice president and general attorney of RCA, argued vigorously against Dill's proposal before the Senate Interstate Commerce Committee.[21]

Though the antimonopoly features of the 1927 radio act were not modified, support in Congress for more severe antitrust legislation was minimal. The prevailing attitude among legislators was that the Couzens Communications Bill, which sought to bring all aspects of communication under one regulatory agency, would be the best method of dealing with communications problems. But the Couzens bill, which eventually included stronger antitrust language, frightened the broadcast industry and never had enough support to become law.[22] Such a reorganization of radio would have to wait until the political climate allowed for a new deal.

Though the FRC had achieved considerable success in reducing the interference problem, by January 1930, Dill's patience with the FRC was growing thin.[23] He now accused the commission of ignoring the Davis amendment, saying, "I would like to know the legerdemain whereby a law passed to ensure equalization has left the power allotments as uneven as they were before."[24] Frustrated as Dill was with the work of the commission, he recognized the political realities of the time and compromised on the makeup of the commission with the Republican administration. He was content with two of the five commissioners being in general agreement with his views, one swing commissioner, and two who favored the networks.[25]

Dill knew of the sentiment among some people in the country for a government-owned radio system. He had been to Europe on several occasions and studied the European system while listening to Europeans complain about it. He used the possibility of such a system as a threat against those who would monopolize the industry. However, he argued for privately owned radio from a unique perspective. Dill believed the listening tax in Europe was too high and constituted a hardship on the poor. He said,

> poor people on the other side of the Atlantic object to the listening tax as too high. Radio should be free to all…the air belongs to all the people and radio programs that are transmitted through it should be available to everybody. If the government collected a listener's fee, it would immediately begin to try to control programs and that would mean censorship and government interference, which is the last thing we want in radio here.[26]

In early 1932, Dill offered or supported several amendments to the Radio Act of 1927. In January he introduced legislation that would have reduced the right-of-way "cleared" channels enjoyed to 2,300 miles, thus opening a number of channels in the West and making diverse programming more likely. In February he discussed limiting the number of stations one corporation or individual could own, and he also advocated the institution of fees for licenses to make the industry pay for its own regulation. Finally, Dill, along with Republican Senator James Couzens of Michigan, began calling for restrictions on the amount of time stations could devote to advertising, which was probably of greater interest to the public than the other issues that troubled the new industry. A survey of radio stations conducted in 1932 revealed that radio advertising revenue was approaching $25 million.[27] Abuse of advertising was raising enough criticism that those fighting for nonprofit radio used the issue to raise sympathy for their cause.[28]

In an effort to deal with the various complaints about radio, especially control of advertising, Dill and Couzens called on the FRC to prepare a report on the state of the industry. Opposition to Dill's effort to regulate advertising came from radio's business leaders and, of course, advertising agencies. They were a persuasive group. When the FRC issued its report, it cited the fact that only 6.5 percent of air time was devoted to advertising and recommended government not interfere with that aspect of radio. But the FRC's report did not stop Dill from calling for limits on radio advertising and criticizing the FRC for failing to allocate more air time for small or independent stations.[29]

Nor did Dill forget about his idea to have broadcasters pay for their own regulation. He was not happy with the fact that the regulation of broadcasting cost the federal government more than $700,000 in 1933. More importantly, even that sum was not enough to adequately fund the work of the commission. Indeed, the FRC and its offspring the Federal Communications Commission had generally suffered from inadequate resources.[30] Consequently, Dill proposed that the government institute a system of broadcasting license fees that would raise the revenue necessary to cover the cost of regulation. In this effort, radio's vested interests again opposed the senator. Henry Bellows, vice president of CBS, appeared before the subcommittee and argued that broadcasters simply could not afford the fees. Dill engaged Bellows in a lengthy cross-examination, which clearly delineated their differences concerning radio legislation. Unfortunately for Dill's licensing scheme, the necessity of holding time-consuming hearings required dropping the licensing fee amendment from the radio bill of 1933. Even had Dill's ideas survived the legislative process in 1933, it would have made no difference because President Hoover vetoed the 1933 Radio Bill. This bill contained the essential concept of a comprehensive communications commission eventually adopted in 1934. Those who would strengthen government regulation of radio, then, faced their greatest challenge from conservatives, as most of Dill's efforts to strengthen and direct the FRC were defeated from that quarter. Radio's big business interests usually saw eye to eye with the Republican administration of Herbert Hoover, but they were very suspicious of the man who would become president in March of 1933—FDR.[31]

Though Hoover vetoed the Radio Bill of 1933, it is worth noting that Dill had managed to include in that bill an amendment odious to business, and another that would have brought better radio service to the sparsely populated West. Business objected in vain to the Washingtonian's idea to give the FRC power to levy fines for violations of various radio regulations. Republican Senator Wallace White of Maine, the co-author of the 1927 Radio Act as a member of the House, led the fight to get the fines removed from the 1933 bill. Dill prevailed. His idea to provide the West with better radio service took advantage of the vast distances often separating the small towns of the region. Dill argued that licensing stations of 100 watts would not interfere with the frequencies of stations already in existence, especially in regions that had too few stations anyway. The signals of such small stations would travel only a few miles, thus serving local inhabitants. Approving Dill's idea required waiving the Davis amendment of 1928 in regard to these small stations. Congress agreed, but Hoover did not.[32]

Dill also addressed the relatively minor issue of government-owned stations versus private radio. He published an article in the *Congressional Digest* in which he argued that the American way of regulating the airwaves was superior to the government-owned European way. Dill extolled the virtues of the 1927 Radio Act, especially its refusal to allow private enterprise to accrue vested rights to a frequency. He implied that whatever abuses existed were not primarily the fault of the law, but of the FRC which—though it held broad powers—did not act in the public interest. Nevertheless, Dill was firmly on the "American way" side, and thus those favoring a state-owned system considered him an opponent, no different and no better than those who would monopolize the industry.[33]

From 1927 to 1934 Dill unsuccessfully, except for the Davis amendment, proposed significant legislation that would have given the federal government greater power in regulating radio and brought better and more diverse radio both to the United States as a whole and to the West in particular. The primary issues in this period were the extent to which chain broadcasters would be allowed to dominate the medium and the complaints the abuse of advertising was generating amongst radio listeners. A secondary issue was the struggle among nonprofit broadcasters to retain a niche in the industry. Dill sought legislation that would have restricted the networks and made it easier for nonprofit broadcasters to survive. Specifically, he sought to balance the number of stations and the wattage of stations throughout the country, thus making more frequencies available to broadcasters. He also sought to limit the right of way of "cleared" channels, which again would have provided more frequencies to broadcasters. Finally, he sought to limit the number of stations any group of broadcasters could own, thus opening the medium to more voices.

By 1934 there was a new attitude in the White House toward communications legislation. In that year, President Roosevelt asked Secretary of Commerce Daniel C. Roper to organize a committee to study the problems of the communications industry. The report recommended that communications regulation be revised and all authority be given to one commission.[34] In a typical Rooseveltian strategy, the report was leaked to the press so that public opinion could be weighed. FDR eventually agreed with the report and decided to place communications regulation in one commission.[35]

Dill and Representative Sam Rayburn of Texas (chairman of the House Committee on Interstate Commerce) now took up the president's desire for communications legislation.[36] The new legislation combined all communications commissions under one authority as the Roper Report had suggested.[37] Up until the creation of the FCC, responsibility for regulation of the various forms of communications had been divided amongst a number of government agencies; telephone and telegraph regulation fell to the Interstate Commerce Commission which, preoccupied with railroad rates, did a poor job of regulating communications. Numerous other agencies had specified responsibilities for some aspect of communications regulation. There were even state agencies attempting to deal with communications problems. By 1934, then, there was a growing belief that one all-encompassing regulatory commission would create efficiency of regulation and allow for a more ordered growth of a dynamic industry.[38] Though the administration, with Dill's help, attempted to sell the new bill as merely an administrative measure, Dill now hoped to gain much the Republicans had denied him.[39]

Dill, following administration strategy, explained the president's purpose in proposing the new commission:

> It is far wiser…to let the proposed commission have power to make these studies than try to have Congress legislate on intricate and complex aspects of the communications program at this time. My idea is simply to bestow the present authority of the ICC and the radio commission upon the new set-up. Existing law is all the power necessary to give at this time…if we leave out the controversial matters the bill can be passed at this session of Congress, otherwise it cannot.[40]

Dill's comment concerning the elimination of "controversial matters" reflected more posturing than reality as the bill, especially his version, contained much that generated controversy.[41] But it is true that framers of the Communications Act of 1934 did set out to avoid controversy as Dill suggested: no new laws regarding monopoly were included in the beginning;

moreover, the supporters of the legislation, Roosevelt among them, contemplated no further safeguards for nonprofit broadcasters. Dill and Rayburn introduced communications bills to their houses on February 27, 1934. Both men expected fairly quick passage as the legislation was similar to the thrust of the New Deal in other areas: banking, commerce, securities, etc. That thrust was essentially an effort to save the capitalist system, under attack from both left and right, through government regulation.[42]

Though Dill and Rayburn hoped for minimal opposition, radio's business interests opposed the measure, especially Dill's version, which repealed the Radio Act of 1927.[43] But Rayburn, who thought himself a conservative, also received what he considered inordinate pressure from radio's business leaders to leave well enough alone. Rayburn's biographers wrote, "The wrath of conservative business interests fell upon Rayburn as he fought in committee and on the House floor for the administration's plan to create an FCC."[44]

If radio's magnates did not appreciate Rayburn, then they must have loathed Dill. For the Dill bill was widely regarded as being much more harsh than the Rayburn measure.[45] If Dill had gotten his way, Congress would have provided the FCC with highly restrictive guidelines on broadcasting rates; Rayburn's bill merely required that those rates "should be just and reasonable."[46] Henry A. Bellows, chairman of the Legislative Committee of the National Broadcasters Association, castigated the bill for going far beyond the president's intent. No doubt the act did go beyond the president's published intent. Roosevelt was usually content to let others take the political heat when possible. Moreover, Bellows opposed repeal of the 1927 Act because that law had created a number of court cases, the results of which provided broadcasters sure grounds of operation. In addition, Bellows believed repeal of the 1927 law would necessarily place an enormous amount of power in the hands of the new commissioners. Of course this is exactly what Dill hoped for: free the new commission, a commission appointed by FDR, to act in the best interests of the American people. Bellows also criticized the proposed limitation of licenses to one year, the idea of increasing fines for rules violations, the requirement to make available equal time for any person wanting to speak on behalf of a political candidate, and the restriction of the right to appeal commission decisions. Bellows was particularly upset with Dill's proposal to place more than one station on cleared channels.[47] It is important to note that all of the above ideas had been on Dill's agenda for some time; many of them were in the Radio Bill of 1933.

William S. Paley, head of the Columbia Broadcasting System, also fired broadsides at the administration's communications bill. He argued that the industry had "proved itself capable in the few years of its existence of regulating itself and the medium could go on working out its own problems in the public interest without having the 'throttling hands of a too rigorous regulation laid upon it.'" Paley went on in an effort to stake out the moral high ground for the broadcast industry: "Columbia has persistently, despite 'temptations of added revenue' declined to take programs which it felt would be contrary to the public interest. The public would be astonished if it knew of the income sacrificed by the leading broadcast enterprises in the interest of good taste, good morals, and honest business."[48] Irritated that Paley and Bellows characterized his legislation as unnecessary censorship, Dill responded, "there isn't any foundation either in theory or in fact for such an idea."[49]

Nor were those interested in other aspects of communications silent. Walter Gifford, president of American Telephone and Telegraph Company, charged the new bill created "government management" of communications, not regulation. Gifford was particularly upset that Dill's bill allowed the new commission to set telephone rates and investigate contracts between the various components of the telephone system. So hostile was business to the Communications Act that Dill found that most of the Democrats on the Interstate Commerce Committee were being pressured to oppose the bill. Indeed, opposition to the bill was so intense that *Variety*, a broadcast industry mouthpiece, predicted in April that the chances of its passing were nil.[50]

Dill responded to Gifford with that time-honored Senate tradition—threat of a Senate investigation; AT&T provided the target. The *New York Times* captured the essence of Dill's remarks:

> Senator Dill said that during hearings on his bill he had become particularly interested in the nature of contracts binding its numerous subsidiaries to the top company of the Bell system. He cited the testimony of Walter Gifford...that it might prove ruinous to the company to have a federal commission, such as the administration proposes, delving into its many private transactions.[51]

The communications bill that emerged from Dill's Interstate Commerce Committee hearings had been modified in accord with some of the criticism from the radio and telephone industries. Though most of the alterations were technical in nature, the leaders of the communications industry did manage to change the bill. The new commission was directed to study the contracts between communications companies (parents and subsidiaries) to ascertain if it should recommend to Congress that the commission be given the power to regulate such contracts in the public interest, rather than be given such power outright. The size of the commission was reduced from seven to five members, making it more likely the commission would be overworked. Nevertheless, the bill retained significant power to regulate the communications industry and was still unpopular among that industry's leaders. Dill's bill would bring potential rate regulation to the telephone industry, its primary goal. It also reduced the duration of radio licenses from three years to one, reduced the avenues of appeal of commission decisions, reduced the range of cleared channels to 2,200 miles, provided for equal time for political candidates, repealed the Radio Act of 1927 and reenacted most of its provisions, and called for an investigation of the allocation of broadcast facilities for educational and religious purposes.[52]

Still facing opposition from the communications industry, Dill now demonstrated his determination to pass his legislation. He made good on his threat to seek a Senate investigation of AT&T. His purpose was clear:

> If Congress fails to pass the communications bill, this investigation will furnish necessary facts upon which to base legislation with broader powers over communications at the next session. If Congress passes the communications bill we should make this investigation anyhow to furnish to Congress further information which the commission will not have time to secure.[53]

The last half of Dill's declaration was pure posturing: he had no intention of pursuing the investigation if Congress passed the communications act. If, however, opposition remained strong, the Senate Interstate Commerce Committee would conduct the investigation; Dill was the chairman.

While Dill was busy fighting critics of his bill from the business sector, church and educational groups with the help of many journalists and intellectuals agitated for assurances that their place in radio would be protected or expanded. With the aid of Senator Henry D. Hatfield (R) of West Virginia, a vociferous critic of the New Deal, and Senator Robert F. Wagner (D) of New York, nonprofit broadcasters had brought before the Senate an amendment to the communications act that called for 25 percent of a station's air time to be reserved for special interest programming. In the early thirties, these groups had formed organizations devoted to promoting the interests of nonprofit broadcasters: the National Committee on Education by Radio and the National Advisory Council on Radio in Education. NCER preferred nonprofit broadcasters to own their stations, and NACRE advocated mandating that commercial broadcasters provide time for special interest programming. By 1934 the concerns of nonprofit broadcasters were being mentioned in newspapers and periodicals.[54]

Meanwhile, the Rayburn version of the communications act, which lacked the more drastic features of the Senate bill, received the endorsement of the National Association of Broadcasters when Henry Bellows gave his stamp of approval.[55] The fight over radio would be waged in the Senate. Thus Clarence Dill would play the central role in reconciling the different interests of the various groups concerned with radio and in shaping the final legislation.

And shape it Dill intended to do. The day after Bellows threw his support behind the Rayburn version, Dill proposed an amendment to his own radio bill. The amendment substantially strengthened the antimonopoly language of the bill, thus fulfilling a long-term Dill goal. The amendment made it illegal for any one company to control all of the broadcast facilities of any community, city, state, or the nation. Dill's amendment would become one of the chief targets of Rayburn's faction.[56]

Dill was sympathetic to the plight of nonprofit broadcasters. In a speech on the Senate floor he said, "The difficulty probably is in the failure of the present commission to take the steps that it ought to take to see to it that a larger use is made of radio facilities for educational and religious purposes."[57] Senator Couzens of Michigan wanted to know if the antimonopoly statute of the Radio Act of 1927 had been retained. Dill assured him it had. After consideration of a few other minor subjects, the Senate moved on to consideration of the Wagner-Hatfield amendment.

Wagner-Hatfield was a direct rebuke of the FRC and its policy of denying licenses to special purpose stations in favor of the general public interest. While the broadcasting industry had become both concerned and incensed over the amendment, which would have provided 25 percent of a station's air time to religious, educational, labor, agricultural, and other similar nonprofit associations, support for the bill was not strong.[58] Both Senators Dill and White argued against the amendment. Dill had also been critical of the FRC policy, but believed Wagner-Hatfield would require micro-management of radio by the commission—or Congress—and would lead to intractable discussions as to who or what qualified as a nonprofit association. In short, Dill believed that Wagner-Hatfield would open Pandora's Box: how would the commission decide the allocation of stations between Protestants, Catholics, and Jews; between labor and education? Wagner-Hatfield made no provisions for such decisions.[59] However, Dill included a provision in his bill that instructed the commission to study the problems of nonprofit radio with an eye toward making adjustments. That report agreed with NACRE and eventually recommended that nonprofit organizations seek expression through general interest radio.[60]

Senate discussion of the communications act was not lengthy. The Wagner-Hatfield amendment was defeated by a 42 to 23 vote. Dill's legislation passed by voice vote.[61]

Communications historians have made more of Wagner-Hatfield than was ever made of it at the time.[62] No doubt the banality of radio in the interceding years has helped prompt such attention. Dill, with his proposal to study the nonprofit issue, has been accused of diverting a rising tide of sentiment for Wagner-Hatfield. However, educators themselves were divided as to how best to pursue their goals (the ACER/NACRE split). Many members of the latter group believed that having educational programs on popular general purpose stations was essential if a large audience was to be reached.[63] Indeed, this split among educators no doubt hurt the cause of educational radio.[64] Regardless, there was no rising tide in favor of Wagner-Hatfield.

Those who expressed disapproval of the Radio Act of 1927, primarily on the grounds that it did not adequately reserve to the United States ownership of the ether, numbered twenty-nine in 1927; those who voted for Wagner-Hatfield in the roll call vote numbered twenty-three in 1934. The issue voted on in 1927 was not synonymous with Wagner-Hatfield, but it was ideologically close enough to demonstrate that whatever sentiment there was for Wagner-Hatfield had more to do with long-term ideological differences in the Senate, than with a specific concern for nonprofit radio. For a good many years, the Senate had a group who could be counted on to support almost any measure that would ostensibly control big business. George Norris, William Borah, David Walsh, Burton Wheeler, and Gerald Nye represented this insurgent wing, and all voted for Wagner-Hatfield, just as they had voted against the Radio Bill of 1927 when nonprofit radio was not an issue. These senators were serious about protecting nonprofit radio if they could. Such legislation fit their political ideology. But their efforts did not constitute a rising tide of sentiment for nonprofit broadcasting. Wagner-Hatfield had actually drawn less support than the opponents of the Radio Act of 1927 had garnered. Further, thirty-one senators were so disinterested in the Wagner-Hatfield amendment they failed even to vote. Key Pittman, who had so strenuously opposed the

Radio Act of 1927, was among those failing to voice an opinion on Wagner-Hatfield.[65] The House was even less interested in such legislation.

In summary, Wagner-Hatfield was a secondary issue in 1934. It drew only modest attention from the press, and it commanded very little of the Senate's time. Only the more radical or insurgent members of the Senate voted for it, just as many of the same senators had voted against the Radio Act of 1927.

Ironically, Dill himself was often counted among those insurgent senators, sometimes referred to as the "Sons of a Wild Jackass."[66] But Dill had one quality that many of them lacked; he knew what was possible and what was not, and he was willing to work toward the possible. A strain of practicality modified his idealism, setting him apart from many other senators, such as William Borah.[67]

After Dill's communications bill passed the Senate, a conference committee began working out the differences between it and the Rayburn communications bill that had passed the House. The Rayburn bill had received the approbation of radio's business leaders in general. *Variety* voiced the hopes of these people: "Outlook is that the most obnoxious Senate amendments will go by the boards and the new act will correspond pretty much with existing legislation."[68] Nevertheless, *Variety* believed Dill would put up a fight for his bill.[69]

Unfortunately for Clarence Dill, *Variety*'s prediction was fairly accurate. The Washingtonian could not get enough votes in conference to retain his stronger antimonopoly language. In addition, the Senate provision calling for equal time for political candidates and their supporters was thrown out. And the educational and religious broadcasting issue was sidestepped by calling for the new commission to study the plight of such broadcasters. Perhaps most disappointing to Dill was his inability to convince the conference committee that restricting cleared channels to a 2,200-mile effective broadcast range was in the best interests of the industry. Such a restriction would have opened the airwaves to more voices, but the conference committee felt the matter was best left in the hands of the new commission.[70] Dill lost on these issues to his more conservative Democratic colleague in the House, Sam Rayburn. Rayburn's biographers described their subject's efforts in the conference committee: "Working against the pressure of adjournment, the Texan pressed the Senate to accept his version rather than a more stringent and, some thought, more punitive measure written by Senator C.C. Dill of Washington."[71] In short, the votes for Dill's more coercive communications bill simply did not exist, especially not in the House where the conference committee's report sailed through with opposition only from those opposed to any new clauses concerning radio.[72] However, Dill salvaged his less controversial idea for expanding the number of voices with access to radio. The Communications Act of 1934 provided the commissioners with the authority to authorize low-wattage stations in the West as long as they did not cause interference with existing broadcasters.[73]

Despite these defeats, there was still cause for optimism. Dill had always believed that the real problem with radio was not the law—though he was willing to admit it had deficiencies—but the make-up of the commission. The FRC operated under intense pressure from radio's business interests and their allies in Congress.[74] But Dill believed that a new Democrat-controlled Congress, combined with a sympathetic president, would result in a changed political and social milieu that would give rise to a commission truly dedicated to regulating radio in the public interest. Consequently, he now hoped an FDR-appointed commission would regulate more justly than had the Coolidge and Hoover tribunals. Perhaps this faith was naive; but it had yet to be tried in 1934. It is worth noting that in the thirties radio's business leaders used the courts to challenge the FCC on the notion that the "public interest and necessity" clause mandated a consideration of a station's programming in determining the fate of a license renewal request. The courts upheld the FCC's interventionist interpretation and rejected the owner's free speech argument.[75] Essentially, the court ruled that the interests of the public came before the free speech concerns of the radio station owners.

In addition, Dill did not see the 1934 Communications Bill as a finished product. During the debate he made clear his intent to revisit communications legislation in 1935 after the new commission had been given a chance to perform and the report on nonprofit radio had been written. Dill was serious in this intent. Throughout the late twenties and early thirties he had been constantly attempting to rewrite radio law. He envisioned no change in that effort.[76]

Historians have recognized Dill's role in the history of broadcast regulation. Their assessments have, on the whole, been positive. However, it is going too far to call Dill's work a victory for progressivism.[77] At best, Dill achieved a standoff with radio's wealthy and powerful business interests; indeed, he may have lost the battle.

On the other hand, Dill fought for the public's interest in regard to radio in areas he thought he could win: reducing the right-of-way of cleared channels, more equitable distribution of wattage throughout the country, and safeguards against radio monopoly. All of these measures made diverse broadcasting more likely without inserting the federal government into the moment-by-moment operation of radio stations.

Nevertheless, the impression lingers that Dill might have agreed to more strict government regulation of radio in the interest of nonprofit broadcasters had there been any hope Wagner-Hatfield might have passed. But because Dill recognized it had no chance of passage he chose to create legislation, rather than merely oppose it, and has consequently sometimes been criticized as being less than a progressive in regard to his radio work. This criticism is valid if by progressive one means someone who would rather be right and accomplish little, like William Borah. But if by progressive one means someone who stands for a philosophy similar to Jeremy Bentham's utilitarianism (the greatest good for the greatest number) then Dill—with his ability to compromise—was an effective progressive: more Americans had better access to diverse radio programming as a result of the Radio Act of 1927 and the Communications Act of 1934 than would have been the case had radio's business leaders been allowed to create a broadcasting system controlled by a few powerful individuals.[78]

Dill comes in for much of the same criticism as his choice for president in 1932, Franklin Roosevelt. Arthur Schlesinger Jr. wrote of FDR: "To the real radicals Roosevelt seemed at best warm-hearted but superficial, at worst glib and insincere, in any case hopelessly committed to the capitalist system."[79] Neither Dill nor Roosevelt would have been offended at the last part of that assessment.

From 1927 to 1934, the American people responded to the problems and potential of an amazing development: radio. They created a combination of private ownership and government regulation, which survives to this day. They rejected both a government-owned system and private monopoly of the airwaves. They chose the middle way. Given the political traditions cherished in this country, and the political realities of the era, it seems unlikely that a government-owned system could have been created. On the other hand, private enterprise had a very real opportunity to monopolize the airwaves. "The interests" were held at bay by a coalition of progressive Republicans and Democrats who sought to protect what they perceived to be the public interest.

President Franklin D. Roosevelt waves good-bye as the train leaves the Great Northern station at Ephrata following his first visit to the Grand Coulee Dam site, August 7, 1934. Also on the platform are Senator Dill and FDR's two sons. *Cheney Cowles Museum/Eastern Washington State Historical Society, Spokane, WA*

Chapter Eleven

Signing Off

I N THE SUMMER OF 1934, Clarence Dill shocked the people of Washington State and changed the rest of his life: he decided to retire from the U.S. Senate. This decision, made just after his success with Grand Coulee and so unusual for politicians who have risen to Dill's stature, reveals much about him.

The senator had been an extremely busy man in the winter of 1933–34. Between Grand Coulee and the communications bill were sandwiched a number of lesser responsibilities. He continued to guide the Roza Reclamation Project (to provide irrigation water for the Yakima area) and the Skagit Dam (to provide electricity for Seattle) while fighting for a railroad pension bill and a labor mediation bill.[1] The Great Depression was a hydra-like problem, the New Deal a demanding taskmaster. The pace of life in Washington was cruel: anyone associated with government often worked well into the night. Dill, a man who identified with place, longed for the solitude of a trout stream in the Kettle River Range. He also missed friendships that did not have politics as the common bond. He said on one occasion, "I find more of a neighborly spirit in the garage man and the small corner grocery man than I do in many of the people with whom I associate daily in the capital."[2]

In June 1934, Dill mentioned to J.D. Ross his strong inclination to forgo reelection, though he hoped to finalize the Skagit Project before his term ended.[3] Late in the month, he returned to Spokane and was surprised to find a large crowd waiting to meet him at the Northern Pacific station. The crowd had convened specifically to urge him to run for reelection. But Dill, in an impromptu speech, declared:

> I am tired of the Senate. I am not physically tired but the Senate has lost its thrill for me. And when a job has lost its thrill, I feel it is time to get another one....
>
> When I retire from the Senate I will make my home in Spokane....I landed in Spokane the first time in July 1908 and I decided right then I would make Spokane my home.[4]

The next day the *Spokesman-Review*, in a plot twist worthy of Dickens, tried to persuade Dill his talents were indispensable. The paper argued the state needed him to ensure completion of Grand Coulee Dam. Dill responded that the completion of the dam was up to Roosevelt, and he believed the president would build the high dam.

Spokane's citizens were not content with Dill's decision to retire. An organization formed to persuade him to run again. Its members argued that his talents were needed in Washington, D.C., as part of the New Deal, that he owed public service to those who had supported him in previous campaigns, and that no statesman had more thoroughly "won the confidence of the people of the Northwest than has Senator Dill." Even William LaFollette, a former Republican colleague of Dill's in the House, urged him to seek a third term.[5]

Dill left for Seattle shortly after his arrival in Spokane. Positive receptions followed him into the Puget Sound country as well. Everywhere he went, pressure increased on him to run, but he refused.[6] Finally, he made his decision irrevocable. In a radio address on July 11, 1934, he announced his decision to retire from the U.S. Senate. Dill told the people of Washington he was retiring because the Senate had a way of capturing a man for life, making him fit for only one role—senator. He sincerely believed most politicians did not know when to quit. Furthermore, he was quitting when he was popular because he thought that preferable to the alternative, and he reminded his listeners that political popularity rises and falls quickly. Dill also argued that the state confronted no pressing issue that mandated his return to the Senate. Then he criticized the political process, claiming he could not afford to mount Senate campaigns since he was not wealthy and campaigns had become so expensive. He further mentioned that he had begun to long for home and the joys of living in the Pacific Northwest. Finally, he admitted he had just had enough of public life.[7]

The speech was not one of Dill's best. He was beginning to develop a habit of bombast, of extended historical allusions, in his oratory. The seeds of these problems had always been there. These oratorical problems would grow in later life and result in listeners thinking less of him.

Dill also retired to make some money. He frankly confessed this fact in *Where Water Falls*. "I have no money, and never will if I stay there [the Senate]. What little I accumulate in six years, I spend in each campaign. That may sound materialistic but I don't want to be a broken down politician with no money in my old age."[8] Dill's concern about money provides insight into his relationship with Rosalie in 1934.

Though all of these reasons probably played a part in Dill's decision to retire, there were two other major factors that no doubt fell under the category of the "personal reasons" that he cited in his memoirs. The first had to do with an old friend of Dill's, William E. Humphrey. On July 25, 1933, President Roosevelt asked for the resignation of Humphrey, who sat on the Federal Trade Commission. Humphrey had been a congressman from Washington State and a colleague of Dill's in the teens. Though he was a Republican, Dill helped him obtain his seat on the FTC in the mid-twenties. After receiving Roosevelt's request for his resignation, Humphrey wrote to Dill asking him to intercede on his behalf. He recalled to Dill their "many years of friendship" and the favors each had previously done the other. Meanwhile, Humphrey asked the president for time in which to put his affairs in order. FDR agreed to give him two and a half weeks.[9]

On August 11, Humphrey informed FDR of his intention to fight removal from the FTC on the grounds that the president had no authority to remove a member of an independent commission.[10] One week later, Humphrey wrote to Dill:

> Never in my life have I reminded a person that I had done him a favor, but I am going to do so now—as this is an unusual case and under the circumstances I feel I am fully justified. You will remember when certain parties were insisting upon your being indicted in the matter of the Colville Indian Claims, and it accidentally came to my knowledge. While the parties argued that it was impossible for you to escape conviction and that the only course would be to throw yourself upon the mercy of the court, I argued with them that even if this were true, that such action on your part carried no moral turpitude and that you were innocent of any intentional wrong doing, that you were a young man and it would tend largely to discredit you and would be a disgrace through life—and that I would not consent to it. Just recently I have seen one of the men who attended that conference, and without any prompting from me, when I mentioned the subject, he stated the facts as I recalled them and he recalls the plea that I made for you. He thought that this plea stopped further proceedings. At any rate, they were stopped.
>
> When Mr. Bell seemed likely to involve you in certain unfortunate real estate transactions, I heard of the matter and immediately notified you, so that you were able to protect yourself....
>
> I think there is the making of a lot of trouble for the accomplishment of so little a purpose.[11]

Dill responded to Humphrey's letter:

> I have your letter of recent date, together with a copy of the letter to the President which I have read carefully. I note particularly what you say about the favors you did for me politically. I have always felt deeply grateful to you for this and as you know I have tried to repay in a small

way as far as I could. If it had not been for the fight I made on you, you would not have been confirmed by the Senate the first time your name came to the Senate, nor do I think you would have been confirmed the second time had I not fought for you.

I would not mention these things except that you go back and mention the things you have done for me. On two occasions I asked the President not to remove you. I did all I could for you this time when I was there, but after all the President is boss and I can't control his appointments. I want you to know I am anxious to help you in every way I can but I think I have exhausted whatever influence I had in this particular matter. I sincerely hope, however, the letter you wrote will have the effect of causing him not to remove you.[12]

Roosevelt persevered in seeking Humphrey's resignation.[13] The commissioner was equally obstinate. Eventually the president fired Humphrey, who then filed a lawsuit arguing that FDR had no authority to remove a member of an independent commission except for "inefficiency, neglect of duty, or malfeasance in office." The case went to the Supreme Court, but Humphrey died on February 14, 1934, before the court could rule. Though Humphrey was dead, his case remained alive. In May 1935, the court upheld Humphrey's case against FDR, thus limiting a president's authority over independent commissions.[14]

The Humphrey affair occurred in late 1933 and early 1934, precisely when Dill would have been pondering a third Senate campaign. The possibility that an angry William Humphrey might go public with his knowledge during that campaign had to cross Clarence Dill's mind.[15] Even after Humphrey's death in early 1934, Dill could not be sure that Humphrey's papers would not fall into the hands of Republican sympathizers. Had Humphrey gone public, or his papers fallen into the wrong hands, the allegations regarding Grand Coulee graft that were already circulating would have made it impossible to survive politically.

The Humphrey affair, though serious, was secondary to the marital difficulties that plagued Clarence and Rosalie Dill. The first few years of the marriage seem to have gone well. Rosalie proved herself an asset to Dill's campaign in 1928, contributing substantial amounts of money. But as time passed, it became obvious to Dill that his wife's fascination with socialism had been superficial and her sympathy for progressivism was spotty. When asked during the divorce trial in 1936 if Dill had not made clear to her his affinity for the "common people," she replied that she did not know what Dill had meant when he referred to such people: "I always thought the common people were the nouveau riche...people who had been thrust suddenly into unaccustomed places." In brief, she was much more conservative and more ambitious than he was.[16]

The first public rift between the two had occurred at the 1932 Democratic National Convention. Dill had a shot at becoming the vice presidential nominee that year. Rosalie was excited at the possibility and worked hard at the convention to achieve that result. She was not without influence. Her family was well acquainted with the upper class and powerful of New York and had been friends and neighbors with Theodore Roosevelt's family. When she learned that Dill had been party to the deal that made John Nance Garner FDR's running mate, she blew up, called Dill a "crook and coward," and left for New York. From that time forth, the Dills' relationship slipped toward destruction. Beginning in 1933, they did not live together on a regular basis, and in June 1934, days before Dill decided not to seek reelection, their separate living arrangements became permanent. Indeed, Dill's remark that he could not afford to mount political campaigns reflects on his relationship with Rosalie at that time. For Rosalie's wealth, had it been available to him, certainly would have alleviated fears regarding campaign expenditures.[17]

Dill's disintegrating marriage burdened him in the summer of 1934. In testimony given at his divorce trial in June 1936, he emotionally admitted as much:

> She had presented herself as sharing my progressive views. But I came to realize that she differed with me on every progressive issue and she was trying to change me and draw me over to the reactionaries. I've been in public life for a long time and I never broke faith with the men and women who elected me to office. So there was nothing else I could do. I couldn't live with her and I couldn't remain in public life.[18]

Though the statement was clearly self-serving, the rift between Clarence and Rosalie was deep. Within weeks of his official retirement in early 1935, the two had reached a property settlement; Dill initiated divorce proceedings against his wife on March 30, 1936.[19]

Dill asked the Superior Court of Spokane to grant him a divorce on the grounds that Rosalie had engaged in cruelty when she called him a "crook and a coward," and when she had spread rumors that he was drinking heavily, losing his mind, going blind, and intended to marry a high school girl. Apparently Rosalie, in addition to spreading these rumors among Dill's friends and associates, wrote to his parents with the same accusations. This brought the relationship to a crisis in September 1935. Rosalie testified that Dill told her one morning, "Get out of my house. My poor old parents—my poor old mother—you're killing them. It was a terrible day I let you in their lives. I don't know why I married you. If I ever made up my mind you'd deceived me, I'd kill you and I'd kill you dead." Rosalie left the house to ask an old friend for advice, but by the time she returned Dill had regained his composure. The incident was not mentioned again until the trial. The trial itself was front-page news even in the state's western dailies. Judge William A. Huneke ruled on July 9, 1936, that Rosalie's actions constituted grounds for divorce, which became final in January 1937.[20]

Dill's retirement at the height of his political career has interested Pacific Northwest historians for years.[21] It is probable that all the above, especially his marital problems, combined to make the thought of another political campaign unbearable in the fall of 1934. In the face of such pressure, Dill persuaded himself that private life would bring him substantially more money, more time to relax and enjoy living in Spokane, would help preserve his public image, and would lessen the publicity surrounding a potential divorce.

CHAPTER TWELVE

THE LONG ROAD HOME

F ROM 1935 TO 1940, CLARENCE DILL created a law practice that brought him financial success. However, he also came to the conclusion that his political career was not finished, that he still had the fire of political ambition left within himself. In the effort to revive his public career Dill faced old ghosts, old enemies, and an opponent seemingly determined to win at all costs.

Dill retired in March 1935 confident that President Roosevelt would see Grand Coulee finished as a high dam and eventually a reclamation project. Scarcely more than a month after he left the Senate, the Supreme Court threatened the existence of Grand Coulee. On April 29, 1935, the Court, not a Roosevelt ally in that year, ruled in regard to the Colorado River's Parker Dam project that the Public Works Administration had no authority to construct the dam without Congress' prior approval.[1] Roosevelt had begun Grand Coulee just as he had Parker: using existing PWA funds to circumvent Congress.

After hearing the devastating news about Parker Dam, James O'Sullivan advised Representative Sam B. Hill of Washington's Fifth District that it would be wise to gain congressional approval of Grand Coulee. Hill agreed and organized support for the dam. It was the hardest legislative fight he had ever undertaken. Private power interests and those opposed to reclamation—especially from the East—tried to block Grand Coulee. However, Hill's coalition of Western congressmen and public power advocates survived the charges of boondoggle and graft heaped on the dam's supporters and won the fight. The vote in the House favored the dam 199 to 126; Grand Coulee was on sure footing.[2]

Ironically, the man who had played the leading role in securing the president's support of the dam was not sure of his own footing in the winter of 1934–35. After Christmas Dill returned to the Senate chamber to gather some papers. The hall was dark and empty. The retiring senator looked over the gallery, the platform, sat in his chair for the last time, remembering battles won and lost. A "tinge of deep regret" overwhelmed him. As if ashamed of himself for dwelling upon what had been, he remembered Lot's wife and that he had lived his dream and chosen of his own accord to move ahead. He quickly left the chamber.[3]

Dill opened a law office in Washington, D.C., and retained his law office in Spokane. For the next few years he split time between the two cities, gradually spending more time in his western home as his practice grew. One of the reasons Dill left the Senate was to make money. Within two months of leaving the Senate, he had received more than $10,000 in legal fees.[4]

Dill even entertained an offer from Clarence Darrow to join the celebrated trial lawyer in his practice. However, the ex-senator turned the offer down because he did not hold Darrow's belief "that every person who commits a crime is justified in his own mind and that society or big business practices are to blame." Dill said to Darrow, "I can't go along with that doctrine."[5] Brought up in a Methodist home, educated in a Methodist school, Dill was steeped in the doctrine of free will and thus personal responsibility. Darrow's philosophy was antithetical to Dill's upbringing, though the latter was no longer a devout Methodist.

Dill's experience in radio procured several cases for him. However, he had always intended eventually to live full time in Spokane. It took love to finally move him west for good. Not long after Dill divorced Rosalie, he met Mabel Dickson, who was working as the National Supervisor of Home Economics for Land Grant Colleges in Washington, D.C.[6] Though Dill was twenty years older, they were married in April 1939.

Neither of the newlyweds was particularly fond of life in Washington, D.C. Mabel longed for her childhood home, the West, and soon persuaded Dill to liquidate his practice in the nation's capital and return to Spokane later that year.[7] Shortly after their arrival, the Dills began building a large home on the cliffs south of downtown Spokane. The home had a commanding view of the Spokane Valley; on a clear day one could see the Selkirk Mountains in Canada one hundred miles to the north. The couple built the house in 1940, but before he had finished it, the restless ex-senator had his eyes on another residence.

Speculation concerning Dill's political plans arose in May 1940 when work on his cliffside home inexplicably came to a halt. Questioned as to his political future, the former senator was not forthcoming until nearly one month later when he announced his candidacy for governor.[8] In his announcement he pledged to bring efficiency and economy to state government, thus eliminating the state's budget deficit, while adding to old age pensions and providing a secure funding base for schools. Dill also claimed it would be possible to reduce state taxes and accused Democratic Governor Clarence Martin of arrogating to himself too much power. The would-be governor proposed to decentralize that power by dividing it among other elected officials and returning some of it to county governments. Finally, he advocated maximum development of the state's hydroelectric power resources through public power administration. Publicly, Dill's desire to secure cheap electrical power for Washington was his primary motive in running for governor; privately, he was responding to Governor Martin's threat to expose his alleged involvement in Columbia Basin land graft if he ran against the governor. Martin's threat enraged Dill, who was already weary of the rumors to which the governor referred. He resolved to run against Martin, a Democrat less devoted to public power, in the primary election.[9]

In mid-July Dill learned that Arthur Langlie had entered the race on the Republican side. He was pleased as he hoped the charismatic Langlie would draw some of Martin's Republican supporters away (Washington

Dill (center left) standing next to Washington State Governor Clarence Martin (center right) and other dignitaries. *Box 4, file #35, Cheney Cowles Museum/Eastern Washington State Historical Society, Spokane, WA*

allowed crossover primary voting). Dill said, "I feel more secure of the Democratic nomination now than ever."[10]

In keeping with his support of public power, Dill opposed the highly controversial private power sponsored Initiative 139. This bill would have made it difficult for public utility districts (PUDs) to purchase or build power plants and distribution systems.[11] Dill also capitalized on his record as a builder. In a handbill, he cited his opening of the Colville Indian Reservation and his role in building Grand Coulee Dam, among other accomplishments. If elected he promised to expand Washington's rural road network, enhance the state's public power system, and work for state help in raising teachers' salaries. The old progressive was still alive and well.[12]

For his part, Martin worked to retain labor's support. He reminded workers that his appointments had often met with their approval. Dill responded that Martin's labor record was pathetic compared to his own work in Congress. He claimed that in the years he had represented Washington, he had voted on labor issues 320 times and on every occasion had voted with labor. Such, indeed, seems to have been the case. Dill even secured a letter from William Green, president of the American Federation of Labor, substantiating his favorable record on labor issues.[13] To secure the support of the AFL, Dill promised James Taylor, president of Washington State's AFL, that if elected he would appoint a person acceptable to labor to head the Department of Labor and Industries.[14]

Of course gaining the support of the AFL did not necessarily mean Dill would garner all the votes of laboring men. Washington was in the thick of the battle between the AFL and the new Congress of Industrial Organizations for control of the American labor union movement.[15] Even so, under normal circumstances, Dill could have hoped for the support of both major union organizations. However, during the 1940 gubernatorial campaign, the CIO, led by John L. Lewis, split dramatically over Lewis's decision to support Republican Wendell Wilkie for president instead of FDR. William Green sought to take advantage of the split in the CIO declaring the organization was "torn with dissension, divided politically because its leaders seek to compel it to support a political party."[16] Thus, after Lewis left the Democratic camp, little was certain concerning the support of the CIO.

Governor Martin failed to stop the hemorrhaging of his labor support. Straw polls revealed that labor backed Dill in large numbers regardless of the opponent, though Dave Beck, vice president of the International Brotherhood of Teamsters in 1940, supported Martin in the primary. Dill also received the nod from farmers at this point in the campaign. Langlie was the businessmen's favorite despite his advocacy for increased pensions.[17]

Late in the campaign, with another European war possible, Martin attacked Dill's World War I voting record. The ploy failed, or perhaps the summer of 1940 was too early for such an appeal. Regardless, Dill received 186,008 votes to Martin's 114,484. Langlie easily won the Republican primary as expected with 160,551 votes.[18]

Both Dill and Langlie had campaigned on the theme that Martin's administration was wasteful and inefficient, a traditional concern of both progressives (Dill) and conservatives (Langlie), though before the campaign Langlie had complimented the governor on his stewardship of the state's finances. As his biographer has noted, Langlie could be boldly hypocritical at times.[19] The crossfire from Dill and Langlie cut Martin to pieces; thus the politics of caution fell to the promise of reform and change. The only questions remaining were who would implement that change and how drastic would it be? Unfortunately, less weighty issues obscured that question during the fall campaign.

The two candidates relaxed for a few days after the primary. Dill went fishing, which allowed him to recoup his strength and ponder the coming campaign. The Democratic nominee well knew his adversary was a worthy opponent. Victory would require mustering all potential support. Dill realized that only with a united Democratic Party could he hope to win the governor's seat. To that end, Dill reconciled with Governor Martin, who agreed to campaign for the party's nominee. Thus were the Democrats united, at least publicly.[20] Langlie did not delay in attacking Dill or in ridiculing the new Democratic solidarity:

> This was not an ordinary fight [the primary contest between Dill and Martin]...vast sums of money were spent—and yet now we are treated to a scene that puts Romeo and Juliet to shame.
> The people of the state were forgotten last night. They didn't count. All that mattered was the machine.[21]

Then Langlie addressed the theme of preparedness, accusing liberals like Dill of being less than supportive of adequate defense measures."[22] He finished his opening attack on Dill with a broadside at the Department of Labor and Industries and at the Democratic Party leadership:

> It [the department] is costing such a high rate that it is forcing small industries out of operation. It needs a thoroughgoing reorganization...
> I don't want to see this state taken over by any machine-controlled gang. Democratic government can be the rottenest form of all government when its [sic] improperly administered.[23]

Dill's new opponent, unlike Clarence Martin, would not hesitate to make Dill's ties to labor a campaign issue. Indeed, Langlie cast those ties in the shadows of criminal behavior (machine politics).

Such a characterization was not difficult to accomplish. Labor leaders such as William Green were fighting to keep criminal activity out of unions, but organized crime had nevertheless infiltrated some unions. In the midst of the 1940 campaign, Green felt it necessary to announce that the AFL would take action against "gangster penetration of affiliated unions," and he had already done so in Chicago and New York. The labor movement in Washington also had an aura of criminal activity. In the general election, Dill had the support of Dave Beck, whose activities as a Seattle labor leader had gained him a reputation for ruthlessness and illegal activity. In addition, officers of the four large railroad brotherhoods endorsed Dill unequivocally, as they had the entire Democratic ticket. The Washington State Federation of Labor had previously endorsed the Democrats as well.[24]

These circumstances, combined with Dill's unblemished labor voting record, were enough to convince a number of voters that he was a labor puppet. Indeed, Langlie purposely planted in the minds of voters the idea that labor's support of Dill constituted old-fashioned machine politics. The Republican particularly attacked Beck's support of Dill declaring, "honest government is vital to the protection of honest labor." Beck fired back, calling Langlie "the man with the automatic mouth." Such name calling tactics were typical of Langlie, who had learned them well as a member of Seattle's Cincinnatus Club and as a candidate for Seattle City Council.[25] Moreover, the old rumors concerning Dill's alleged profit from Grand Coulee land schemes further prepared the public to accept the idea he was for sale. The polish of the messenger delivered a few more votes to the Republican column. In late September Langlie said:

> Bear these facts well in mind—it is the governor who is the highest administrative officer of our state, it is he to whom we must look for the firm hand to guide us in the unpredictable days to come, it is he to whom the aged must look for fulfillment of their pension needs, it is he to whom the schools must look for fulfillment of financial obligations. It is he to whom the people must look for proper supervision of the military draft act, it is he to whom the people must trust the spending of nearly one hundred millions of their tax dollars annually.
>
> Do you want to put these obligations and privileges in the hands of a political machine?[26]

Thus did Langlie serve notice that the governor's race of 1940 would be a completely different campaign than any in Dill's experience.

Nevertheless, the Democrat responded to Langlie's blast with charges of his own. He asserted that a Langlie victory would reduce the financial benefits that public power, properly administered, would one day bring the state. He implied Langlie was a pawn of the power trust:

> The issue in this campaign is: How, by whom and for whom are these new millions [federal war spending] to be employed? Is the program of cheap public power to be enforced? Is the development of our state to be placed in capable and unshackled hands and worked out for the benefit of all the people, or will the power trust and the political rings which in the past have thwarted this development be permitted to resume control?
>
> The inauguration of the policy of boosting water bills in Seattle to make up for any shortage in the city's budget leaves no doubt as to my opponent's stand. That policy of bleeding a publicly owned utility to meet a political need, if applied throughout the state, will sabotage the entire public ownership program and destroy instantly any benefits of the public power program in this state.[27]

The candidates now fought like two Roman gladiators chained together, but Langlie's attack seemed to possess more power, seemed to make more indelible impressions on the citizens. His use of names in support of his "machine" accusations lent credence to those charges; in contrast, Dill was vague.[28]

As September gave way to an emerald and gold October, the candidates toured the state in an effort to convince the confused and energize the lethargic. Langlie typically campaigned from 7:00 a.m. to 10:00 p.m., drumming up support in small towns and large. Political pundits predicted a Dill victory. However, the combatants took nothing for granted, though Dill's speeches reflected his frontrunner status in avoiding inflammatory rhetoric.[29]

Langlie accepted the underdog role and campaigned accordingly. In mid-October he appeared to provide substance to his machine charge when he asserted that a Democratic campaign official pressured Spokane city employees for money arguing, "It is better to give up a month's salary than be unemployed for four years." Langlie commented on the alleged activity, "That's what I mean by machine politics." Of course he meant a great deal more, but the money-pressuring story served his purpose nicely; it allowed him to expand on his idea for a merit system for government employees that would reduce party patronage. Thus a minor issue briefly captured the attention of the state and further substantiated Langlie's "machine" charges.[30]

A few days later, Dill categorically denied soliciting funds in the manner Langlie described and further stated that his campaign workers were under strict orders not to engage in any such tactics. The *Wenatchee Daily World*, a fiercely Republican newspaper, reported that it had actually been Martin loyalists who were putting the squeeze on city employees: "Local Central Committee Democrats said they knew of several instances where job-holders had been asked to contribute money, ostensibly for the Dill campaign, but in reality to cover a Martin primary deficit."[31]

Langlie's blows and the grind of the campaign wore on Dill. At fifty-six, he was no longer the young man who had driven the dusty roads of northeastern Washington during his 1914 campaign. Yet he maintained the same arduous schedule he had nearly thirty years earlier. On Thursday, October 10, he made seven speeches on the west side of the state, where rain muffled his voice and the enthusiasm of the crowds. By 3:00 p.m. he was in Wenatchee, and by eight the next morning he was shaking hands again. In the afternoon, he spoke in Leavenworth, Entiat, Ardenvoir, and Cashmere. Saturday he delivered nine speeches in Whitman County.[32] In the midst of this mind-numbing schedule, he confessed to the *Wenatchee Daily World*, "This is the last political campaign I will ever make." The words were a promise to himself, in the throes of physical exhaustion, that he would never suffer such affliction again. Like the miler who tells himself he can go still faster because he can rest soon, it was a means of summoning his last reserves of strength for the task at hand.

In his speeches, Dill asked the people of Washington to defeat Initiative 139, which would have required PUDs to earn a majority vote in a special election if they desired to expand, with the majority required to be based on the number of votes cast in the last general election, a difficult task for a single issue. In his fight for the governor's chair, Dill received the support of Senator Homer Bone, who campaigned strongly against Initiative 139 and for Dill. But Langlie came out against 139 as well and thus stole some of Dill's thunder. Nevertheless, Dill continued to color Langlie as the "nominee of the private power crowd" while Bone reminded voters of Dill's work for Grand Coulee and his impeccable public power record.[33]

Langlie was both relentless and masterful. He turned Dill's promise to bring efficiency to state government into a program to deprive "good men and women" of their jobs. Then he charged that Dill had promised every job on the state payroll three times over to those involved in the Democratic "machine." According to Langlie, Dill was either taking good jobs from innocent, hard-working people (who were previously part of Martin's "machine"), or promising jobs to "political has-beens."[34]

With three weeks left in the campaign, Langlie decided to focus his attack on labor's "self-centered leaders." In a Tacoma speech, he emphasized his support for labor in general, collective bargaining, and workmen's insurance. He cast himself as labor's protector against the exploitive tactics of "some" greedy employers and a "few" labor leaders.[35]

Nor did Langlie forget to hammer away at his opponent's private life and public policies. He challenged Dill, who had made a considerable amount of money in the previous five years, to make public his recent income tax returns, thus again implying unethical conduct on Dill's part. Langlie also attacked Dill's tax-cutting ideas, leaving the wholly erroneous impression that the Democrat would not provide for old-age pensions, school funding, or other essential services.[36]

However, these were side shows. Always, Langlie returned to his theme that Dill was a machine politician. How ironic that the man so often and deeply reviled in his own party for being an independent, the man who had been out of politics for six years, the man who had caught George Norris's attention as an independent, the man whom the Martin Democrats—the Democrats who did have political power—bent every muscle to defeat, should be cast in the role of the ultimate party hack.[37] But the thirties and forties were decades in which labor was flexing its muscles—sometimes violently. Moreover, politicians had grown up with the graft associated with prohibition, and government often seemed unable or unwilling to cope with the problems engendered by the Depression. Strong men like Huey Long, if not common, were certainly possible. In such conditions, conservatives were often described as being firmly controlled by the big money interests and those sympathetic to the working man were customarily described by their opponents as being firmly in the grasp of a "political machine" controlled by organized labor.

It was even more ironic that the master campaigner from the teens and twenties should prove so ineffectual in 1940. However, Dill's response to Langlie's vituperative and visceral onslaught lacked the sting of the Republican's charges. Instead of attacking Langlie, Dill accused the newspapers of covering only half the campaign: the Republican half; and argued they ought to give equal time to other political candidates. Though true to a point, Dill's charge was essentially irrelevant, and more importantly, failed to parry Langlie's blows. Nor did it make any friends in the media; the next day, the *Wenatchee Daily World* resurrected the enforced campaign contribution story.[38]

The *Wenatchee Daily World* was not the only paper bent on the demise of Dill's political career. Indeed the state's major dailies were either for

Langlie or chose to remain aloof. The *Seattle Times* left no story untold in its effort to defeat the Democrat while the *Spokesman-Review* and *Bellingham Herald* all pushed the Langlie candidacy ardently. The *Everett Daily Herald* and *Tacoma News Tribune* confined themselves to urging their readers to vote. The latter paper believed partisanship was ruining the country and reminded readers of George Washington's admonition against party spirit. The *Seattle P.I.*, which had supported Dill in 1922 and 1928, was also fairly even-handed in its campaign coverage but refused to endorse Dill.[39]

The Republican's assault on Dill gained new energy as November approached. Albert Goss, who had been master of the Washington State Grange, had worked with Dill to gain FDR's approval of Grand Coulee Dam, and had become a federal land bank commissioner in the Roosevelt administration in 1933, attacked Dill on two fronts. Goss had served as a land bank commissioner until March 1940 when he resigned. He claimed that Roosevelt's Secretary of Agriculture at that time, Henry Wallace, was guilty of a "shameful effort to change the farmers' cooperative credit system into a political organization." However, during the election of 1940, Goss accused Dill of placing the land bank under a spoils system when he was a senator back in the mid-thirties. Goss asserted that in so doing, Dill had created a political machine. Apparently, Goss had no problem working as a land bank commissioner under "Dill's machine," but balked at the Roosevelt administration's alleged politicizing of the land bank in 1940. In short, the former commissioner's comments made little sense but did provide great headlines. Goss also declared Dill had been "cold on the proposition" to build Grand Coulee Dam before FDR approved the $63,000,000 dollars in PWA funds. Goss's remarks about Grand Coulee drew a heated response from Dill. He called Goss little more than an interloper in the effort to build the dam, which was an accurate if uncharitable assessment. Goss's version of how the dam gained approval does not bear scrutiny.[40]

Days before the election, Dill decided his strategy of ignoring Langlie's charges had been unwise. He now vehemently denied that he owed jobs to campaign workers or labor figures or was a tool of labor leaders.[41] He called Langlie's charges "silly" and caustically replied that his "machine had apparently given Herbert Hoover 145,000 more votes in 1928 than it had him." Dill went on: "My election was won by the people in the little towns, the neighborhood areas and the farming communities. That 'machine' never wants anything but honest government and the election of a man who is on the side of the people who need help."[42]

In the last days of the campaign Dill took to the radio to put his program before the people. He answered Langlie's charges, explaining his solutions to the state's problems. He also responded to Langlie's assertion that he was a "radical" (thus opposed to preparedness):

> Of course, I know that my opponent's intention and the intention of the *Seattle Times* is to give the impression that I am in favor of the kind of radicalism that would overturn our system of government. They would have the people believe that I sympathize with the fifth columnists who would sabotage preparedness and national solidarity and would wink at and overlook subversive activities of various kinds throughout the country. They do not dare make these statements openly. That would be too brazen a lie about me. So they try to insinuate it by shouting Dill is a "radical."[43]

The next day Dill returned insult for insult, accusing Langlie of being a tool of the "entire special privilege machine that has fought me ever since I have run for public office." Then Dill associated Langlie with the forces attempting to pass Initiative 139, the "last stand of the private power interests in Washington."[44]

The 1940 gubernatorial campaign in Washington had been a political brawl. On November 5, the people of the state went to the polls to cast their score cards. In Spokane voters crunched through fresh snow; winter's early entombment of the eastern Washington city was not a good omen for Clarence Dill.

In the national election the American people did not keep FDR in suspense long. It was soon obvious the Squire of Hyde Park would become the first man elected to serve three terms as President of the United States. In addition, Democrat Mon Wallgren became one of Washington's senators.[45] Thus Dill had reason to hope that his own election was imminent. However, the electorate was not as kind to Arthur Langlie or Clarence Dill; the two men were locked in a contest that refused to end.

The election returns for the 1940 governor's race in Washington took both candidates on a roller coaster ride. Ballot counting went into the night: first Dill led, then Langlie, then Dill again. In the early hours of Wednesday, Pierce County, Dill's most reliable base of support on the west side of the mountains, had given him a substantial 11,000 vote lead. When morning broke, Langlie, stone-faced, refused to comment.[46]

By Wednesday afternoon, however, the Republican had surged to a 2,734 vote lead. Langlie had taken the majority of eastern and rural counties, offsetting Dill's strength in the cities. As those returns came in his lead increased, eventually cresting at 7,000 votes. Then other returns from King and Pierce counties siphoned away the Republican's lead all through Wednesday night: when morning came Langlie's lead was only 1,580.

Officials now predicted that absentee ballots would decide the election. Both sides expressed confidence in the result, though they would have to wait a week to learn it. It had been thirty years since the governor's race had been so close.[47]

In the meantime, political observers analyzed the election. Unable to wait for the result, they assumed Langlie's lead, though precarious, would hold. Thus the task at hand was to account for Langlie's stunning upset victory. Conventional wisdom held that Langlie's Scandinavian heritage mitigated Dill's strength in the Puget Sound region, home to many of Scandinavian descent. The argument went that Langlie had taken many Democratic or liberal Republican Scandinavian voters who would other-wise have voted for Dill. This argument would seem to have some merit, though it would be impossible to gauge how much.

Some argued Langlie's solid organization and cunning campaign strat-egy were key.[48] There is no doubt Langlie's staff was excellent, his cam-paign near flawlessly executed. He early on removed public power as a galvanizing issue by opposing Initiative 139, though he did not emphasize his opposition. He agreed with Dill that the head of the social security department, Charles Ernst, had to go (Dill had castigated Martin for re-fusing to fire Ernst, alleging the latter was responsible for waste in the department). Thus another of the Democrat's issues died quietly. Langlie also turned Dill's plan to reorganize state government against him, arguing that though the state needed to reorganize, it could not afford to lose qual-ity people. The state's workers all thought he meant them, and many worked diligently for his election (thus further discrediting Langlie's "machine" allegations).[49] The two men's views on old-age pensions were indistinguish-able, but that did not stop Langlie from scaring the elderly when he said Dill's tax cuts might affect pensions.

Observers also believed that Albert Goss's pronouncements on Dill's role in regard to farm loans probably delivered votes to Langlie. There is more to this hypothesis than even those who put it forward realized. In previous elections, Dill had always been able to count on reasonable sup-port in rural counties. But in 1940, Dill lost twenty-three out of thirty-five rural counties. His rural wins were narrow victories and generally in tim-ber-oriented counties (Grays Harbor, Mason, Kitsap, etc.), and his losses were generally in farming counties and by massive numbers. Yakima County went for Langlie by nearly 7,000 votes, Whitman 4,000 votes (2-1), and Walla Walla 5,000 votes (more than two to one). Dill, of course, won in the cities. However, his home, Spokane, gave him only 1,500 more votes than Langlie. There were bright spots; Pierce County held firm providing a 9,000 vote plurality while King County provided 7,000 votes to the good, Snohomish 3,000. Had Dill carried most of the agricultural counties, as he always had before, he would have won. Thus Langlie's biographer George Scott was correct when he cited central Washington's agricultural counties as being the key to Langlie's win.[50]

There are several explanations as to why Dill lost so many of the farm counties. First, Langlie devoted a great deal of time to the region.[51] There was good reason. His "machine" charges would have found the most receptive ears in Washington's rural agricultural counties. Accusations of "machine" politics and labor ties would not have seriously shaken Dill's support in the cities, nor would they have been effective in timber camps and mills. Workers were accustomed to hearing such charges. But farmers were very suspicious of politicians tied to the big city, as Al Smith had found in 1928. Then, too, there was the question of Dill's "radical" politics, the mention of which was meant to remind voters of his obstructionist voting record during World War I. This argument, too, carried more weight in the wheat fields of eastern Washington than in the labor halls of Seattle, as there was greater inclination among labor factions to view the Great War as a capitalist's money-making scheme. Finally, one must remember that FDR's farm program under the Agricultural Adjustment Administration simply never solved America's farm problem. As a Democrat, Dill would have borne some of the anger farmers felt. However, Democrat Mon Wallgren won in his bid for the Senate, and FDR himself was victorious in Washington; so it would seem that the nature of Langlie's campaign—featuring his "machine" charges and Goss's aspersions on Dill's record—were the most important factors in the Democrat's defeat.

It is also possible that Dill's forces had been overconfident. Before the election, Dill had presumptuously included in his account of his life for *Who's Who In America* the claim that he had been elected Washington's governor in 1940.[52] Overconfidence may account for Dill's reluctance to respond to Langlie's "machine" charges with the requisite vigor. Not until the last week of the campaign did Dill consistently and energetically rebut Langlie's assertions.

However, none of the above would have mattered if Dill could have found just a few thousand more votes than Langlie in the absentee ballots. It was not to be; the absentee ballots increased Langlie's lead. Nine days after the election Langlie's victory was certain, with nearly 4,000 votes more than Dill.[53] Langlie's assassination of Dill's character had been just effective enough to ensure the Republican's election.

There is no record of Dill's emotions regarding his defeat, but his trip to Ohio to see his mother after the campaign must surely be seen as an attempt to put it all behind him. After much time had passed, he wrote in his memoirs that he came to believe he had a bigger job to do.[54] He returned to Spokane, his law practice, his new cliffside home, and mountain stream trout.

On December 7, 1941, the Japanese government altered the course of American history and drastically changed the lives of all Americans. Many, especially women, took jobs they would not otherwise have done and engaged in charity work they might not have considered in other circumstances, but the war had brought a sense of urgency and importance to the most mundane tasks and created a severe labor shortage. Clarence Dill shared this desire to serve. After his defeat in the gubernatorial race of 1940, he was through with politics—at least that was his determination at the time—but the war and President Roosevelt changed his mind.

FDR asked Dill to run for Congress in the Fifth District in 1942. The president believed his Democratic support in Congress was in jeopardy; he also wanted to be sure a public power man represented that district; finally, he believed Dill could win despite the growing Republican sentiment. The idea appealed to Dill because it provided a means for a very patriotic man to serve his country in time of crisis. At one point Dill remarked that it was the war alone that brought him into the race.[55]

Dill won the 1942 Fifth District congressional primary. In the general election, he faced Walt Horan, a public-power Republican. Thus one of Dill's primary reasons for running no longer existed. Still, he campaigned on the theme that his familiarity with Washington, D.C., and relationship with Roosevelt would maximize the Fifth District's chances for war-based industrial development. Dill was still a builder at heart. Moreover, his argument concerning his ability to help the Fifth District grow was made more powerful because Horan had never held elective office.[56]

Horan's campaign was well suited to wartime. He hammered away at Dill's World War I activities and called him an obstructionist in regard to his voting record on major war issues in 1917–18. It was not an unfair characterization.[57]

It requires no intricate logic to argue Dill would have been the better choice that November, but it was not to be. Horan won easily, following the state and national trend of Republican rejuvenation.[58] Nor need analysts work overtime to discover the cause of Dill's defeat. Republicans throughout the district had made Dill's World War I voting record the primary issue.[59] Thus northeastern Washingtonians well knew his work in

Congress during the last war—he was not the man they felt comfortable with in representing their interests in Washington, D.C., during this war.[60] Dill never had a chance to return to Congress in 1942; it may just as well have been 1918.

Clarence Dill was a resilient man. He would eventually find a way to serve the region he had come to love and call home. In so doing, he would return to an old friend, the Columbia River, and help open a new frontier. In the meantime, he returned to his home and legal practice in Spokane, and made some money.

After his defeat in the congressional race of 1942, Dill enjoyed considerable success in his private law practice in Spokane. He often represented eastern Washington public utility districts (PUDs) and was considered an expert in that area of law. The war made tremendous demands on Grand Coulee and Bonneville power. It was fairly obvious that power production would be substantially enhanced if some method could be devised to restrain the Columbia's flood waters—which roared unproductively over Grand Coulee's spillway in spring and summer—for release in the fall and winter when the river was low. Clarence Dill devoted a substantial portion of the next twenty years of his life to finding a way to harness those flood waters.

As early as 1940, Dill advocated building flood storage dams in Canada, especially at a place known as Arrow Lakes. He also firmly supported a Columbia Valley Authority modeled after the Tennessee Valley Authority. But the idea did not gain enough support among Westerners. After World War II, he became more vocal in his advocacy of Canadian storage and often mentioned the concept during his frequent speaking engagements. Nevertheless, his voice remained unaccompanied for several years. He described his singular agitation for Canadian storage dams at the time as reminding him of John the Baptist—preaching in the wilderness.[61]

Eventually, that voice found listeners. Mon Wallgren, Washington's governor, appointed Dill to the Columbia Basin Commission (CBC) in time for the January 1947 meeting in Wenatchee. At the meeting, Dill outlined the basics of his Canadian storage plan and persuaded the commission to pass a resolution encouraging the International Joint Commission (IJC) to complete its survey and report on the feasibility of the project. The IJC consisted of three Canadians and three Americans appointed by their governments to resolve differences between the two nations, which generally had to do with rivers and lakes. In addition, the CBC made clear its support of the project on the basis of sharing with Canada the power that Canadian storage dams would generate on the lower Columbia.[62]

Dill now began keeping Washington Senator Warren Magnuson informed of the efforts of the CBC in regard to Canadian storage. Magnuson always showed Dill the greatest respect, and in August 1948, Magnuson assured Dill of his support for the Canadian storage project.[63]

Dill related to Magnuson how he had been working to persuade members of British Columbia's Parliament to propose a storage dam at Arrow Lakes. He hoped British Columbia would propose the project to the IJC. Dill explained his belief that the project could be approved on the basis of a trade of power rights for flood storage. He also emphasized what the agreement would mean to the Columbia Basin:

> They can store 10 million acre feet in the Arrow Lakes without serious damage. That, in addition to the storage in Montana and Idaho, would mean that we could install a third set of nine generators at Coulee by a short tunnel around the east bank of the river. Then the dam would produce 3 million KWH instead of 2 million. Every other dam down the river would of course benefit to the same extent.[64]

Magnuson now promised to contact the IJC and touch base with President Harry Truman.[65] Then, discovering there was an opening on the American side of the IJC, Magnuson recommended Dill for the position. He wrote of Dill:

> I think his suggestion [Canadian storage] is an excellent one. He is able, well versed in these matters and would be a definite asset to the commission. I am sure Senators Stanley and McWhorter would be more than pleased to have him as an associate. Approximately half of the problems of the commission arise in our area and are directly connected with power. Senator Dill is very well informed and qualified to deal with these questions.
>
> Such an appointment would be well received in the Senate and would meet with considerable enthusiasm from the thousands of persons in our area, who are vitally interested in power and its further development.[66]

Though Truman did not appoint Dill to the IJC, the latter continued his work for Canadian storage. The power shortage in the winter of 1948–49 helped advance his cause. Northwesterners were being asked to curtail electricity use during peak hours, turn off unnecessary lights, and cook meals at unusual hours. The Bonneville Power Administration even cut 82,000 KW to aluminum plants, and emergency power was transported from Montana. Even so, generators were blowing out due to overloads, and there were no prospects for new power sources over the next four years. Canadian storage represented the quickest solution.[67]

In January 1949, Dill traveled to Victoria, B.C., to speak with Premier Byron Johnson about Canadian storage. He found Johnson willing to study the proposal in detail.[68] At this meeting, Dill first mentioned the idea of splitting the power that Canadian storage dams would create on the lower Columbia on a fifty-fifty basis with Canada as payment for flood water storage.[69] But little came of the meeting with Johnson.

Dill continued to write letters, bend ears, and generally agitate for the project, but the lack of progress frustrated him.[70] Though study of the projected site above Revelstoke went forward, the ex-senator lamented that what was really needed was for

> the B.C. power commission or some privately owned organization, with the approval of the B.C. government, to offer to store five million acre feet somewhere in the upper Columbia. Dr. [Paul] Raver, Bonneville Power Administrator, has repeatedly said he would be glad to enter into negotiations for an agreement satisfactory to British Columbia and the governments of Washington and Ottawa, to be submitted to the IJC for approval.[71]

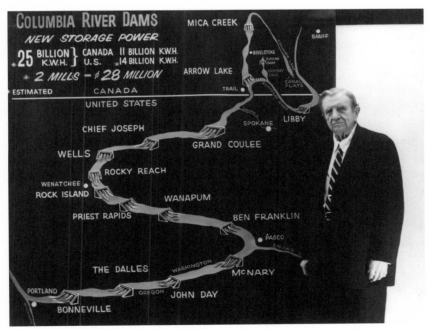

Former Senator Dill explains how to enhance Columbia River power production. *Box 2, file #2, Cheney Cowles Museum/Eastern Washington State Historical Society, Spokane, WA*

But years were to pass before any appreciable progress occurred. Dill wrote Magnuson in September 1951 that the project was not as complicated as the Canadians had led President Truman to believe. All that was needed was an incentive to move the premier of British Columbia off dead center. "How about if we loan them the money to build the dam?" Dill suggested to Magnuson. Dill also wrote to Secretary of Interior Oscar Chapman in October 1951 in an effort to promote Canadian storage. The secretary responded that the IJC was considering half-a-dozen projects, none of which could be isolated and quickly advanced. Canadian storage was just one of the projects. On the American side, Dill's ideas were gaining popularity as brown-outs increased. Moreover, Army engineers claimed the Vanport flood of 1948 would have been substantially reduced if flood control dams had been in existence. Still, the Department of the Interior advised patience and essentially abdicated responsibility.[72]

Two years later, Dill was still working for the project but now from a different angle. If straightforward efforts had proven ineffective, how about an end run around governments? Dill now spent more than a year trying to convince private firms to build a dam at Arrow Lakes on the basis of contracts with PUDs in Washington and with the Bonneville Power Administration (BPA). The BPA and the PUDs were to pay the owner of the Canadian storage dams for the increased power generated by the flood waters released through those dams. Though Dill's proposal would still require permits of various kinds from the governments involved, he believed it was a considerably less complicated route than having the Canadians build the dam. Dill actually gained tentative agreement from the BPA and several PUDs and found some businesses initially interested in building the dams. But one by one they all dropped out. Finally, he persuaded Kaiser Aluminum of Spokane to build Arrow Lakes Dam. But the Canadian government would have none of it. The Parliament in Ottawa passed a law making it illegal for a foreign company to build a dam on a stream in Canada without Parliament's consent. There were no Canadian firms willing to undertake the project; the only alternative lay with governments.[73]

Three more years passed while Dill pushed Canadian storage whenever possible. New dams built on the Columbia made the potential payoff for properly released flood waters even greater. In November 1957, he sent a proposal to the British Columbian government outlining his fifty-fifty split idea.[74] Neither this overture nor a similar one to U.S. Secretary of the Interior Frederick A. Seaton bore fruit. It should be noted that Dill was now under contract to the Grant County PUD for his work on Canadian storage. Should Dill's efforts have succeeded in securing Canadian storage dams, his contract with Grant County would have been very lucrative.[75]

Time was catching up with Dill, once regarded as the most handsome man in the Senate. In those days he had sported a Gable-esque mustache. In 1958 he preferred to send out pictures of himself—when speaking engagements so required—that were representative of a younger Clarence Dill. He joked about this "vain" proclivity. He was seventy-four.[76]

Though Dill felt himself losing a little strength as age pressed upon him, his Canadian storage proposal along with his idea to split the run-off power fifty-fifty was gaining it.[77] American and Canadian officials were finally discussing a flood water storage agreement in earnest. The only negative was that they were taking the project out of the hands of the man who had agitated for it for so long. However, it must have been gratifying for Dill to read—when the IJC agreement was made public—that one of the key provisions in the agreement was "the power added to downstream dams would be split fifty-fifty between the two countries." The United States and Canada concluded negotiations on the storage issue on October 18, 1960. President Dwight Eisenhower announced the agreement from Palm Springs, California, and indicated he intended to send the treaty to the Senate in January 1961. The treaty called for storing more than fifteen million acre-feet of water behind Canadian dams—enough water to ensure that a third powerhouse at Grand Coulee would be economically feasible and that more generators could be added to other dams.[78]

There were several benefits from the agreement. Power production at Grand Coulee from Canadian storage would increase as much as 50 percent. The key to this downstream power bonanza was to be the giant dam at Mica Creek—two hundred miles north of the international border. Preliminary plans called for a 740-foot high dam at the Mica Creek location. Engineers also predicted half of the storage benefit could be functional by 1965. But perhaps the greatest benefit from the treaty was that it meant the Columbia would no longer send its waters rampaging into farm lands and cities downstream.[79]

When the United States Senate received the bill, senators wasted little time in discussion. Hearings were held, but they were a mere formality. However, they did provide the opportunity for one of the Pacific Northwest's builders to speak formally before senators one more time. Dill seemed to enjoy the opportunity to relate how he had worked on the project for so long and how he had hit upon his fifty-fifty idea. He made the point that this treaty would allow for the completion of Columbia River development that he, James O'Sullivan, FDR, and so many others had struggled so long to accomplish. The senators addressed the now gray-haired river development advocate as "Senator" and allowed Dill to read a rather lengthy recount of the battle for Grand Coulee and the hope for the Columbia Basin. The treaty was approved 90 to 1.[80]

The final agreement called for the United States to buy British Columbia's half of the new electrical power created by the storage dams. The United States also paid for flood control benefits. Finally, the treaty passed the Canadian Parliament. President Lyndon Johnson attended the ceremony in Blaine, Washington, honoring Canadian-American cooperation in the West. Canadian storage and Clarence Dill's hope for the Columbia Basin became reality.[81]

While Dill spent a significant amount of time on the Canadian storage project, he maintained a successful law practice in Spokane. During the forties, fifties, and sixties, Dill's practice centered around his work for various eastern Washington PUDs. Beginning in 1961, he represented Pend Oreille County PUD in its fight with Seattle over the Z Canyon dam site in northeastern Washington. Pend Oreille County PUD owned the Z Canyon dam site and intended to build a dam there, though the PUD had experienced difficulty raising the funds to proceed. In 1961 Seattle filed an application with the Federal Power Commission for a dam at a place known as Boundary, about one mile down river from Z Canyon. If Seattle were allowed to build Boundary dam, the Z Canyon site would be put under water and thus be worthless for power production.[82]

On July 10, 1961, the Federal Power Commission ruled in favor of Seattle and granted a license to build Boundary Dam. Pend Oreille County PUD filed a lawsuit claiming state law prohibited a municipality from condemning the property of a PUD. The state superior court ruled in April 1963 that the commerce clause of the federal constitution took precedence over the state law barring a municipality from condemning the property of a PUD. Eventually Boundary Dam was built.[83]

Clarence Dill's fight for Canadian storage is symbolic of the man. He made a comfortable living through his law practice. But he began his campaign for Canadian storage as a project that would primarily benefit others and as something to do in his spare time. From more efficient electrical production to flood control, the project had many positive aspects. Through the forties and well into the fifties, the idea remained for Dill one that would benefit his fellow Pacific Northwesterners. In fact, it cost him a considerable amount of money and time to sustain his agitation for the project. Unlike most of the West's entrepreneurs, who usually figured a profitable angle before they began a project, Dill did not figure his until the project entered the stage in the mid-fifties when he was trying to arrange for an agreement between various PUDs, the BPA, and a private builder. At this time he entered into a contract with Grant County PUD, and possibly other PUDs, which would have paid him on a per kilowatt basis for achieving Canadian storage. Though Dill played a significant role in promoting the project, he had faded from the main picture by the time the treaty was actually put into operation in 1964. Nevertheless, when the Canadian-held waters actually increased power production on the Columbia River, he informed the Grant County PUD it was time to begin making payments. The PUD disagreed. Thus followed a lawsuit between Dill and the PUD, which caused some observers to perceive the aging senator as a money-grubbing old has-been, largely out to enrich himself at the expense of the public. The courts did not view the case as simplistically as Dill's critics. After several years of litigation, Grant County PUD agreed to settle for a $20,000 payment to Dill.[84]

Clarence Dill played a prominent role in promoting Canadian storage. He espoused the idea when few were listening, putting the concept of Canadian storage in the public domain. For that reason, he deserves the thanks of those who benefit from the increased power, flood control, and irrigation Canadian storage generates.

Dedicating the first concrete pouring at the site of Grand Coulee's new third power plant, October 21, 1970. From left to right: Senator Henry M. Jackson, Congresswoman Catherine May, Commissioner Ellis L. Armstrong, former Senator C.C. Dill, and Congressman Thomas S. Foley. *#99-149, Washington State University Libraries, Pullman, WA*

Epilogue
The Author's View

I N MARCH 1969, AT THE AGE of sixty-three, Mabel Dill died of heart failure at the Dills' Spokane home.[1] Dill had always imagined that he would be the first to die; he was devastated. On one occasion, he told Ken Billington, "I pray each day that I will not awaken. My wife is gone; my brother is taken care of; any other living relative is of no avail."[2] Dill spoke these words to Billington in relation to his desire to establish a trust fund that would award yearly prizes to high school students for outstanding achievement in public speaking or debate. The trust fund was established as Dill desired. However, his prayer was not answered in the timely fashion he had hoped for. He lived nearly nine more years after his wife's death in 1969; the ex-senator died on January 15, 1978, at the age of ninety-three.

Dill had retired too early from the Senate and lived too long afterward for his death to receive a great amount of attention. However, extended obituaries did appear in the state's major papers, which mentioned his work on radio legislation and on Columbia Basin development. By the time of his death, most Washingtonians were probably not impressed that he had been the Senate's driving force behind radio legislation in the 1920s and early 1930s. They simply could not relate to what radio had meant to the people of that era. The idea that listening to radio helped bring the nation closer together and began to unify East and West in a cultural and psychological manner would never have occurred to most of those who read his obituary in 1978. The vast majority of us live in the modern world without possessing an understanding of how that world was made possible. Dill played a significant role in shaping our reality.

Clarence Dill was one of the first modern senators. He understood the necessary course of the federal government's relationship to commerce, especially commerce based on new technology, in a way that few of his peers did. Indeed, the Supreme Court demonstrated the gulf between future and past, between Dill and his learned contemporaries on the bench, when it adopted an interpretation of interstate commerce in the Schechter

Clarence Dill in his elder statesman years. *#L93-66.97, Cheney Cowles Museum/Eastern Washington State Historical Society, Spokane, WA*

case of 1935, which FDR caustically described as a "horse and buggy" definition.[3] Dill's colleagues, even those who supported his radio legislation, admitted they knew little concerning the ramifications of radio technology or radio law. They simply supported Dill because public clamor for legislation was so great.

Most Washingtonians reading Dill's obituary were probably surprised to learn of his role in bringing about Grand Coulee Dam's construction and Columbia River development. Many have seen the dam, and all of us benefit from the power and irrigation water it provides. Nevertheless, we all more or less take for granted the benefits the Columbia River dams provide. Some of us do this even to the extent of arguing that they be dismantled. But for the vast majority of Pacific Northwesterners, the benefits the dams provide—flood control, water storage and irrigation, electric power, soil erosion prevention, extended transportation, recreation, and market development—far outweigh their negative aspects, which we will hopefully continue to work to mitigate.[4]

But we do see the dams differently than Dill's generation. Murray Morgan wrote of Grand Coulee in 1954: "There are parts of our culture that stink with phoniness. But we can do some wonderful things too. That dam is one of them. If our generation has anything good to offer history, it is that dam. Why, the thing is going to be completely useful. It is going to be a working pyramid."[5]

We no longer think of the dams in those terms. For us they are tools, not wonders, tools that require constant adjustments and maintenance. We do not share our forebears' enthusiasm because we are desensitized to amazing things in our culture due to their abundance; from medicine to entertainment, we are constantly confronted with the near miraculous. Another reason for our lack of amazement at the Columbia's dams is that they are not visually inspiring, not even Grand Coulee. Stewart Holbrook wrote of this paradox in *The Columbia:* "It is big all right, but it has to contend with too much space to look big. Set in the midst of appalling distances, it appears like a play dam of children, lost in the terrifying wastes."[6]

Just as the vast landscape diminishes our appreciation for Grand Coulee, the passage of time diminishes our appreciation for Dill and other Columbia River developers. I suppose this is as it should be; we need to make room to honor those who make new contributions to life in this region. But why did Dill's contemporaries deny him, except for a brief period in 1934, the credit due him for his work in bringing Grand Coulee to reality? There are several reasons. One of them is that he occupied a unique and pioneering niche in Washington State politics. As far as the western part of the state was concerned, he was an Easterner—not one of them—thus he did not receive generous coverage from the large western papers. Moreover, he was something of an outcast in Spokane as well. As a Democrat, he was not particularly welcome among the Republican power brokers of that city. William H. Cowles, publisher of the Inland Empire's dominant newspapers, was particularly venomous to Dill. Finally, the grassroots group centered in Ephrata and Wenatchee that had agitated for the dam since 1918 was leery of anything and anyone coming from Spokane—and with good reason usually—so that even when the whole project rested on Dill's relationship with FDR, they were suspicious that he would betray the dam. One of the leaders of this group, Rufus Woods, was a diehard Republican and publisher of central Washington's most important newspaper, the *Wenatchee Daily World*. All things considered, it is remarkable that Dill's importance in relation to Grand Coulee can be discerned from extant sources.

Just as some denied Dill recognition for his work in developing the Columbia River, there are some today who criticize Dill and his generation for building dams in the first place. Donald Worster, one of these critics, advocates small community living, doing nothing more than the basics for survival. He writes:

> Relieved of some of its [the West] burdens of growing crops, earning foreign exchange, and supporting immense cities, it might encourage a new sequence of history, an incipient America of simplicity, discipline, and spiritual exploration, an America in which people are wont to sit long hours doing nothing, earning nothing, going nowhere, on the banks of some river running through a spare lean land.[7]

For Worster, the dams, and the reclamation they made possible, epitomize the evils of the capitalist system in the West. His solution requires nothing less than the complete transformation of human nature. When water is scarce, human beings as we know them, as history reveals them, respond quite differently than Worster's idyllic man. Stewart Holbrook described that response when he wrote, "men fought, sued, and shot each other because of water. Communities warred and split because of water."[8]

Contrary to Worster, in the real West, populated with real people, irrigation was a prerequisite for survival. One either irrigated land in the arid regions or moved away. The very first white settler in the arid region of eastern Washington, Marcus Whitman, possessed his share of idealism but was practical enough to see the necessity of irrigation. There was no other way the land could support significant numbers of people.[9] The fact of the West's aridity, then, was a significant factor in molding the lives of Westerners and their society. Wallace Stegner wrote of the West's pioneers, "Most of the changes in people's lives—which I am quite sure in most of their lives were unintended—were forced upon them by the condition of aridity."[10] In short, Worster, and those who believe as he does, have little concept of what life would really be like if they were to implement their philosophy and even less understanding of the human suffering that implementation would require.

Aridity, then, dictated the nature of life in much of the West in Dill's early days and is even more powerful today given the scarcity of good farmland. The need for irrigation in the West, in Dill's Inland Empire, is a constant that ties the past to the present and makes us very much like our forebears. So too our dependence on electrical power. There are other continuities as well.

Despite assertions to the contrary, the West is still a place of open spaces and extended distances.[11] The task of those who came here before us was to conquer that wilderness and overcome the distance to make a non-nomadic civilization possible. Our task may well be to preserve that wilderness that remains to make temporary escape from the pressures of modern life possible. Thus the problem before us concerning the wilderness is very different than the one our forebears faced. Let us not criticize our ancestors because they faced a different challenge.

The answer to our dilemma does not lie in disavowing the progress of the past as Donald Worster would have us do. He argues that the West is trapped by its past. Because of its reliance on irrigation, it is ruled by a concentrated power hierarchy based on the command of scarce water. The great evil for Worster—after the capitalist economy—is irrigation and how it is used to allow a small group to dominate others and the land.[12] But surely it was not the dams and irrigation canals that were the basis for this alleged power structure, but the reality that water was scarce. Even without dams and irrigation, the fact would remain that whoever controlled the water possessed great power. It would only have meant concentrating a more limited resource in fewer hands, with the result of even fewer people living in arid areas. The problem is aridity, not man's ancient solution to it. Thus Worster continues in error when he writes that the basic problem is "the apparatus and ideology of unrestrained environmental conquest which lies at the root of the Joads' affliction."[13]

The people of Dill's generation, including the Joads of John Steinbeck's *The Grapes of Wrath*, would not have understood Worster's solution to their problem. In fact they would have thought him crazy, for Worster has their affliction exactly backwards. Isn't the cause of the Joads' desperation the failure to control the dust bowl environment of Oklahoma? And didn't irrigation, far from being their nemesis in the West, offer them some hope that they might find a new home? Hasn't the West offered that new home to millions? And without irrigation where might those millions have gone? What would have become of them? Though it is true that only a small percentage of those who came west now live on an irrigated farm, all Westerners benefit from the cornucopia irrigation makes possible and from the power the Columbia River's dams generate. Stegner analyzed correctly the role of irrigation and the federal government in the West when he said, "I think the West would have been impossible without federal intervention [which brought vast irrigation projects]."[14] What might have happened to the country had not the West absorbed so many displaced persons in the thirties? Worster's "solutions" to society's problems do not address those problems: they eliminate the society. Though Stegner was no admirer of the modern West—he identified too closely with the West of his youth for that—he understood what irrigation meant to the region.[15] And in that recognition, he leads us to a more interesting question: how did the West come to be a region built, to a large extent, on irrigation?

The effort to irrigate extensive sections of western land was largely unsuccessful until the federal government passed the Newlands Act in 1902. Under this act, money derived from selling public lands in the West was to be used to construct irrigation projects. Land reclaimed through these projects was then to be sold in 160-acre parcels or less, depending on the needs of family farmers. The Newlands Act was a significant milestone in the region's history in that it marked the intrusion of the federal government into two of the defining elements of western life: water supply and agriculture. Out of the Newlands Act came the Bureau of Reclamation, which held the power to pass judgment on the hopes and dreams of Westerners. But even the federal government found conquering the vastness of the West a challenge. The Newlands Act failed to reclaim lands to the degree its proponents had envisioned.[16]

Thus intense development of the West's reclaimable lands did not begin until Franklin Roosevelt became president. When FDR spoke to the 20,000 people assembled at Grand Coulee on August 4, 1934,[17] he looked forward to vast development of the region, fully aware that New Deal dollars were coming west in disproportionate amounts. He pointed out to his Grand Coulee audience that he "had allocated to the three states, Washington, Oregon, and Idaho a 'much larger share of the public works than the population justifies.'"[18] There were many reasons for this, but surely one of the reasons was reclamation's ability to provide homes and jobs for thousands of the nation's unemployed once agricultural commodities returned a fair profit. FDR shared Thomas Jefferson's romantic notions concerning farm life. If he could put people on farms as part of the solution to the Great Depression, he would do it.

Other reasons the West received New Deal dollars in disproportionate amounts were the extent of poverty and suffering in the region and many federal aid programs' favoritism for large, sparsely populated areas. Donald Reading has made a fascinating study of this issue in which he argues that the federal government tended to spend money in states where it owned a higher percentage of land and where real per capita personal income had declined the sharpest.[19] Reading further argues that an important factor in determining whether New Deal funds would be spent in a state was the willingness of state and local units to set up machinery for disbursing such funds. Moreover, the vigor with which state officials lobbied for programs seems to have had a significant effect on the flow of funds.[20] Reading is correct. Funds for Grand Coulee came to the Pacific

Dill signs copies of his autobiography, *Where Water Falls*, ca. 1971. *#L93-66.44, Cheney Cowles Museum/Eastern Washington State Historical Society, Spokane, WA*

Northwest because the region, led by Clarence Dill, lobbied so effectively for them and because Dill had placed himself in a persuasive position with the president.

One question remains: Why were Westerners so determined to secure New Deal dollars? The answer has to do with the builder mentality so typical of the West in the first half of the twentieth century. Recognizing their region possessed vast resources but was underdeveloped, western congressman and senators, Dill chief among them, went after New Deal dollars like Sooners after new land. The Washingtonian brought to his quest for Grand Coulee a long-term plan and a refusal to take no for an answer in addition to an army of Westerners of the same mind. There was little of the squabbling that beset other regions over whether the West wanted federal help. The peculiar western mind, then, had much to do with securing New Deal dollars, which in turn helped create the modern dam-based West.

Though the reclamation aspect of Grand Coulee did not become a reality until the 1950s, the Pacific Northwest benefited enormously from the other aspect of the project: cheap electricity. In the 1920s, the Pacific Northwest was an economic and social hinterland, a colony. The region's failure to gain a significant tariff on wood products in the late 1920s suggested that it was a political colony as well. Dill understood how the rest of the country was using the Pacific Northwest and how the immense Grand Coulee project could help develop the region.[21] He saw clearly that cheap power and reclamation could help bring prosperity to the region and that prosperity would help make Washington more powerful politically. Indeed, he fought for the project on the grounds that other parts of the nation were benefiting from large federal projects (Muscle Shoals on the Tennessee and Boulder Dam on the Colorado) while the Pacific Northwest was being rebuffed in regard to Grand Coulee.[22] Thus it was no surprise to Clarence Dill when the development of the Columbia River, especially Grand Coulee Dam, began to change Washington's relationship to the rest of the country. The cheap and abundant electricity Grand Coulee provided made possible vast increases in manufacturing during World War II. Shipbuilding, aircraft construction, and aluminum production increased dramatically in the region as a result of the war. The latter two remain important aspects of the region's economy.

Then there is Hanford. Because of the vast open spaces and the existence of cheap electricity, southeastern Washington was a logical site for nuclear experimentation. One might argue Hanford was the price the Pacific Northwest paid to become an equal member of the Union. However we view Hanford, the nation's defense needs and the region's electrical power combined with Boeing's commercial aircraft industry have formed the backbone of the region's postwar economy. It was no accident that in the third quarter of this century another senator from Washington, Henry Jackson, rose to the top echelons of the Senate as an expert on defense.

Clarence Dill was extremely proud of his region's importance, due largely to Grand Coulee, during the war. He smiled when he heard people say the great dam may have won World War II because it supplied the energy that produced the aluminum for 60 percent of America's planes.[23] He was prouder still of the region's increasing prosperity, made more evident with each passing decade. He accepted completely the idea that development was good, that prosperity defined as a rising standard of living was a worthy goal. Thus he would have shaken his head in dismay at the trend in western literature that sees the present West as not worthy of the past, that the West of today has lost its allure, its romance.

We come, then, to Clarence Dill the man and his contribution to Pacific Northwest history. In his prime, Dill was an accomplished politician, adept at presenting a carefully crafted image to the public. A historian, however, must not allow a politician's image to obscure the man. As John Clive has written, history is "to a great extent a process of penetrating disguises and uncovering what is hidden."[24]

Clarence Dill believed firmly in what Stegner calls "three of the American gospels: work, progress, and the inviolability of contract," though perhaps it is fair to say he believed in them in inverse order.[25] Dill was a lawyer and a politician; on more than one occasion he sued for failure to fulfill a contract. Moreover, the work of lawyers and politicians rests on the strength of the contracts they make. Nor did work scare the Methodist-raised Dill, though he learned early on that one hour with his nose behind the rear end of a mule was less enjoyable than two with his nose in a book. Then there is progress; Dill believed in three kinds of progress and came to believe that they might be mutually exclusive. First, he believed in progressive political principles: the idea that government could and should make society better for the majority of people. Second, he believed in progress for individuals, the people of his district and state. He wanted to see those people do better for themselves and the government do better by them. Finally, he believed in progress for Clarence Dill; he did not want to spend his life in public service and have little to show for it. Wesley Jones' defeat in 1932 and quick subsequent death profoundly affected Dill. From the time Dill chose to retire in 1934, and probably much earlier, to the end of his lawsuit against Grant County PUD over his Canadian storage work,

Dill wrestled with the conflict between making money and serving the public interest.

There are other aspects of Dill's personality worth remembering, especially his attachment to the Pacific Northwest, his chosen home. Dill loved eastern Washington, with its azure sky, sparkling waters, and majestic landscape. Reminiscent of the first President Roosevelt, he loved to hunt and fish; the outdoors was his sanctuary from politics.

Dill was also a student of history, and though he studied it without great depth, he learned that change was a given in human society. Thus there was no sense looking back to some mythical Golden Age, as many of his progressive brethren did. He believed in taking from the past what was useful—the solid principles and wisdom of men like Thomas Jefferson and Abraham Lincoln—and moving forward, progressing. In that adaptability, Dill was unlike many people both past and present, who, partly as a result of their lack of historical perspective, are reluctant or unable to adapt to new realities. Without a knowledge of history, many people know only their own lives, thus they are prisoners of the present and afraid of what lies ahead. Dill was never afraid of the future.

Dill used history to provide a philosophical base for his politics and material for his oratorical performances. The spoken word was his lifelong love, but it was a blind romance. He did not notice when the oratorical style that had made the Great Commoner so popular, the style he had adopted as his own, lost its ability to impress most Americans. One of the last things he did was set up high school prizes for oratorical achievement. Dill's persistence in speaking in the oratorical style that had helped send him to the Senate in 1922 caused many later observers to esteem him lightly and believe he had significantly exaggerated his accomplishments. Indeed, for many he became the living stereotype of the old-time machine politician: tainted with graft, a blowhard, and a has-been, not the much more complicated political maverick presented in these pages. Those who remembered him as he had truly been regarded him differently from those who knew him only in his later years. The correspondence between Dill and Warren Magnuson is full of the latter's respect for the old senator.

Nevertheless, Dill did feel the need to tell people of his accomplishments. Part of this need was rooted in his political personality: successful politicians must find a way to make their constituents aware of their accomplishments; but the greater cause of this self-promotion was his unique position in the history of Washington State politics. Dill was nothing less than a pioneer in his own right: a progressive Democrat in a state full of progressive Republicans and conservative Bourbons. This circumstance forced him to distance himself from the state's Democratic party to appeal to enough progressive Republicans to get elected. The result was a state Democratic party that was always suspicious of its most prominent member in the 1920s and early 1930s. Seldom did the party credit Dill for his accomplishments. Adding to his isolation was his east-side origins. Washington's major newspapers—along with most of the population—were located in the Puget Sound area. These newspapers, almost always Republican in sympathy, tended to ignore the rest of the state. They especially ignored successful Democrats whenever possible. Nor were the two primary papers on the east side of the mountains, the *Wenatchee Daily World* and the *Spokesman-Review,* any more forthcoming in praise. Thus did Dill's unique political position in the state contribute to his propensity for self promotion. If he hadn't promoted himself through his vast letter writing and public appearances, his constituents would seldom have heard about his efforts in their behalf. As his life continued into its post-political period, this self promotion, once so politically necessary, became a habit that resulted in some unfavorable impressions.

The epic length of Dill's life presents other problems. He lived so long, and was involved in so many different events, that it is difficult to bring structure and balance to his biography. In that sense, he is very much like the region he made home—the West. In truth, Dill was the archetypal Westerner: he never stopped building, never questioned whether or not building was progress.

We might excuse this optimistic boosterism if we could say that Dill was an honest man, always guarding the public interest. But the evidence suggests that he had moments of weakness, moments when his own enrichment became more important to him, moments when he violated the public trust.

Nevertheless, there was much good in Clarence Dill. His life is one of those that substantially contributed to the molding of the United States into one nation. Inasmuch as our national identity consists of both East and West—is a mingling of the two—Dill helped establish the mix. Born and raised in the Midwest, Dill emigrated to the West, as had most Westerners of the era. Once there, he energetically pursued a political career, making a place for himself in his new home. Sent to Washington, D.C., in the 1920s as a senator, he made his mark in the East through his work on radio legislation, which had a profound effect on the unification of the nation. Thus Dill's life and work can be seen as strengthening the ties that bound the nation together, ties that have held in tough times. Energized by a dream of cheap power and reclaiming otherwise marginal frontier land, Dill sought and secured the aid of the federal government in developing the Columbia Basin. As a result, Westerners grew to look more often to Washington, D.C., for solutions to their problems than in the past.

Dill embodied the more robust western version of the American spirit of his time in another way as well: he rose from being dirt poor to entering the upper middle class by his own exertions. At the same time, he avoided developing contempt for those who failed to follow his example. He was always sympathetic to the less fortunate among his constituents, as his voting record on farm and labor issues attests. In his efforts on behalf of the less prosperous members of society, Dill was an advocate of change. He understood the changes that were coming and wanted to be a part of the inevitable transformation they would bring. Indeed, he wanted to lead in that transformation.

Dill's life links East and West and demonstrates the mutability of American social classes. It also serves as a bridge between past and present. The West of today, in many ways, is still very much like the West of Clarence Dill's youth: vast open spaces, wilderness, populations centered in cities, and, of course, the condition of aridity in most of the region. Consequently, life in the modern Pacific Northwest depends to a great extent on irrigation and hydroelectric power, two developments in which Dill played a leading role. Few of us would be willing to renounce these developments, which brings us to the question posed much earlier. Is it more instructive for Pacific Northwesterners of today to view themselves as essentially similar to their antecedents of the first half of the twentieth century or have we become so different that those differences define who we are? There can be no question that there are differences. But the overwhelming fact remains that we share an abiding faith in progress with those who came before us in this region; we still believe government can be a tool in that progress, and we feel that building and development are good if carefully managed. Careful management implies cooperation and compromise among competing interests; it has always been so. In the best western tradition, the tradition Clarence Dill embodied, cooperation will remain the path to progress.

ENDNOTES

Endnote Abbreviations

In the following list of endnote abbreviations, UW refers to collections held by the Manuscripts Division of the University of Washington Libraries, Seattle.

ABLC—Arthur B. Langlie Collection, UW
AGC—Arthur Gunn Collection, UW
CDP—Clarence C. Dill Papers, Eastern Washington State Historical Society, Spokane
CMP—Clarence Martin Papers, Manuscripts, Archives and Special Collections, Washington State University Libraries, Pullman
DNCR—Democratic National Committee Records, Franklin D. Roosevelt Library, Hyde Park, New York
EDR—Edith Dolan Riley Collection, UW
FDRL—Franklin D. Roosevelt Library, Hyde Park, New York
HCCSP—Houghton, Cluck, Coughlan, and Schubat Papers, UW
HMP—Hugh Mitchell Papers, UW
HSP—Henry Suzzallo Papers, UW
JBP—John Ballaine Papers, UW
JDRP—J.D. Ross Papers, UW
JOSP—James O'Sullivan Papers, Gonzaga University, Spokane
MC—Warren Magnuson Collection, UW
MRL—Merrill and Ring Lumber Company Collection, UW
NBC—Naomi Benson Collection, UW
NPPAP—Northwest Public Power Association Papers, UW
RBP—Reclamation Bureau Papers, National Archives, Washington, D.C.
RWP—Rufus Woods Papers, *Wenatchee World,* Wenatchee
SHP—Saul Hess Papers, UW
SLP—Seattle Light Papers, UW
SPTL—St. Paul and Tacoma Lumber Company Collection, UW
WHC—William Humphrey Collection, UW

Chapter One, pages 1–11

[1]Biographical entry, CDP.

[2]*Spokesman-Review*, 4 July 1937.

[3]Biographical entry, CDP.

[4]Clarence Dill, *Where Water Falls* (Spokane: Self published, 1970), 16.

[5]*Ibid.*, 17.

[6]*Ibid.*, 19.

[7]*Ibid.*, 21. *Inland Empire News*, 11 March 1915.

[8]Dill, *Where Water Falls*, 22. *Journal Herald* (Delaware, Ohio) n.d., CDP.

[9]*Journal Herald*, 16 May 1916.

[10]*Ibid.*, 25.

[11]*Ibid.*, 24.

[12]Lloyd Spencer and Lancaster Pollard, *A History of the State of Washington* (New York: American Historical Society, 1937), 443.

[13]Dill, *Where Water Falls*, 28.

[14]Robert D. Saltvig, "The Progressive Movement In Washington" (Ph.D. diss., University of Washington, 1966), 343.

[15]Carl Lorenz, *Tom L. Johnson: Mayor of Cleveland* (New York: A.S. Barnes, 1911), 88–89.

[16]Saltvig, "The Progressive Movement in Washington," 343. Lorenz, *Tom L. Johnson*, 138. Arthur S. Link and Richard L. McCormick, *Progressivism* (Arlington Heights, Ill.: Harlan Davidson, 1983), 96–104. Dill, *Where Water Falls*, 30.

[17]Lorenz, *Tom L. Johnson*, 20.

[18]*Ibid.*, 30, 33.

[19]Dill, *Where Water Falls*, 27.

[20]*Ibid.*, 28.

[21]Wallace Stegner, *Angle of Repose* (New York: Doubleday and Co., 1971), 383.

[22]Spencer and Pollard, *History of the State of Washington*, 443.

[23]In 1915 Seattle had a population of over 300,000, while Portland was larger still. Spokane had about 125,000 people. Spencer and Pollard, *A History of the State of Washington*, 444.

[24]Dill, *Where Water Falls*, 33.

[25]Lucille Fargo, *Spokane Story* (New York: Columbia University Press, 1950), 258.

[26]John Fahey, *The Inland Empire: Unfolding Years, 1879–1929* (Seattle: University of Washington Press, 1986), 217. In addition to the quote, I am indebted to Fahey for most of the information in this paragraph.

[27]*Ibid.*, 217.

[28]*Ibid.*, 5.

[29]Dill, *Where Water Falls*, 33.

[30]Ralph Dyar, *News for an Empire: The Story of the Spokesman-Review of Spokane, Washington and of the Field It Serves* (Caldwell, Id.: Caxton Printers, 1952), 144–145. Dill, *Where Water Falls*, 34–35.

[31]*Spokesman-Review*, 27 August 1908. Dyer, *News For An Empire*, 145.

[32]*Ibid.*, 145.

[33]Dill, *Where Water Falls*, 35.

[34]Spencer and Pollard, *History of the State of Washington*, 443.

[35]Dill, *Where Water Falls*, 38.

[36]*Seattle Star*, 28 January 1913.

[37]*Seattle P.I.*, 10 March 1912.

[38]*Spokesman-Review*, 31 August 1912.

[39]Dill's address at the Democratic State Convention, Walla Walla, Washington, 6 May 1912, CDP.

[40]*Seattle P.I.*, 7 May 1912.

[41]*Ibid.*, 8 May 1912.

[42]Notes on Democratic National Convention, CDP.

[43]*Ibid.*

[44]*Spokesman-Review*, 3 September 1912; 27 September 1912.

[45]*Seattle P.I.*, 19 October 1912.

[46]Secretary of State, *Abstract of the Votes Polled in the State of Washington in the General Election 5 November 1912* (Olympia: Government Printing Office).

[47]*Seattle Star*, 28 January 1913. Dill, *Where Water Falls*, 41.

[48]Dill, *Where Water Falls,* 42.

[49]*Seattle P.I.,* 21 February 1913. *Olympia Daily Recorder*, 20 February 1913.

[50]*Olympia Daily Recorder,* 20 February 1913.

[51]*Spokesman-Review*, 25 May 1913. Clarence C. Dill to Mr. B.F. Kunkel, 30 July 1913. CDP.

[52]Jim Ford's column, *Spokesman-Review*, 31 August 1912.

Chapter Two, pages 13–27

[1]"Election Returns," CDP.

[2] Robert D. Saltvig, "The Progressive Movement in Washington" (Ph.D. diss., University of Washington, 1966), 344.

[3]*Spokane Chronicle*, 10 August 1914.

[4]*Ibid.*, 30 April 1914.

[5]Arthur S. Link and Richard L. McCormick, *Progressivism* (Arlington Heights, Ill.: Harlan Davidson, 1983), 21–26. Richard Hofstadter, *The Age of Reform* (New York: Alfred A. Knopf, 1989), 84–85, 131–134. Dill's progressivism is clearly substantiated in his long congressional voting record and in his many speeches. A reference to himself as a progressive can be found in Dill, *Where Water Falls* (Spokane: Self published, 1970), 30, 31.

[6]Alan Dawley, *Struggles for Justice: Social Responsibility and the Liberal State* (Cambridge: Belknap Press, 1991), 99.

[7]*Ibid.*, 99, 113–116. John M. Cooper, *Pivotal Decades: The United States, 1900–1920* (New York: W.W. Norton and Co., 1990), 18–30. Hofstadter, *The Age of Reform*, 84–85, 131–134. Link and McCormick, *Progressivism*, 21–26.

[8]Benjamin Kizer, "May Arkwright Hutton," *Pacific Northwest Quarterly* 57 (April 1966): 54.

[9]Dill, *Where Water Falls*, 45.

[10]*Ibid.*, 46.

[11]In fairness to the newspapers of the Inland Empire, it should be noted that while the coverage they gave Dill was seldom favorable, it was not nonexistent as he sometimes claimed. *Spokesman-Review*, 10 July 1914. *Spokane Chronicle*, 10 July 1914.

[12]*Spokane Chronicle*, 5 August 1914.

[13]Dill, *Where Water Falls*, 46–47.

[14]*Spokane Chronicle*, 3 September 1914.

[15]*Spokesman-Review*, 24 September 1914. Secretary of State, *Abstract of the Votes Polled in the State of Washington in the Primary Election September 8, 1914* (Olympia: Government Printing Office).

[16]*Spokesman-Review*, 20 September 1914; 24 September 1914; 3 October 1914. *Spokane Chronicle*, 24 September 1914; 30 September 1914.

[17]*Spokane Chronicle*, 25 September 1914.

[18]*Spokesman-Review*, 7 October 1914.

[19]*Spokane Chronicle*, 6 October 1914.

[20]*Republic Journal*, 8 October 1914.

[21]*Spokesman-Review*, 10 October 1914.

[22]*Colville Examiner*, 11 October 1914.

[23]*Ibid.*

[24]*Ibid.*

[25]*Spokane Chronicle*, 22 October 1914. *Spokesman-Review*, 25 October 1914; 18 October 1914.

[26]*Ibid.*, 23 October 1914; 25 October 1914.

[27]*Spokane Chronicle*, 25 October 1914.

[28]*Oroville Gazette*, 16 October 1914.

[29]*Seattle Times*, 2 November 1914. *Spokane Chronicle*, 30 October 1914.

[30]*Spokane Chronicle*, 2 November 1914.

[31]Secretary of State, *Abstract of the Votes Polled in the State of Washington in the General Election November 3, 1914* (Olympia: Government Printing Office).

[32]*Ibid.*

[33]*Spokane Chronicle*, 5 November 1914.

[34]*Spokane Press*, 24 November 1914.

[35]Secretary of State, *Abstract of the Votes Polled in the Primary Election in the State of Washington September 8, 1914. Spokesman-Review*, 5 November 1914; 12 November 1914.

[36]*Spokesman-Review*, 5 November 1914.

[37]Secretary of State, *Abstract of the Votes Polled in the General Election, State of Washington, November 3, 1914.*

[38]Robert E. Ficken, *The Forested Land...* (Seattle: University of Washington Press, 1987), 85.

[39]Cooper, *Pivotal Decades*, 147, 178–179. David Burner, *The Politics of Provincialism: The Democratic Party in Transition, 1918–1932* (New York: Alfred A. Knopf, 1968), 28–39.

[40]*Spokesman-Review*, 15 November 1914.

[41]*Ibid.*, 29 November 1914. Dill, *Where Water Falls*, 50.

[42]*Congressional Record* (31 January 1916) vol. 53, pt. 2, 1922–25.

[43]Note and receipt, CDP.

[44]Dill, *Where Water Falls*, 50–51.

[45]*Ibid.*, 52.

[46]*Wenatchee Daily World*, 16 June 1913.

[47]*Ibid.*, 30 December 1914.

[48]*Spokesman-Review*, 12 November 1914.

[49]Link and McCormick, *Progressivism*, 33.

[50]Hofstadter, *The Age of Reform*, 9, 210.

[51]*Omak Chronicle*, 6 May 1965; 11 March 1971. *Spokesman-Review*, 20 February 1955. The agreement was named after James McLaughlin, a U.S. Indian inspector at the time. The Colville Indians received directly only a fraction of the $1.5 million promised to them. The rest was apparently used by the Indian Bureau.

[52]*Wenatchee Daily World*, 18 December 1915.

[53]*Ibid.* Dill, *Where Water Falls*, 53.

[54]*Ibid.*

[55]*Ibid.*, 54. *Spokesman-Review*, 9 April 1916.

[56]*Congressional Record* (8 February 1916) vol. 53, pt. 3, 2303–2305.

[57]Speech of Clarence Dill to the House in Committee of the Whole House, 28 March 1916, CDP.

[58]*Ibid.*

[59]*Wenatchee Daily World*, 9 December 1915; 3 May 1916. Howard Allen, *Poindexter of Washington: A Study in Progresive Politics* (Carbondale: Southern Illinois University Press, 1981), 162.

[60]*Wenatchee Daily World*, 3 May 1916.

[61]Dill to Arthur Gunn, 16 May 1916, AGC.

[62]William Humphrey to Clarence Dill, 18 August 1933, Clarence Dill to William Humphrey, 21 August 1933, William Humphrey to Clarence Dill, 2 September 1933, WHC.

[63]William Humphrey to Clarence Dill, 18 August 1933, Clarence Dill to William Humphrey, 21 August 1933, WHC.

[64]Dill's relationship with Humphrey is more fully developed in the chapter on Dill's decision to retire from public life.

[65]*Wenatchee Daily World*, 3 May 1916.

[66] *Okanogan Independent*, 18 July 1916; 1 August 1916.

[67] *Spokesman-Review*, 7 November 1967. Dill, *Where Water Falls*, 54–55.

[68] *Spokesman-Review*, 14 June 1933.

Chapter Three, pages 29–42

[1] *Spokesman-Review*, 24 October 1916; 15 February 1916.

[2] Letter of 26 April 1916 from C.C. Dill to Arthur Gunn, AGC.

[3] Arthur S. Link, *Woodrow Wilson and the Progressive Era, 1910–1917* (New York: Harper Bros., 1954), 180.

[4] *Congressional Record* (31 May 1916), vol. 53, pt. 9, 8969.

[5] *Ibid.*

[6] *Spokesman-Review*, 24 October 1916.

[7] Link, *Woodrow Wilson and the Progressive Era*, 185. Nathan Miller, *Theodore Roosevelt: A Life* (New York: William Morrow and Co., 1992), 550.

[8] *Spokesman-Review*, 15 November 1916.

[9] *Ibid.*

[10] Link, *Woodrow Wilson and the Progressive Era*, 183.

[11] *Spokesman-Review*, 13 February 1916.

[12] Link, *Woodrow Wilson and the Progressive Era*, 186.

[13] *Spokesman-Review*, 11 February 1916.

[14] *Ibid.* Link, *Woodrow Wilson and the Progressive Era*, 192–194. *Congressional Record* (10 July 1916), vol. 53, pt. 11, 10768.

[15] *Omak Chronicle*, 22 September 1916. *Okanogan Independent*, 17 October 1916.

[16] *Ibid.*

[17] Norman Clark, *The Dry Years: Prohibition and Social Change in Washington* (Seattle: University of Washington, 1965), 86, 134.

[18] *Spokesman-Review*, 16 October 1916.

[19] *Okanogan Independent*, 28 October 1916.

[20] *Spokesman-Review*, ? October 1916.

[21] *Ibid.*, 17 October 1916; 2 November 1916.

[22] *Okanogan Independent*, 7 October 1916. *Spokesman-Review*, 17 October 1916. *Seattle Daily Times*, 8 November 1916. Secretary of State, *Abstract of the Votes Polled in the State of Washington in the General Election of 7 November 1916* (Olympia: Government Printing Office).

[23] Robert Saltvig, "The Progressive Movement in Washington" (Ph.D. diss. University of Washington, 1966), 399.

[24] *Seattle Daily Times*, 8 November 1916.

[25] Secretary of State, *Abstract of the Votes Polled in the State of Washington in the General Election of 7 November 1916*. Saltvig, "The Progressive Movement In Washington," 399.

²⁶*Spokesman-Review*, 3 November 1916; 5 November 1916. Further demonstrating the new importance of women, in 1916 Montana elected the first woman, Jeannette Rankin, ever sent to the U.S. Congress. National woman suffrage would not be long in coming.

²⁷ *Spokesman-Review*, 24 October 1916. *Wenatchee Daily World*, 27 March 1917.

²⁸*Ibid.*, 2 April 1917.

²⁹Winston Churchill, *The World Crisis* (6 volumes), III, (New York: Scribner's, 1927), 234.

³⁰August Heckscher, *Woodrow Wilson* (New York: Charles Scribner's Sons, 1991), 433–434.

³¹*Ibid.*

³²Arthur S. Link, *Wilson: Campaigns For Progressivism and Peace, 1916–1917* (Princeton: Princeton University Press, 1965), 414, 439.

³³*Congressional Record* (5 April 1917), vol. 55, pt. 1, 344–347.

³⁴*Spokesman-Review*, 6 April 1917.

³⁵Letter from Dill to Alfred J. Schweppe, 6 October 1916, CDP. Letter from Clarence Dill to Henry Suzzallo, 6 April 1917, HSP.

³⁶H.C. Peterson and Gilbert C. Fite, *Opponents of War, 1917–1918* (Madison: University of Wisconsin Press, 1957), 3–6.

³⁷Saltvig, "The Progressive Movement in Washington," 446.

³⁸Peterson and Fite, *Opponents of War*, 5.

³⁹Clarence Dill, *Where Water Falls* (Spokane: Self published, 1970), 63. Richard Lowitt, *George W. Norris: The Persistence of a Progressive, 1918–1933* (Urbana: University of Illinois Press, 1971), 72. One cannot help but wonder what circumstances would have had to arise to compel the more timid members of Congress to straighten their backbones and vote their conscience. Dill, at least, was worthy of the office.

⁴⁰Peterson and Fite, *Opponents of War*, 5, 10. Letter from Dill to Alfred J. Schweppe, 6 October 1916, CDP. Letter from Clarence Dill to Henry Suzzallo, 6 April 1917, HSP.

⁴¹*Ibid.*

⁴²*Spokesman-Review*, 11 April 1917.

⁴³*Ibid.*, 16 April 1917. *Seattle Times*, 1 November 1918.

⁴⁴*Spokesman-Review*, 16 April 1917.

⁴⁵*Wenatchee Daily World*, 8 May 1917.

⁴⁶Peterson and Fite, *Opponents of War*, 21–22.

⁴⁷*Congressional Record* (27 April 1917), vol. 55, pt. 2, 1408–1411.

⁴⁸*Spokesman-Review*, 27 March 1917; 6 January 1918.

⁴⁹*Ibid.*, 1 January 1918; 6 April 1917.

⁵⁰*Wenatchee Daily World*, 8 August 1917. *Spokesman-Review*, 6 April 1917; 15 November 1917; 29 December 1917; 1 January 1918.

⁵¹*Wenatchee Daily World*, 31 October 1918.

⁵²Dill's notes on his trip, October-November 1917, CDP.

[53]*Spokesman-Review*, 3 January 1918. *San Poil Eagle*, as quoted in Dill, *Where Water Falls*, 75.

[54]*Spokesman-Review*, 31 December 1917; 30 December 1917; 3 January 1918.

[55]*Seattle P.I.*, 22 October 1918; 24 October 1918. *Spokesman-Review*, 22 July 1918.

[56]Dill, *Where Water Falls*, 76. Drumheller's assessment of Dill as a "builder" derived from Clarence's work in opening the Colville Reservation.

[57]Speech before the Spokane Democrats, July 1918, CDP. *Seattle P.I.*, 24 October 1918.

[58]Saltvig, "The Progressive Movement in Washington," 445.

[59]John M. Cooper, *Pivotal Decades: The United States, 1900–1920* (New York: W.W. Norton and Co., 1990), 320.

[60]Dill, *Where Water Falls*, 76.

[61]*Seattle P.I.*, 24 October 1918.

[62]*Wenatchee Daily World*, 31 October 1918. *Seattle P.I.*, 22 October 1918; 24 October 1918.

[63]*Wenatchee Daily World*, 24 October 1918.

[64]*Seattle Times*, 1 November 1918. *Wenatchee Daily World*, 31 October 1918. *Seattle P.I.*, 22 October 1918.

[65]Cedric Larson and James Mock, *Words That Won the War: The Story of the Committee on Public Information, 1917–1919* (New York: Russell and Russell, 1939), 3–10.

[66]*Seattle P.I.*, 8 November 1918.

Chapter Four, pages 43–55

[1]Clarence Dill, *Where Water Falls* (Spokane: Self Published, 1970), 78.

[2]*Spokesman-Review*, October 1916. Dill, *Where Water Falls*, 79. When he first went to Congress, Dill had hoped to land seats on four committees: irrigation, public lands, Indian affairs, and weights and measures. He gained positions on all four committees.

[3]*Seattle P.I.*, 20 March 1920.

[4]*Ibid.*

[5]*Ibid.*

[6]*Spokesman-Review*, 30 April 1920.

[7]*Ibid.*, 2 May 1920.

[8]*Ibid.*, 29 June 1920; 30 June 1920. Dill, *Where Water Falls*, 80.

[9]Alan Dawley, *Struggles for Justice: Social Responsibility and the Liberal State* (Cambridge: Belknap Press, 1991), 211. Robert Ferrell, *Woodrow Wilson and World War I, 1917–1921* (New York: Harper and Row, 1985), 98–117.

[10]John M. Cooper, *Pivotal Decades: The United States, 1900–1920* (New York: W.W. Norton and Co., 1990), 365–372. Dawley, *Struggles for Justice*, 239.

[11]*Ibid.*, 233, 243.

[12]William E. Leuchtenburg, *The Perils of Prosperity, 1914–1932* (Chicago: University of Chicago Press, 1958), 128–129.

[13]Dawley, *Struggles For Justice*, 231–241.

[14]David Burner, *The Politics of Provincialism: The Democratic Party in Transition, 1918–1932* (New York: Alfred A. Knopf, 1968), 78–102. *Seattle P.I.*, September 1922. Robert E. Ficken and Charles P. LeWarne, *Washington: A Centennial History* (Seattle: University of Washington Press, 1988), 98–100. Norman Clark, *The Dry Years: Prohibition and Social Change in Washington* (Seattle: University of Washington, 1965), 179–206. Frederick Merz, *The Dry Decade* (New York: Doubleday and Doran, 1931), 130–159.

[15]Burner, *Politics of Provincialism*, 99.

[16]Ficken and LeWarne, *Washington: A Centennial History*, 96.

[17]Burner, *The Politics of Provincialism*, 103–104.

[18]Speech at the Jackson Day Banquet, Colfax, Washington, 13 January, 1922, CDP.

[19]*Seattle Star*, 28 January 1922. *Tacoma News-Tribune*, 11 October 1922.

[20]Mary Lou Krause, "Prohibition and the Reform Tradition" (M.A. thesis, University of Washington, 1963), 138. Howard Allen, *Poindexter of Washington: A Study in Progressive Politics* (Carbondale: Southern Illinois University Press, 1981), 566. Dill's speech before the Jackson Day banquet at Tekoa, Washington, 15 March 1922, CDP.

[21]Allen, *Poindexter of Washington*, 238. *Seattle P.I.*, 4 June 1922. Hamilton Cravens, "A History of the Washington Farmer-Labor Party, 1918–1924" (M.A. thesis, University of Washington, 1962), 170. *Seattle P.I.*, 20 July 1922.

[22]Allen, *Poindexter of Washington*, 6–12, 85. Krause, "Prohibition and the Reform Tradition," 33–34.

[23]Krause, "Prohibition and the Reform Tradition, 166. Richard Hofstadter, *The Age of Reform* (New York: Vintage, 1960), 218–222. Allen, *Poindexter of Washington*, 246, 247.

[24]Cravens, "A History of the Washington Farmer-Labor Party," 176.

[25]Allen, *Poindexter of Washington*, 251.

[26]Cravens, "A History of the Washington Farmer-Labor Party," 180, 182. Clark, *The Dry Years*, 187. Allen, *Poindexter of Washington*, 226, 251. *Seattle Union Record*, 18 October 1922; 19 October 1922. *Tacoma News Tribune*, 27 October 1922.

[27]*Seattle P.I.*, 1 November 1922.

[28]*Everett Daily Herald*, 23 October 1922. *Seattle P.I.*, 1 November 1922.

[29]*Ibid.*, 17 October 1922. *Seattle Star*, 27 October 1922. Cravens, "A History of the Washington Farmer Labor Party," 173. *Labor Journal*, 5 March 1920. *Seattle P.I.*, 17 October 1922; 1 November 1922. Allen, *Poindexter of Washington*, 248.

[30]*Seattle Union Record*, 11 October 1922. *Labor Journal*, 20 October 1922. Cravens, "A History of the Washington Farmer-Labor Party," 180.

[31]*Spokesman-Review*, 7 November 1922. *Seattle Times*, 2 November 1922.

[32]*Everett Daily Herald*, 6 November 1922.

[33]Allen, *Poindexter of Washington*, 248–249. Krause, "Prohibition and the Reform Tradition," 137–138.

[34]Allen, *Poindexter of Washington*, 238, 241.

[35]Krause, "Prohibition and the Reform Tradition," 47.

[36]Robert L. Cole, "The Democratic Party in Washington State, 1919–1933: Barometer for Social Change" (Ph.D. diss., University of Washington, 1972), 78.

[37]*Literary Digest*, 26 August 1922, vol. 74, no. 9, 9. Krause, "Prohibition and the Reform Tradition," 58–62.

[38]Krause, "Prohibition and the Reform Tradition," 107–111.

[39]Cole, "The Democratic Party in Washington State, 1919–1933," 68.

[40]Cravens, "A History of the Washington Farmer-Labor Party," 180.

[41]*Ibid.*, 179. Terry Slatten, "Homer T. Bone, Public Power, and Washington State: Progressive Politics in the Mid 1920's" (M.A. thesis, University of Washington, 198?, date unavailable from library records), 21, 36, 37, 39, 40.

[42]Cravens, "A History of the Washington Farmer-Labor Party," 181. *Seattle Union Record*, 30 September 1922. Krause, "Prohibition and the Reform Tradition," 148, 155.

[43]*Seattle P.I.*, 2 November 1922. Allen, *Poindexter of Washington*, 252. *Tacoma News Tribune*, 2 November 1922.

[44]*Seattle P.I.*, 6 November 1922.

[45]*Seattle Times*, 2 November 1922; 3 November 1922.

[46]*Seattle P.I.*, 6 November 1922.

[47]*Tacoma News Tribune*, 8 November 1922.

[48]Secretary of State, *Abstract of the Votes Polled in the State of Washington in the General Election 7 November 1922* (Olympia: Government Printing Office).

[49]Leuchtenburg, *The Perils of Prosperity, 1914–1932*, 128–129.

[50]Dill, *Where Water Falls*, 78.

Chapter Five, pages 57–66

[1]*Congressional Record*, 11 December 1923, vol. 65, pt. 1, 235. Clarence Dill, *Where Water Falls* (Spokane: Self published, 1970), 101.

[2]Richard Lowitt, *George Norris: The Persistence of a Progressive, 1918–1933* (Urbana: University of Illinois Press, 1971), 372.

[3]*Congressional Record* (14 January 1927), vol. 68, pt. 2, 1642. *New York Times*, 15 January 1927.

[4]Lowitt, *George Norris*, 373.

[5]*New York Times*, 21 January 1928.

[6]William Dietrich, *Northwest Passage: The Great Columbia River* (New York: Simon and Schuster, 1995), 265.

[7] Lowitt, *George Norris*, 434. *New York Times*, 10 December 1926, 1–2. *Congressional Record* (3 January 1927), vol. 68, pt. 1, 989.

[8]*New York Times*, 10 December 1926. Frank L. Smith's right to take his seat was also being challenged.

[9]*Ibid.*, 12 December 1926. *Congressional Record* (3 January 1927), vol. 68, pt. 1, 989.

[10]Lowitt, *George Norris*, 434–435.

[11]Gilbert Fite, *George N. Peek and the Fight for Farm Parity* (Norman: University of Oklahoma Press, 1954), 8–10. James H. Shideler, *Farm Crisis, 1919–1923* (Westport, Ct.: Greenwood Press, 1976), 5.

[12]William E. Leuchtenburg, *The Perils of Prosperity, 1914–1932* (Chicago: University of Chicago Press, 1993), 100–101. Robert E. Ficken, and Charles P. LeWarne, *Washington, a Centennial History* (Seattle: University of Washington Press, 1988), 99.

[13]Leuchtenburg, *Perils of Prosperity, 1914–1932*, 101. Gordon B. Dodds, *The American Northwest: A History of Oregon and Washington* (Arlington Heights, Ill.: Forum Press Inc., 1986), 222.

[14]Leuchtenburg, *Perils of Prosperity*, 2.

[15]Richard S. Kirkendall, *The United States 1929–1945: Years of Crisis and Change* (New York: McGraw-Hill, 1974), 6.

[16]Fite, *George N. Peek*, 5, 11. Shideler, *Farm Crisis*, 40–41.

[17]Donald McCoy, *Calvin Coolidge: The Quiet President* (New York: Macmillan Co., 1967), 307.

[18]Fite, *George N. Peek*, 5–6.

[19]Leuchtenburg, *The Perils of Prosperity*, 101–102.

[20]John D. Hicks, *Republican Ascendancy: 1921–1933* (New York: Harper and Row, 1960), 198.

[21]McCoy, *Calvin Coolidge*, 308. Richard Hofstadter, *The Age of Reform* (New York: Alfred A. Knopf, 1989), 96–97.

[22]David Burner, *The Politics of Provincialism: The Democratic Party in Transition, 1918–1932* (New York: Alfred A. Knopf, 1968), 169. Hicks, *Republican Ascendancy*, 198. *Congressional Record* (23 May 1928), vol. 69, pt. 9, 9557.

[23]Lowitt, *George W. Norris*, 408.

[24]McCoy, *Calvin Coolidge*, 234, 308, 310.

[25]Hicks, *Republican Ascendancy*, 198.

[26]*Ibid.*, 198–199. *New York Times*, 19 February 1927.

[27]Fite, *George N. Peek*, 164.

[28]McCoy, *Calvin Coolidge*, 323, 324.

[29]*Ibid.*

[30]*Ibid.*, 325. *New York Times*, 19 February 1927.

[31]*Ibid.*, 20 February 1927. Lowitt, *George Norris*, 298–299.

[32]Hicks, *Republican Ascendancy*, 199.

[33]McCoy, *Calvin Coolidge*, 325.

[34]*New York Times*, 26 February 1927.

[35]McCoy, *Calvin Coolidge*, 198, 326. *New York Times*, 2 April 1928; 9 April 1928.

[36]*New York Times*, 12 April 1928.

[37]*Congressional Record* (11 April 1928), vol. 69, pt. 6, 6217.

[38]*New York Times*, 12 April 1928. McCoy, *Calvin Coolidge*, 327. *Congressional Record* (April 12, 1928), vol. 69, pt. 6, 6283.

[39]McCoy, *Calvin Coolidge*, 327.

[40]*New York Times*, 24 May 1928. *Congressional Record* (25 May 1928), vol. 69, pt. 9, 9880.

[41]Leuchtenburg, *The Perils of Prosperity*, 102.

[42]Fite, *George N. Peek*, 199.

[43]*Ibid.*, 200.

[44]Hicks, *Republican Ascendancy*, 200, 201.

Chapter Six, pages 67–82

[1]Erik Barnouw, *A History of Broadcasting in the United States*, (vol. 1), (New York: Oxford University Press, 1966), 10–12, 16–17, 28–32. Joel Rosenbloom, "Authority of the Federal Communications Commission with Respect to the Programming of Radio and Television Broadcasting Stations" (unpublished legal brief, 1961), 5, CDP.

[2]Congress, House of Representatives, Committee on the Merchant Marine and Fisheries, *Hearings before the Committee on the Merchant Marine and Fisheries on H.R. 11964*, 67th Congress., 4th sess., 1923, 29.

[3]Rosenbloom, "Authority of the Federal Communications Commission," 7–10.

[4]*Hearings on H.R. 11964*, 29. As quoted in Rosenbloom, "Authority of the Federal Communications Commission," 10.

[5]C.C. Dill, *Radio Law* (Washington, D.C.: National Law Book Company, 1938), 78.

[6]Congress, House of Representatives, Committee on the Merchant Marine and Fisheries, *Hearings before The Committee on Merchant Marine and Fisheries on H.R. 7357*, 68th Congress, 1st sess., March 11,12,13,14, 1924, 40–51, 52–63, 70–98, 157–207.

[7]*Congressional Record* (16 February 1924), vol. 65, pt. 3, 2572–2573.

[8]Congress, House, Committee on the Merchant Marine and Fisheries, *Hearings before the Committee on Merchant Marine and Fisheries on H.R. 5589*, 69th Congress, 1st sess., January 6–7, 14–15, 1926, 37.

[9]Congress, Senate, Committee on Interstate Commerce, *Hearings before the Committee on Interstate Commerce on S.1 and S.1754*, 69th Congress, 1st sess., January 8–9, 1926, 37, 216–283.

[10]Rosenbloom, "Authority of the Federal Communications Commission," 16.

[11]*Ibid.*, 17. *New York Times*, 20 December 1925; 9 January 1926.

[12]Clarence Dill, *Where Water Falls* (Spokane: Self published, 1970), 106–108.

[13]*New York Times*, 10 January 1926; 2 May 1926. David Burner, *Herbert Hoover: A Public Life* (New York: Alfred A. Knopf, 1979), 161, 169, 183, 184.

[14]*New York Times,* 2 May 1926. Rosenbloom, "Authority of the Federal Communications Commission," 18.

[15]*New York Times*, 9 May 1926.

[16]*Ibid.*, 13 May 1926; 14 May 1926.

[17]*Ibid.*, 18 May 1926.

[18]*Ibid.*

[19]*Congressional Record* (23 June 1926), vol. 67, pt. 11, 11803. W. Jefferson Davis, *Radio Law* (New York: Parker Stone and Baird, 1929), 31. Rosenbloom, "Authority of the Federal Communications Commission," 18. *New York Times*, 12 December 1926.

[20]*New York Times*, 12 December 1926.

[21]*Congressional Record* (30 June 1926), vol. 67, pt. 11, 12335.

22*Ibid.* (1 July 1926), vol. 67, pt. 11, 12501.

23*Ibid.* (3 July 1926), vol. 67, pt. 11, 12959.

24*New York Times*, 15 September 1926; 12 December 1926.

25*Ibid.*, 12 December 1926. Donald Godfrey, "A Rhetorical Analysis of the Congressional Debates on Broadcast Regulation in the United States" (Ph.D. diss., University of Washington, 1975), 103.

26*Congressional Record* (12 January 1927), vol. 68, pt. 2, 1481; (15 January 1927), vol. 68, pt. 2, 1704.

27*New York Times*, 16 January 1927; 13 February 1927.

28Robert B. Horwitz, *The Irony of Regulatory Reform* (New York: Oxford University Press, 1989), 118.

29Godfrey, "A Rhetorical Analysis," 43.

30*Ibid.*, 259.

31Walter B. Emery, *Broadcasting and Government: Responsibilities and Regulations* (East Lansing: Michigan State University Press, 1971), 30.

32*Congressional Record* (3 February 1927), vol. 68, pt. 3, 2869.

33*Ibid.*, 2870.

34*Ibid.*

35*Ibid.*, 2870–2873.

36*Ibid.*, 2873.

37*Ibid.*, 2882.

38*Ibid.*, 2877, 2878.

39Emery, *Broadcasting and Government*, 43–44.

40*Congressional Record* (3 February 1927), vol. 68, pt. 3, 2880–2881.

41*Ibid.* (5 February 1927), vol. 68, pt. 3, 3026, 3027.

42*Ibid.*, 3028.

43*Ibid.*, 3030.

44*Ibid.*, 3033.

45*Ibid.*, 3034.

46Godfrey, "A Rhetorical Analysis," 91–94.

47*Congressional Record* (5 February 1927), vol. 68, pt. 3, 3027; (7 February 1927), vol. 68, pt. 3, 3118.

48*Ibid.*, 3122.

49*Ibid.* (8 February 1927), vol. 68, pt. 3, 3257.

50*Ibid.*

51*Ibid.*, 3258.

52*Ibid.*, 3262; (9 February 1927), 3336.

53*Ibid.* (18 February 1927), vol. 68, pt. 4, 4111.

54*Ibid.*

55Godfrey, "A Rhetorical Analysis," 151. *Congressional Record* (18 February 1927), vol. 68, pt. 4, 4154.

[56]*Ibid.*, 4155.

[57]*Ibid.*

[58]*New York Times*, 20 February 1927.

[59]Christopher H. Sterling and John M. Kittross, *Stay Tuned: A Concise History of American Broadcasting* (Belmont Ca.: Wadsworth Publishing Co., 1990), 127.

[60]Donald McCoy, *Calvin Coolidge: The Quiet President* (Lawrence: University of Kansas Press, 1988), 285–286.

[61]George H. Gibson, *Public Broadcasting: The Role of the Federal Government* (New York: Praeger Publishers, 1977), 9.

[62]*New York Times,* 2 October 1927. *Congressional Record* (13 March 1928), vol. 69, pt. 4, 4608, 4609.

[63]Robert McChesney, *Telecommunications, Mass Media, and Democracy: The Battle for the Control of U.S. Broadcasting, 1928–1935* (New York: Oxford University Press, 1993), 17.
Dill's role in passing the Radio Act of 1927 has attracted considerable attention from scholars from various fields. McChesney, a leading scholar on the subject, argues Congress should have been discussing a public versus private radio system but failed to do so. [*Ibid.*] He is correct in his opinion that the nation, and Congress, failed to engage in such a debate. However, failure to openly debate this issue was not due, as McChesney implies, to a lack of American awareness concerning it. It was because Americans had held the debate already in countless other forms, the role of government in the progressive era being only the most recent. Moreover, government-owned radio was perceived as being a foreign system. Dill himself stood in the Senate in 1924 and compared the rapid development of radio in America to the moribund European system. [*New York Times,* 4 March 1924. *Congressional Record* (4 March 1924), vol. 65, pt. 4, 3546.] Even had the Europeans been more dynamic with their system, it is unlikely that it would have changed the debate. By 1924, and on through the decade, Americans were dubious about anything from the old world: Europeans seemed to learn little from their wars and settle less; they also failed to pay their bills. American attitudes toward Europe, combined with the distinctive American psychology, made adoption of a European-style government-owned radio system unlikely. Wallace Stegner beautifully captures the American mind in *Angle of Repose:* "One of the charming things about nineteenth century America was its cultural patriotism–not jingoism, just patriotism, the feeling that no matter how colorful, exotic, and cultivated other countries might be, there was no place so ultimately right, so morally sound, so in tune with the hopeful future, as the USA." [*Angle of Repose* (New York: Doubleday and Co., 1971), 319.

What was true of Americans in the nineteenth century was no less true in the America of the 1920s; it may have been more so. Thus the failure to consider a state-run radio system grew out of what the United States was in the twenties and where it was going. [Emery, *Broadcasting and Government,* 40.] McChesney's criticism of the path the nation took in regard to radio amounts to criticizing the people of the era for not being wholly other than what they were and not perceiving clearly what path the development of radio would take in the future.

Moreover, McChesney does not take note of the strenuous efforts on the part of progressives to defeat Dill's radio bill, to reshape it along lines that were at least conceivably attainable in that day and age. Pittman and his colleagues argued vociferously for government ownership of the air and strict guidelines to the commission. To imply as McChesney does that the Senate rushed the debate and that there was little disagreement on substantial issues does not bear scrutiny. For the Radio Bill of 1927 was definitely not rushed:

Congress had been considering radio legislation since 1923. Moreover, Dill's own bill had been before the Senate for more than a year when it was finally passed. And certainly the progressives in the Senate believed important issues were at stake; by the end of the radio debate, every progressive senator had abandoned the conferees' report except Dill, who alone fully understood what it had taken to get it as far as he had. The majority of the nation's legislators were opposed to the commission and had only acquiesced in the face of public demand for regulation. Those who were in favor of a government-owned system were waging the battle on grounds they thought winnable. George Norris clearly preferred a government-run radio system, but realized the hopelessness of that cause and thus fought Dill on other related issues. [Gibson, *Public Broadcasting*, 7. Godfrey, "A Rhetorical Analysis," 218.] In the end, the progressives could not force change in any aspect of the radio bill. Government-owned and operated radio was never possible.

McChesney is no doubt right, however, in taking to task Donald Godfrey and Sydney Head, among others, for their view that the 1927 Radio Act was a progressive victory. [Donald Godfrey, "Senator Dill and the 1927 Radio Act," *Journal of Broadcasting* 23 (1978): 485. Sydney W. Head, *Broadcasting in America* (Boston: Houghton-Mifflin, 1956), 134.] Clearly the progressives lost the fight over radio in 1927. Dill gained all he could.

McChesney's argument that the 1927 Radio Act was not a progressive victory suggests a force that caused the progressive defeat. Though the progressives realized government-owned radio was virtually impossible, they did go to great lengths to gain provisions in the radio bill they considered attainable. They were defeated. The victors were the conservatives, primarily in the House, who refused to compromise any further on radio legislation. In his work, Godfrey slights the power of these representatives and emphasizes the divisions within the ranks of radio interests as contributing to the conferees' compromise and the creation of progressive legislation. As we have seen, the Radio Act of 1927 cannot be characterized as progressive; Dill himself would not have used that word. The House conferees, especially White, fought tenaciously to enervate the commission as much as possible and ultimately relied on President Coolidge to frustrate Dill's hopes for the commission, even to denying funds for the commission to operate. [*New York Times*, 2 October 1927.]

Thus McChesney and Godfrey slight the role of politics in the Radio Act of 1927. Godfrey fails to see the hand of the conservative Republicans in shaping the legislation before it reached the Senate floor; McChesney ignores the battles progressives waged in fighting for government ownership of the air, and other concerns. However, McChesney's assessment of the legislation seems more accurate given the subsequent history of radio, but his identifying Dill with commercial interests is too vague. [McChesney, *Telecommunications, Mass Media, and Democracy*, 125–127.] Dill was an unequivocal believer in the American free enterprise system, but he was a fervid advocate of government regulation to improve the lot of the common people. Moreover, he was unhappy with much of what the FRC did and sought to amend the Radio Act of 1927 on several occasions.

[64]Robert E. Ficken and Charles P. LeWarne, *Washington: A Centennial History* (Seattle: University of Washington Press, 1989), 97.

Chapter Seven, pages 83–97

[1]*New York Times*, 9 March 1927; 31 March 1936. *Seattle P.I.*, 30 June 1936. *New York Times*, 31 March 1936.

[2]*Ibid.*, 9 March 1936.

[3]John M. Cooper, *Pivotal Decades: The United States, 1900–1920* (New York: W.W. Norton and Co., 1990), 184, 308.

[4]*New York Times*, 9 March 1927.

[5]*Ibid.*, 31 March 1936; 10 July 1936.

[6]*Ibid.*, 9 March 1927; 31 March 1936.

[7]*Ibid*, 31 March 1936. *Seattle P.I.*, 7 July 1936; 27 June 1936; 30 June 1936.

[8]*New York Times*, 16 March 1927.

[9]*Ibid.*

[10]*Seattle P.I.*, 7 July 1936; 26 June 1936; 4 July 1936; 2 July 1936.

[11]*Ibid.*, 12 April 1928; 13 April 1928.

[12]*New York Times*, 28 October 1928. Robert L. Cole, "The Democratic Party in Washington State, 1919–1933: Barometer of Social Change" (Ph.d. diss., University of Washington, 1972), 199–200. *Seattle P.I.*, 27 June 1928.

[13]*New York Times*, 20 July 1927.

[14]*Inland Empire News*, 11 July 1928.

[15]Ibid., *Everett Daily Herald*, 11 July 1928. *New York Times*, 13 July 1928.

[16]Secretary of State, *Abstract of the Votes Polled in the State of Washington in the Primary Election, September 11, 1928* (Olympia: Government Printing Office).

[17]Robert E. Ficken, *The Forested Land...* (Seattle: University of Washington Press, 1987), 168–180.

[18]*Ibid.*, 174.

[19]John Fahey, *The Inland Empire: The Unfolding Years* (Seattle: University of Washington Press, 1986), 211. Ficken, *The Forested Land...*, 177. Robert E. Ficken, *Lumber and Politics: The Career of Mark E. Reed* (Seattle: University of Washington Press, 1979), 165–181.

[20]Letter from C.C. Dill to the Merrill and Ring Lumber Company, 23 January 1924, MRL.

[21]*Congressional Record* (9 January 1928), vol. 69, pt. 1, 1170. Box 22, Folder C.C. Dill, SPTL.

[22]*Congressional Record* (31 January 1928), vol. 69, pt. 2; (20 February 1928), vol. 69, pt. 3. Richard Lowitt, *George Norris: The Persistence of a Progressive, 1918–1933* (Urbana: University of Illinois Press, 1971), 426–427.

[23]*Seattle Times*, 8 October 1928.

[24]*Tacoma News Tribune*, 12 October 1928. Ficken, *Lumber and Politics*, 167. *Seattle P.I.*, 19 October 1928.

[25]*Ibid.*, 9 October 1928.

[26]*Tacoma News Tribune*, 12 October 1928. *Everett Daily Herald*, 5 November, 1928. *Seattle P.I.*, 12 October 1928.

[27]*Ibid.*, 26 June 1936; 30 June 1936.

[28]*Spokesman-Review*, 13 October 1928. *Seattle Times*, 14 October 1928; 17 October 1928.

[29]*Ibid.*, 13 October 1928. *Seattle P.I.*, 13 October 1928.

[30]*Ibid.*, 14 September 1928.

[31]*Ibid.*, 21 September 1928. *Seattle Times*, 14 October 1928. *Everett Daily Herald*, 5 November 1928.

[32]*Spokesman Review*, 15 October 1928. *Seattle P.I.*, 18 October 1928.

[33]*Seattle Times*, 19 October 1928.

[34]*Labor World*, 12 October 1928; 19 October 1928. *Labor Journal,* 12 October 1928.

[35]*Spokesman-Review*, 19 October 1928; 27 October 1928.

[36]*Seattle P.I.*, 20 October 1928.

[37]*Tacoma News Tribune*, 20 October 1928.

[38]*Ibid. Seattle P.I.*, 27 October 1928. *New York Times*, 28 October 1928. *Spokesman-Review*, 21 October 1928.

[39]*Ibid.*, 27 October 1928.

[40]*Seattle P.I.*, 29 October 1928; 26 October 1928; 30 October 1928. *Seattle Times*, 1 November 1928.

[41]*Seattle P.I.*, 2 November 1928; 1 November 1928.

[42]*Ibid.*, 3 November 1928.

[43]*Ibid.*

[44]*Ibid.*, 6 November 1928; 5 November 1928.

[45]*Ibid.*, 6 November 1928. *Spokesman-Review*, 7 November 1928.

[46]*Seattle Times*, 7 November 1928.

[47]*Everett Daily Herald*, 7 November 1928; 12 October 1928. *Seattle P.I.*, 7 November 1928.

[48]*Spokesman-Review*, 8 November 1928.

[49]Fayette Krause, "Democratic Party Politics in the State of Washington during the New Deal" (Ph.D. diss., University of Washington, 1971), 25.

[50]Secretary of State, *Abstract of the Votes Polled in the State of Washington in the General Election Held 6 November 1928* (Olympia: Government Printing Office). Secretary of State, *Abstract of Votes Polled in the State of Washington in the General Election Held 7 November 1922* (Olympia: Government Printing Office).

[51]*Seattle Times*, 14 October 1928; 17 October 1928; 22 October 1928; 26 October 1928; 30 October 1928.

[52]James Kreiss, "A County by County Analysis of Voting Trends in the State of Washington from 1920 to 1962" (Master's thesis, University of Washington, 1964), 28.

[53]Robert E. Ficken and Charles P. LeWarne, *Washington: A Centennial History* (Seattle: University of Washington Press, 1988), 110, 111.

[54]*New York Times*, 17 April 1929. Lowitt, *George Norris*, 299.

[55]*Congressional Record* (14 June 1929), vol. 71, pt. 3, 2880.

[56]*Ibid.*, 2886.

[57]*Congressional Record* (14 June 1929), vol. 71, pt. 3, 2880.

[58]Lowitt, *George Norris*, 421.

[59]*Congressional Record* (12 November 1929), vol. 71, pt. 5, 5454, 5460, 5461.

[60]*Ibid.*, 5466–5469.

[61]Ficken, *Lumber and Politics*, 173–175.

[62]*Congressional Record* (13 November 1929), vol. 71, pt. 5, 5509.

Chapter Eight, pages 99–111

[1]Bruce Mitchell, *Flowing Wealth: The Story of Water Resource Development in North Central Washington, 1870–1950* (Wenatchee: Wenatchee Daily World, 1967), 8. Paul C. Pitzer, *Grand Coulee: Harnessing a Dream* (Pullman: Washington State University Press, 1994), 10–18.

[2]*Wenatchee Daily World*, 18 July 1918.

[3]*Ibid.*, 3 December 1918. Robert E. Ficken, *Rufus Woods, The Columbia River, and the Building of Modern Washington* (Pullman: Washington State University Press, 1995), 60–61.

[4]*Spokesman-Review*,? 1920.

[5]*Congressional Record* (12 December 1927), vol. 69, pt. 1, 474. Transcript of John Fahey's interview with Clarence Dill on 24 April 1948, in the possession of the author. The Secretary of War, *Columbia River and Minor Tributaries* (Washington, D.C.: U.S. Government Printing Office, 1933), 1064.

[6]*Wenatchee Daily World*, 4 June 1929.

[7]*Ibid.*, 6 July 1929; 14 December 1929. Mitchell, *Flowing Wealth*, 30.

[8]*Wenatchee Daily World*, 6 November 1930; 7 November 1930.

[9]*Grange News*, 20 November 1928. *Congressional Record* (11 June 1929), vol. 71, pt. 3, 2636.

[10]Bernard Bellush, *Franklin D. Roosevelt as Governor of New York* (New York: Columbia University Press, 1955), 259–260.

[11]*Seattle P.I.*, 3 July 1936.

[12]*Grange News*, 2 October 1931. Mitchell, *Flowing Wealth*, 33.

[13]*Wenatchee Daily World*, 19 January 1931.

[14]Mitchell, *Flowing Wealth*, 33.

[15]*Ibid.*, 34.

[16]The phrase quoted is from Stegner, *Angle of Repose*, 367.

[17]Clarence Dill to Franklin Roosevelt, 7 December 1928, DNCR, FDRL. *Seattle P.I.*, 4 July 1936.

[18]Clarence Dill to Henry Ashhurst, 6 February 1937, President's Personal File, FDRL. Clarence Dill, *Where Water Falls* (Spokane: Self published, 1970), 147–150.

[19]*Ibid.*

[20]James M. Burns, *Roosevelt: The Soldier of Freedom* (New York: Harcourt Brace Jovanovich, Inc., 1970), 233. John Fahey's interview with Clarence Dill, 24 April 1948. Dill, *Where Water Falls*, 147–150. Minor details of the account differ, but Roosevelt agrees to build the dam in both. Roosevelt's promise to the Russian Foreign Minister, Vyacheslav Molotov, concerning a second front in Europe in 1942, is perhaps the best known in a long line of FDR spontaneity.

[21]*Congressional Record* (20 January 1931), vol. 74, pt. 3, 2657.

[22]Franklin Roosevelt to Clarence Dill, 27 January 1931, FDR Governor's Collection, FDRL.

[23]Telegram, Clarence Dill to Franklin Roosevelt, 25 February 1931. Letter from Franklin Roosevelt to Clarence Dill, 18 February 1932, Governor's Collection, FDRL.

[24]Clarence Dill to Henry Ashhurst, 6 February 1937, FDRL.

[25]*Seattle P.I.*, 4 July 1936.

[26]*New York Times*, 13 March 1931.

[27]*Ibid.*, 7 May 1931. *Seattle P.I.*, 14 April 1931.

[28]*New York Times*, 10 June 1931.

[29]*Ibid.*, 6 November 1931.

[30]*Ibid.*, 26 November 1931.

[31]*Ibid.*, 31 December 1931. *Seattle P.I.*, 31 December.

[32]*Congressional Record* (20 February 1932), vol. 75, pt. 5, 4904; (8 April 1932), vol. 75, pt. 7, 7729.

[33]*Spokesman-Review*, 1 February 1932.

[34]Clarence Dill to Mrs. E.D. Riley, 25 April 1928, Edith Riley to Clarence Dill, 1 May 1928, EDR.

[35]Edith Riley to Franklin Roosevelt, 12 January 1931, EDR.

[36]*Seattle P.I.*, 7 February 1932.

[37]*Seattle Times*, 23 June 1932.

[38]*Seattle P.I.*, 7 February 1932. Robert L. Cole, "The Democratic Party in Washington State, 1919–1933: Barometer of Social Change" (Ph.D. diss., University of Washington, 1972), 270.

[39]Frank Freidel, *Franklin D. Roosevelt: The Triumph* (Boston: Little, Brown and Co., 1952–1973), 243.

[40]Clarence Dill to Franklin Roosevelt, 19 February 1932, DNCR, FDRL.

[41]Dill, *Where Water Falls*, 153–154. James Farley, *Behind the Ballots* (New York: Harcourt, Brace and Co., 1938), 89.

[42]Dill, *Where Water Falls*, 154.

[43]Farley, *Behind the Ballots*, 98–99.

[44]*Congressional Record* (8 April 1932), vol. 75, pt. 7, 7729. Clarence Dill to Franklin Roosevelt, 9 April 1932, DNCR, FDRL.

[45]Clarence Dill to J. D. Ross, 6 May 1932, SLP. Dill, *Where Water Falls*, 155–156.

[46]*Seattle Times*, 23 June 1932.

[47]Dill, *Where Water Falls*, 156–157. Farley, *Behind the Ballots*, 112–113.

[48]Frank Freidel, *The Triumph*, 293.

[49]*Seattle Times*, 29 June 1932.

[50]*Ibid.* Dill, *Where Water Falls*, 158. James Farley, *Jim Farley's Story: The Roosevelt Years* (New York: McGraw-Hill Book Co., 1948), 17. *Seattle Times*, 29 June 1932.

[51]Dill, *Where Water Falls*, 159.

[52]Farley, *Behind the Ballots*, 145–152. Frank Freidel, *Franklin D. Roosevelt: Rendezvous with Destiny* (Boston: Little, Brown and Co., 1990), 72.

[53]*New York Times*, 16 June 1932. Freidel, *The Triumph*, 312–313.

[54]Clarence Dill to James Farley, 7 July 1932; James Farley to Clarence Dill, 8 July 1932, DNCR, FDRL. Freidel, *The Triumph*, 338.

[55]James Farley to Clarence Dill, 3 August 1932; Clarence Dill to James Farley, 28 July 1932; James Farley to Clarence Dill, 10 August 1932; Clarence Dill to Franklin Roosevelt, 2 August 1932, DNCR, FDRL.

[56]Franklin Roosevelt to Clarence Dill, 13 August 1932, DNCR, FDRL.

[57]Clarence Dill to Louis Howe, 6 August 1932, DNCR, FDRL.

[58]James Farley to Clarence Dill, 12 August 1932; Clarence Dill to James Farley, 15 August 1932; James Farley to Clarence Dill, 20 August 1932, DNCR, FDRL.

[59]Stephen Chadwick to Franklin Roosevelt, 15 August 1932; Louis Howe to Clarence Dill, 31 August 1932; Clarence Dill to Louis Howe, 12 December 1932. DNCR, FDRL.

[60]Clarence Dill to Louis Howe, 12 December 1932, DNCR, FDRL.

[61]Office memo, Louis Howe to J. O'Mahoney, 27 September 1932. Roosevelt Campaign to Clarence Dill, 6 October 1932. DNCR, FDRL.

[62]Dill, *Where Water Falls*, 161.

[63]*Seattle P.I.*, 21 September 1932.

[64] *Ibid.*, 22 September 1932; 18 October 1932; 5 November 1932. Dill, *Where Water Falls,* 162.

[65]*Seattle P.I.*, 3 November 1932; 5 November 1932; 9 November 1932. Frank Bell to Monrad Wallgren, 29 October 1932, SHP. Cole, "The Democratic Party in Washington State," 283, 291.

Chapter Nine, pages 113–134

[1]Clarence Dill to J. D. Ross, 14 March 1933, JDRP.

[2]Paul C. Pitzer, *Grand Coulee: Harnessing a Dream* (Pullman: Washington State University Press, 1994), 40, 69. *Wenatchee Daily World*, 28 Oct. 1940. Many important backers of Grand Coulee were quick to criticize their representatives in Washington, D.C., for being uninspired supporters of the dam. Wesley Jones, who very much wanted to make Grand Coulee a reality, had no end of criticism from Ralph Horr and others for his alleged reluctance to pursue the dam in 1932 when, as the senior senator and a Republican, he was thought to be the key to persuading Hoover to approve the project. Ironically, in that year Dill received praise for his interest in and support of Grand Coulee. After the election of 1932 Dill became the senior senator and the lead man in securing the dam. His efforts were criticized just as Jones's had been. Nothing could satisfy many of the dam's supporters who had no idea how Washington, D.C., worked and who were prone to think in terms of betrayal and self interest. Wesley Jones to Roy Staley, 16 February 1932, Ralph Horr to Rufus Woods, 20 February 1932, H. R. Smith to Rufus Woods, 22 January 1932, Incoming Correspondence, 1932, RWP.

[3]*Spokesman-Review,* 4 August 1934. Clarence Dill to Ralph Nichols, 7 July 1933, CDP. It would be easy to explain Clarence Dill solely in terms of corruption and greed. However, avarice was only a part of his personality. As earlier chapters have shown, his progressive and liberal politics were early formed and deeply held.

[4]Pitzer, *Grand Coulee*, 67, 68.

[5]Clarence Dill to James O'Sullivan, 1 April 1933, JOSP.

[6]Pitzer, *Grand Coulee*, 67.

[7]Albert Goss to James O' Sullivan, 13 April 1933. Sam B. Hill to James O' Sullivan, 13 April 1933, JOSP. Robert E. Ficken argues in *Rufus Woods: The Columbia River, and the Building of Modern Washington* (Pullman: Washington State University Press, 1995), that Goss pressured a reluctant Dill to make an appointment with FDR. Ficken's argument is based on a 1942 letter from Goss to Woods. Goss's letter written in April 1933 reveals a more complicated situation.

[8]Richard Lowitt, *The New Deal and the West* (Bloomington: Indiana University Press, 1984), 33.

[9] Bernard Bellush, *Franklin D. Roosevelt as Governor of New York* (New York: Columbia University Press, 1955), 238–240.

[10]Lowitt, *The New Deal*, 1–7, 33, 157.

[11]Dill to Rufus Woods, 22 February 1949, CDP. John Fahey's transcript of an interview with Clarence Dill, 24 April 1948. Clarence Dill, *Where Water Falls* (Spokane: Self published, 1970), 167.

[12]Pitzer, *Grand Coulee*, 69. Dill, *Where Water Falls*, 169. Fahey Transcript, 24 April 1948. C.C. Dill to Rufus Woods, 22 February 1949, CDP. *New York Tribune*, 5 August 1934. *Spokesman-Review*, 4 August 1934.

[13]*Ibid*. Dill, *Where Water Falls*, 167–170. My rendition of Dill's conversation with Roosevelt in early April is derived from four sources, Fahey's interview with Dill in 1948, Dill's letter to Rufus Woods in 1949, Dill's autobiography, and, most importantly, Dill's speech at the 4 August 1934 Grand Coulee celebration. This speech was recorded in detail by the many papers represented there that day including the *New York Tribune*. In his speech Dill told his version of the story. The president was seated right behind him and was due to speak next. If Dill's version were not true he was taking an awful chance. Dill related how FDR did not want to build the high dam and reclamation project, Clarence argued for the whole program not realizing the president had a compromise in mind, then FDR proposed a low dam with the larger structure to be built later. In the speech Dill left out his claims—included in later versions—of virtually browbeating FDR into submission. My argument follows this original version supplemented by reasonable details taken from the other sources. *New York Tribune*, 5 August 1934. *Spokesman-Review*, 4 August 1934.

[14]Albert Goss to Clarence D. Martin, 17 April 1933, JOSP.

[15]Historians have made much of this remark by FDR that he did not know enough about the project at this time, implying that Dill's assertion that he had talked to FDR about Grand Coulee in January 1931 was greatly exaggerated. Such an interpretation is not required by the evidence. Dill never claimed to have outlined the project to FDR in the kind of detail the president would require in order to officially support it. Even after the April 17 meeting FDR insisted on seeing more studies on Grand Coulee before he would render a decision. He specifically wanted to know if the low dam idea was feasible. Pitzer, *Grand Coulee*, 70, 399. Ficken, *Rufus Woods*, 132.

[16]Clarence Dill to James O'Sullivan 19 April 1933; Albert Goss to Clarence Martin, 17 April 1933; James O'Sullivan to Louise Lawton, 6 May 1933, JOSP.

[17]Myron Jordan, "The Kilowatt Wars: James D. Ross, Public Power and the Public Relations Contest for the Hearts and Minds of Pacific Northwesterners" (Ph.D. diss., University of Washington, 1991), 250–251.

[18]James O' Sullivan to Albert Goss, 20 April 1933, JOSP.

[19]*Ibid.*

[20]*Spokesman-Review*, 22 April 1933.

[21]*Wenatchee Daily World*, 2 May 1933. *Spokesman-Review*, 3 May 1933.

[22]*Spokesman-Review*, 5 May 1933. As students of FDR know, the president hated confrontations. He would often tell people what they wanted to hear to avoid unpleasant scenes. Thus it is entirely likely the Oregonians believed they had won FDR over to their plans.

[23]James O' Sullivan to Miss Louise Lawton, 6 May 1933; James O'Sullivan (?) to Rufus Woods, 8 May 1933; J.A. Ford to the Spokane Chamber of Commerce, 8 May 1933, JOSP. *Spokesman-Review,* 6 May 1933.

[24]James O' Sullivan to Miss Louise Lawton, 11 May 1933, JOSP.

[25]*Ibid.*, 16 May 1933, JOSP. Thus the fact that Dill made all the official announcements concerning the dam was part of the CBC's strategy. Moreover, it was entirely appropriate since Dill was the leader of Washington's congressional delegation in regard to securing FDR's support of Grand Coulee. However, Dill has suffered no little criticism for his "grabbing the Grand Coulee spotlight." Pitzer, *Grand Coulee*, 40, 76.

[26]James O'Sullivan to Miss Louise Lawton, 16 May 1933, JOSP.

[27]Dill, *Where Water Falls*, 172, 173.

[28]*Spokesman-Review*, 18 May 1933; 20 May 1933.

[29]*Seattle P.I.*, 21 May 1933.

[30]James E. Ford to John Fahey, 18 December 1945, in possession of the author. *Spokesman-Review*, 7 July 1933.

[31]Ralph Dyar, *News for an Empire...* (Caldwell, Id.: Caxton Printers, 1952), 408.

[32]*Spokesman-Review*, 1 June 1933.

[33] James O'Sullivan to Louise Lawton, 7 June 1933. James O'Sullivan to Rufus Woods, 6 June 1933, JOSP.

[34]O'Sullivan to Rufus Woods, 6 June 1933; O'Sullivan to Rufus Woods, 1 June 1933. O'Sullivan to Louise Lawton, 7 June 1933, JOSP. Jordan, "The Kilowatt Wars," 230, 233, 247, 254, 256. *Spokesman-Review*, 1 June 1933.

[35]Pitzer, *Grand Coulee*, 116.

[36]*Bellingham Herald*, 11 July 1933.

[37]*Wenatchee Daily World*, 10 June 1933; 21 June 1933. *Spokesman-Review*, 13 June 1933; 14 June 1933.

[38]Clarence Dill to Ralph Nichols, 12 June 1933, CDP.

[39]Ralph Nichols to Clarence Dill, 16 June 1933, CDP. Minutes of the CBC meeting, 21 July 1933, JOSP. *Seattle P.I.*, 11 April 1932. Ralph Nichols to Mrs. Scott Bullitt, 21 July 1933, SLP. Pitzer, *Grand Coulee*, 73.

[40]*Wenatchee Daily World*, 13 June 1933. *Spokesman-Review*, 13 June 1933.

[41]*Ibid.*, 14 June 1933. Minutes of the CBC meeting 14 June 1933, JOSP.

[42]*Spokesman-Review*, 17 June 1933.

[43]Albert Goss to Rufus Woods, 20 June 1933, JOSP. *Wenatchee Daily World*, 16 June 1933.

[44]Rufus Woods to Clarence Dill, 5 June 1933, Outgoing Correspondence, 1933, RWP.

[45] *Wenatchee Daily World*, 21 June 1933.

[46] *Ibid.*, 22 June 1933. *Spokesman-Review*, 22 June 1933.

[47] *Ibid.*, 23 June 1933; 24 June 1933. Rufus Woods to James O'Sullivan, 23 June 1933, JOSP.

[48] *Wenatchee Daily World*, 27 June 1933; 29 June 1933; 28 June 1933; 30 June 1933; 11 July 1933. *Spokesman-Review*, 30 June 1933; 1 July 1933.

[49] Ralph Nichols to Clarence Dill, 3 July 1933, CDP.

[50] Jordan, "The Kilowatt Wars," 255.

[51] *Hillyard Washington Press*, 19 July 1933.

[52] *Ibid. Wenatchee Daily World*, 17 July 1933. *Almira Herald*, 20 July 1933.

[53] *Ibid.*

[54] *Wenatchee Daily World*, 24 July 1933. It is probable that Dill envisioned himself as head of a TVA-type organization.

[55] *Ibid.*

[56] *Ibid.* Jordan, "The Kilowatt Wars," 251. *Spokesman-Review*, 26 July 1933.

[57] Telegram from Clarence Dill to Governor Clarence Martin, 25 July 1933, CMP. Telegram, Clarence Dill to James O'Sullivan, 25 July 1933, JOSP. The Washington Water Power Company of Spokane did in fact have lobbyists in Washington, D.C., attempting to stop Grand Coulee.

[58] Telegram, Clarence Dill to James O'Sullivan, 26 July 1933, JOSP. *Spokesman-Review*, 26 July 1933.

[59] Telegram, Clarence Dill to James O'Sullivan, 27 July 1933, JOSP.

[60] *Spokesman-Review*, 27 July 1933.

[61] *New York Tribune*, 5 August 1934. *Tacoma News Tribune*, 4 August 1934. Rufus Woods to H.R. Fraser, 19 April 1934, RWP.

[62] Resolution for Special Board, 27 July 1933; telegram, James O'Sullivan to *Wenatchee Daily World*, 27 July 1933, JOSP. *Spokesman-Review*, 28 July 1933. *Wenatchee Daily World*, 28 July 1933. Telegram from Clarence Dill to Governor Clarence Martin 26 July 1933, CMP. This telegram also reveals FDR's instructions to Ickes to approve the project.

[63] *Spokesman-Review*, 28 July 1933.

[64] *Ibid.*, 28 July 1933; 29 July 1933. *Wenatchee Daily World*, 28 July 1933.

[65] *Seattle P.I.*, 21 September 1932; 22 September 1932; 18 October 1932.

[66] *Ibid.*, 18 October 1932. Telegram, James O'Sullivan to *Wenatchee Daily World*, 27 July 1933.

[67] Clarence Dill to V. Hallstane, 28 August 1933. Telegram, Clarence Dill to J.D. Ross, 14 October 1933, SLP. *Bellingham Evening News*, 26 August 1933; 24 August 1933. There was a period in which Dill did not favor the Skagit project because he feared it might compromise Grand Coulee. Once Grand Coulee had been approved, Dill returned to supporting the Skagit project. Clarence Dill to John Ballaine, 6 July 1933, JBP.

[68] *Spokesman-Review*, 13 September 1933; 15 September 1933.

[69] Unfortunately for WWP, the Federal Power Commission denied the company's application for a permanent license to the Kettle Falls site in January 1934, and its Washington state permit expired that July.

[70]Ellsworth French to C.C. Dill, 23 October 1933, JOSP. *Spokesman-Review*, 25 October 1933.

[71]*Ibid.*, 26 October 1933.

[72]Rufus Woods to Willis T. Batchellor, 6 November 1933, Outgoing Correspondence, 1933, RWP. Ficken, *Rufus Woods*, 137, 138.

[73]*Spokesman-Review*, 2 November 1933. *Wenatchee Daily World*, 7 November 1933; 3 November 1933. Lowitt, *The New Deal and the West*, 170–171.

[74]*Spokesman-Review*, 17 November 1933.

[75]*Ibid.*, 26 November 1933. *Wenatchee Daily World*, 27 November 1933. Pitzer, *Grand Coulee*, 78, 79.

[76]Clarence Dill to James O'Sullivan, 31 January 1934, JOSP.

[77]*Ibid.*, 14 February 1934, JOSP.

[78]James O'Sullivan to Clarence Dill, 19 February 1934, JOSP.

[79]S.O. Harper to James O'Sullivan, 21 February 1934, JOSP.

[80]Clarence Dill to James O'Sullivan, 23 February 1934, JOSP.

[81]Telegram, Clarence Dill to James O'Sullivan, 7 April 1934, JOSP. Telegram, James O'Sullivan to Clarence Dill, 6 April 1934, JOSP. George Sundborg, *Hail Columbia: The Thirty Year Struggle for Grand Coulee* (New York: Macmillan, 1954), 262–265.

[82]James O'Sullivan to Ray Clark, 5 July 1934, JOSP.

[83]James O'Sullivan to Rufus Woods, 7 July 1934, JOSP.

[84]Records of the Public Works Administration, Case Files Relating to Investigations of Personnel, 1933–1941, Entry (new number 85, old number 92) box #5, AF-150, reports of agents Brinkman, Grier, and Young, National Archives, Washington, D.C.

[85]Reports of agents Grier and Young, Records of the PWA.

[86]Report of agent Young, Records of the PWA.

[87]Reports of agents Brinkman and Grier, Records of the PWA. Elwood Mead to Harold Ickes, November 7, 1934, Central Classified File, 1907–1936, File No. 8–3, Columbia— Garden City, Dept. of the Interior, Office of the Secretary, Reclamation Bureau, National Archives, College Park, Maryland.

[88]Dill had trouble with another of his former secretaries, Frank Bell. Bell owned substantial parcels of land in the Columbia Basin. Many of the rumors regarding Dill's alleged complicity in a Grand Coulee land scheme emanated from Bell's activities in the Columbia Basin. Apparently William Humphrey warned Dill about Bell's schemes in time for Dill to remove himself from Bell's sphere of operations. Late in life, Bell was indicted by a grand jury in regard to his activities in the construction of the Priest Rapids Dam and later convicted of perjury. William Humphrey to Clarence Dill, 18 August 1933; Clarence Dill to William Humphrey, 21 August 1933; William Humphrey to Clarence Dill, 2 September 1933, WHC.

[89]Elwood Mead to Harold Ickes, November 7, 1934, RBP.

[90]James O'Sullivan to John Smith, 18 July 1934, JOSP.

[91]James O'Sullivan to Albert Goss, 28 July 1934, JOSP.

[92]*Tacoma News Tribune*, 4 August 1934. *Seattle Star*, 5 August 1934. *New York Tribune*, 5 August 1934.

[93]Clarence Dill to Franklin Roosevelt, 25 June 1937, PPF-243, FDRL. Clarence Dill to Knute Hill, 9 August 1956, CDP. *New York Tribune*, 5 August 1934. *Spokesman-Review*, 4 August 1934.

[94]James O'Sullivan to Ray Clark, 8 August 1934, JOSP.

[95]*New York Tribune*, 5 August 1934. *Tacoma News Tribune*, 4 August 1934.

[96]Jalmar Johnson, *Builders of the Northwest* (New York: Dodd, Mead and Co., 1963), 223–224. Sundborg, *Hail Columbia*, 265–270.

[97]Pitzer, *Grand Coulee*, 118.

[98]Dyar, *News for an Empire*, 146.

[99]Sundborg, *Hail Columbia*, 253, 260, 277–284.

[100]Stewart Holbrook argued in *The Columbia* that O'Sullivan was the "father" of the dam, as did Murray Morgan in *The Dam*. Morgan explained that O'Sullivan organized the various advocates of the project into an effective alliance. O'Sullivan, in fact, did more than that. He was, along with Rufus Woods, the heart of the project throughout much of the 1920s, the one who kept the dam alive and the one who had the knowledge to help Dill advocate for the dam. If Murray, Holbrook, and Sundborg had also explained Dill's role, their praise of O'Sullivan would not have distorted the history of the dam. The most recent treatment of this subject is Robert Ficken's *Rufus Woods*. Ficken recognizes that the senator was the "vital link between the Columbia Basin Commission and Franklin Roosevelt." Stewart Holbrook, *The Columbia* (New York: Rinehart, 1956), 307–308. Murray Morgan, *The Dam* (New York: Viking Press, 1954), 30. Ficken, *Rufus Woods*, 131, 132.

[101]Robert E. Ficken and Charles P. LeWarne, *Washington: A Centennial History* (Seattle: University of Washington Press, 1988), 119–120. In April 1934 Rufus Woods received a letter from a Hugh Fraser in which the latter told Woods that Dill's version of how the federal approval of the dam occurred placed the senator in the leading role and relegated Woods to a lesser role (Fraser had received a two-page letter from Dill detailing Dill's version of events. Unfortunately Fraser lost Dill's letter.) Woods responded to Fraser, "You will understand that it was Senator Dill who carried the ball across the line, and although he is a Democrat and I am a Republican, I am going to give him due credit for the job." Moreover, in a speech to Washington's county commissioners in the summer of 1933, Woods commended Dill saying "he had the cards and played them" in convincing FDR to build the dam. Hugh Fraser to Rufus Woods, 8 April 1934, Incoming Correspondence, 1934; Rufus Woods to Hugh Fraser, 19 April 1934, Outgoing Correspondence, 1934; Woods's address to county commissioners, summer 1933, Outgoing Correspondence, 1933, RWP.

[102]It is most appropriate that the recently unveiled FDR memorial in Washington, D.C., features a waterfall theme. The president's work in water power development is unrivaled in the nation's history.

Chapter Ten, pages 135–153

[1]Arthur Schlesinger Jr., *The Crisis of the Old Order: 1919–1933* (Boston: Houghton Mifflin Co., 1957), 455.

[2]*New York Times*, 14 March 1928; 10 March 1934.

[3]Robert McChesney, *Telecommunications, Mass Media, and Democracy: The Battle for Control of U.S. Broadcasting, 1928–1935* (New York: Oxford University Press, 1993), 20–23, 92–120, 126.

[4]Joel Rosenbloom, "Authority of the Federal Communications Commission with Respect to the Programming of Radio and Television Broadcasting Stations" (unpublished legal brief, 1961), 38, CDP.

[5]Erwin Krasnow, Lawrence Longley, and Terry Herbert, *The Politics of Broadcast Regulation* (New York: St. Martin's Press, 1982), 17.

[6]Rosenbloom, "Authority of the Federal Communications Commission," 40, 41.

[7]*Ibid.*, 40.

[8]*Ibid.* McChesney, *Telecommunications, Mass Media, and Democracy*, 20–37.

[9]*New York Times*, 4 February 1928. *Congressional Record* (6 February 1928), vol. 69, pt. 3, 2563.

[10]*Ibid.*, (27 February 1928), vol. 69, pt. 4, 3599. Eric Barnouw, *A History of Broadcasting in the United States* (New York: Oxford University Press, 1966), 247.

[11]*New York Times*, 14 March 1928.

[12]*Ibid.*, 14 March 1928; 22 April 1928. *Congressional Record* (22 March 1928), vol. 69, pt. 5, 5158; (24 March 1928), vol. 69, pt. 5, 5293. *New York Times*, 22 April 1928, sec. 10, 19.

[13]George H. Gibson, *Public Broadcasting: The Role of the Federal Government, 1912–1976* (New York: Praeger Publishing, 1977), 10.

[14]*Congressional Record* (7 January 1929) vol. 70, pt. 2, 1239.

[15]*New York Times*, 8 January 1929; 5 December 1928; 3 March 1929. *Congressional Record* (5 December 1928), vol. 70, pt. 1, 54. *Washington Post*, 16 December 1928, radio section, 1; 14 December 1928; 16 December 1928, radio section, 1.

[16]*New York Times*, 10 March 1929; 17 March 1929; 24 March 1929. *Congressional Record* (29 May 1929), vol. 71, pt. 2, 2185; (21 September 1929), vol. 71, pt. 4, 3835.

[17]*Washington Post*, 26 February 1929. The resolution which extended the life of the FRC included authorization of a general counsel and three assistants, clearly an effort to beef up the legal capabilities of the commission. *Ibid.*, 16 December 1928.

[18]*Ibid.*, 15 December 1928.

[19]*Ibid.*, 14 December 1928; 20 December 1928. *New York Times*, 22 September 1929; 13 October 1929. In December 1928 the Federal Trade Commission dismissed its five-year-old suit against RCA and seven other companies on the grounds that it lacked jurisdiction. The FTC had contended that these companies had illegally restrained trade. *Congressional Record* (21 November 1929), vol. 71, pt. 5, 5884.

[20]Christopher H. Sterling and John M. Kittross, *Stay Tuned: A Concise History of American Broadcasting* (Belmont, Ca.: Wadsworth Publishing Co., 1990), 130.

[21]*New York Times*, 7 December 1929; 22 September 1929; 17 December 1929.

[22]*Variety*, 1 January 1930, 57; 9 April 1930, 74. McChesney, *Telecommunications, Mass Media, and Democracy*, 127.

[23]Walter B. Emery, *Broadcasting and Government: Responsibilities and Regulations* (East Lansing: Michigan State University Press, 1971), 30. Sterling and Kittross, *Stay Tuned*,

130. *New York Times*, 17 December 1929; 18 December 1929; 8 January 1930; 9 January 1930.

[24]*Ibid.*, 11 January 1930.

[25]*Congressional Record* (21 February 1930), vol. 72, pt. 3, 4064.

[26]*New York Times*, 14 June 1931.

[27]Emery, *Broadcasting and Government*, 31.

[28]*New York Times*, 16 January 1932; 18 February 1932; 12 December 1932; 14 June 1931. *Congressional Record* (14 April 1932), vol. 75, pt. 8, 8179; (16 December 1933), vol. 76, pt. 1, 542. *The Nation*, 22 August 1934, 201; 27 September 1933, 340.

[29]*Congressional Record* (16 June 1932), vol. 75, pt. 12, 13121; (10 February 1933), vol. 76, pt. 4,5, 3764–3770, 5203–5204, 5212. *New York Times*, 27 December 1933.

[30]Krasnow, Longley and Terry, *The Politics of Broadcast Regulation*, 13–15.

[31]*Congressional Record* (16 December 1932), vol. 76, pt. 1, 542. Congress, Senate, Subcommittee of the Committee on Interstate Commerce, *Hearings before the Subcommittee of the Committee on Interstate Commerce on S. 5201*, 72nd Congress, 2nd session, January 1933, 3–4, 34–43. *Congressional Record* (16 December 1932), vol. 76, pt. 1, 542. Barnouw, *A History of Broadcasting in the United States*, 264, 273.

[32]*Congressional Record* (28 February 1933), vol. 76, pt. 5, 5207, 5212, 5204, 5212. There seems to be much confusion amongst broadcasting historians concerning White's congressional career. He served in the House from 4 March 1917 to 3 March 1931; elected to the Senate in 1932, he served in that capacity until January 1949.

[33]Clarence Dill, "Should the United States Adopt the British System of Radio Control?" *Congressional Digest* 12 (August-September 1933): 194, 196.

[34]Alan Stone, *Public Service Liberalism...* (Princeton: Princeton University Press, 1991), 276.

[35]*New York Times*, 10 February 1934.

[36]*Ibid.* Gibson, *Public Broadcasting*, 24.

[37]*New York Times*, 11 January 1934.

[38]Emery, *Broadcasting and Government*, 31, 32.

[39]Stone, *Public Service Liberalism*, 276. *New York Times*, 10 February 1934.

[40]*New York* Times, 10 February 1934.

[41]Stone, *Public Service Liberalism*, 276–278.

[42]*New York Times*, 10 February 1934; 28 February 1934. William E. Leuchtenberg, *Franklin D. Roosevelt and the New Deal* (New York: Harper and Row, 1963), 24–25, 248, 275–277. Gibson, *Public Broadcasting*, 23, 24.

[43]*New York Times*, 10 March 1934. Robert B. Horwitz, *The Irony of Regulatory Reform* (New York: Oxford University Press, 1989), 122.

[44]D.B. Hardeman and Donald Bacon, *Rayburn: A Biography* (Austin: Texas Monthly Press, 1987), 160. Alfred Steinberg, *Sam Rayburn* (New York: Hawthorn Books, 1975), 119.

[45]Steinberg, *Sam Rayburn*, 119. Hardeman and Bacon, *Rayburn*, 160.

[46]Steinberg, *Sam Rayburn*, 119.

[47]*New York Times*, 10 March 1934. *Variety*, 13 March 1934, 39.

[48]*Ibid.*, 6 March 1934, 44.

[49]*Ibid.*, 13 March 1934, 39.

[50]*New York Times*, 14 March 1934. Clarence Dill, *Where Water Falls* (Spokane: Self published, 1970), 193–194. *Variety*, 17 April 1934, 33. Stone, *Public Service Liberalism*, 276–278. *Congressional Record* (15 May 1934), vol. 78, pt. 8, 8824.

[51]*New York Times*, 16 March 1934.

[52]*Congressional Record* (15 May 1934), vol. 78, pt. 8, 8822–8826. *New York Times*, 5 April 1934; 14 April 1934; 20 April 1934.

[53]*New York Times*, 27 April 1934.

[54]*Variety*, 8 May 1934, 37,45.

[55]*Ibid.*, 15 May 1934, 38.

[56] *New York Times*, 16 May, 1934.

[57]*Congressional Record* (15 May 1934), vol. 78, pt. 8, 8843.

[58]Gibson, *Public Broadcasting*, 25.

[59]*Ibid.*, 27.

[60] *Congressional Record* (15 May 1934), vol. 78, pt. 8, 8843, 8854. Rosenbloom, "Authority of the Federal Communications Commission," 54–55.

[61]*Congressional Record* (15 May 1934), vol. 78, pt. 8, 8854.

[62]Philip T. Rosen, *The Modern Stentors: Radio Broadcasters and the Federal Government: 1920–1934* (Westport Ct.: Greenwood Press, 1980), 179. McChesney, *Telecommunications, Mass Media, and Democracy*, 16, 21.

[63]Gibson, *Public Broadcasting*, 22, 26.

[64]*Ibid.*, 26, 27.

[65]*Congressional Record* (15 May 1934), vol. 78, pt. 8, 8846.

[66]Ray Tucker, *Sons of a Wild Jackass* (Boston: L.C. Page and Company, 1932).

[67] LeRoy Ashby, *The Spearless Leader: Senator Borah and the Progressive Movement in the 1920's* (Urbana: University of Illinois Press, 1972), 284–294.

[68]*Variety*, 5 June 1934, 35.

[69]*Ibid.*

[70] *Ibid.*, 22 May 1934, 31, 32. *New York Times*, 16 May 1934.

[71]Hardeman and Bacon, *Rayburn*, 160. Dill's inability to get his more strict version of the FCC in 1934 when his party controlled the government makes his accomplishments under previous Republican administrations seem all the more remarkable.

[72]*Variety*, 12 June 1934, 39.

[73]*Ibid.*, 22 May 1934, 32. *New York Times*, 16 May 1934.

[74]Barnouw, *A History of Broadcasting in the United States*, 272, 273. *New York Times*, 10 February 1934; 28 February 1934.

[75]Emery, *Broadcasting and Government*, 48–50.

[76]*Ibid.*

[77]Donald Godfrey, "Senator Dill and the 1927 Radio Act," *Journal of Broadcasting* 23 (1979), 485.

[78]Ashby, *The Spearless Leader,* 284–294.

[79]Schlesinger, *The Crisis of the Old Order,* 435.

Chapter Eleven, pages 155–160

[1]*Spokesman-Review,* 29 June 1934.

[2]Unidentified biographical sketch, CDP.

[3]Clarence Dill to J.D. Ross, 29 June 1934, SLP.

[4]*Spokesman-Review,* 29 June 1934.

[5]*Ibid.*

[6]*Tacoma News Tribune,* 6 July 1934.

[7]Text of radio speech, 11 July 1934, CDP. *The Tacoma Times,* 12 July 1934.

[8]Clarence Dill, *Where Water Falls* (Spokane: Self published, 1970), 200, 201.

[9]Franklin Roosevelt to William Humphrey, 25 July 1933; William Humphrey to Clarence Dill, 25 July 1933; William Humphrey to Franklin Roosevelt, 1 August 1933; Franklin Roosevelt to William Humphrey, 4 August 1933, WHC.

[10]William Humphrey to Franklin Roosevelt, 11 August 1933, WHC.

[11]William Humphrey to Clarence Dill, 18 August 1933, WHC.

[12]Clarence Dill to William Humphrey, 21 August 1933, WHC.

[13]*Ibid.* William Humphrey to Clarence Dill, 2 September 1933, WHC.

[14]William E. Leuchtenburg, in his monograph on the transformation of the Supreme Court in the 1930s, argues that it was the Humphrey case, not the more celebrated Schechter decision, which initially started FDR thinking along the lines of his court-packing plan. William E. Leuchtenburg, *The Supreme Court Reborn* (New York: Oxford University Press, 1995), 52–81.

[15]The accusations themselves are dealt with in chapter three.

[16]*Seattle P.I.,* 30 June 1936; 4 July 1936.

[17]*Ibid.,* 3 July 1936; 4 July 1936; 30 June 1936. Rosalie's "crook and coward" statement was a reference to her belief that the maneuvering which brought FDR John Garner's support was somehow unethical.

[18]*Ibid.,* 30 June 1936.

[19]*New York Times,* 31 March 1936. *Seattle P.I.,* 1 July 1936. Interlocutory Decree of Divorce, Clarence Dill Plaintiff, versus Rosalie Jones Dill defendant, 9 July 1936, Spokane County Superior Court Case no. 97726, 7. Archives, Spokane County Courthouse, Spokane, Washington.

[20]*Seattle P.I.,* 26 June 1936; 8 July 1936; 1 July 1936; 7 July 1936. *New York Times,* 31 March 1936. Interlocutory Decree of Divorce, 1, 3.

[21]George Sundborg, *Hail Columbia: The Thirty Year Struggle for Grand Coulee Dam* (New York: Macmillan, 1954), 272. Paul Pitzer, "Grand Coulee: The Struggle" (unpublished manuscript in author's possession), 368.

Chapter Twelve, pages 161–181

[1]Bruce Mitchell, *Flowing Wealth: The Story of Water Resource Development in North Central Washington, 1870–1950* (Wenatchee: Wenatchee Daily World, 1967), 41.

[2]*Ibid.*

[3]Clarence Dill, *Where Water Falls* (Spokane: Self published, 1970), 203.

[4]*Ibid.*

[5]*Ibid.*, 204.

[6]*Spokane Chronicle*, 21 March 1969.

[7]Dill, *Where Water Falls*, 211.

[8]*Spokesman-Review*, 5 May 1940.

[9]Dill's announcement for governor, 8 June 1940, CDP. Clarence Dill to Franklin Roosevelt, 6 August 1940, President's Personal File 243, FDRL. Dill, *Where Water Falls*, 217.

[10]*Wenatchee Daily World*, 17 July 1940.

[11]Press release to *Grange News*, 17 August 1940, HCCSP.

[12]Handbill, HCCSP. *Everett Daily Herald*, 25 October 1940.

[13]*Seattle P.I.*, 19 August 1940. Telegram, William Green to Clarence Dill, 27 August 1940; letter from William Green to Clarence Dill, 27 August 1940, NBC.

[14]Clarence Dill to James Taylor, 19 August 1940, NBC.

[15]Walter Galenson, *The CIO Challenge to the AFL...* (Cambridge: Harvard University Press, 1960), 494, 552–555. Dave Beck, a teamster organizer from Seattle, would rise through the ranks of the AFL to become one of the most powerful union men in the US.

[16]*Bellingham Herald*, 27 October 1940.

[17]*Wenatchee Daily World*, 2 September 1940; 3 September 1940. George Scott, "Arthur B. Langlie: Republican Governor in a Democratic Age" (Ph.D. diss., University of Washington, 1971), 72.

[18]Secretary of State, *Abstract of the Votes Polled in the State of Washington in the Primary Election 10 September 1940* (Olympia: Government Printing Office). *Seattle Times*, 11 September 1940.

[19]Scott, "Arthur B. Langlie," 68.

[20] Clarence Dill to Franklin Roosevelt, 15 October 1940, President's Personal File 243, FDRL. *Seattle P.I.*, 26 September 1940. *Wenatchee Daily World*, 26 September 1940.

[21]*Seattle P.I.*, 27 September 1940.

[22]*Ibid.* The Washington Commonwealth Federation was organized in Tacoma in 1934. Its purpose was to promote liberal, even radical, political causes such as the "production for use referendum" defeated by Washington's voters in 1936. The WCF was conspicuous in its support for the New Deal and vociferously opposed both Martin's reelection and the Langlie candidacy in 1940. The WCF had developed strong support from both the AFL and CIO. Scott, "Arthur B. Langlie," 69–71, 100.

[23]Scott, "Arthur B. Langlie," 69–71, 100.

[24]Jonathan Dembo, "Dave Beck and the Transportation Revolution," in *Experiences in a Promised Land*, ed. Thomas Edwards and Carlos A. Schwantes (Seattle: University of

Washington Press, 1986), 344, 350. *Labor Journal*, 11 October 1940. *Wenatchee Daily World*, 16 October 1940. *Seattle P.I.*, 26 September 1940.

[25]Scott, "Arthur B. Langlie," 20, 73–74.

[26]*Seattle P.I.*, 30 September 1940.

[27]*Ibid.*

[28]*Ibid.*

[29]Scott, "Arthur B. Langlie," 68. *New York Times*, 14 October 1940.

[30]*Wenatchee Daily World*, 9 October 1940. *Everett Daily Herald*, 18 October 1940.

[31]*Everett Daily Herald*, 12 October 1940.

[32]*Ibid.*, 11 October 1940.

[33]Scott, "Arthur B. Langlie," 75–76. *Seattle P.I.*, 3 November 1940.

[34]*Wenatchee Daily World*, 16 October 1940.

[35]*Seattle P.I.*, 16 October 1940.

[36]*Seattle Times*, 18 October 1940. *Seattle P.I.*, 18 October 1940. *Wenatchee Daily World*, 19 October 1940; 18 October 1940.

[37]*Ibid.*, 21 October 1940; 23 October 1940.

[38]*Ibid.*, 23 October 1940; 24 October 1940.

[39]*Seattle Times*, 3 November 1940. *Spokesman-Review*, 3 November 1940; 2 November 1940. *Bellingham Herald*, 27 October 1940; 11 September 1940. *Tacoma News Tribune*, 29 October 1940; 2 November 1940. *Everett Daily Herald*, October and November 1940. *Seattle P.I.* October and November 1940.

[40]*Bellingham Herald*, 16 October 1940. *Wenatchee Daily World*, 28 October 1940; 31 October 1940.

[41]*Ibid.*, 1 November 1940.

[42]*Seattle P.I.*, 2 November 1940.

[43]Dill radio speech, 1 November 1940, CDP.

[44]*Seattle P.I.*, 3 November 1940.

[45]*Ibid.*, 6 November 1940.

[46]*Ibid. Seattle Times*, 6 November 1940.

[47]*Ibid.*, 6 November 1940. *Seattle P.I.*, 7 November 1940. *Wenatchee Daily World*, 6 November 1940; 7 November 1940; 8 November 1940. *New York Times*, 8 November 1940.

[48]Scott, "Arthur B. Langlie," 66.

[49]*Seattle P.I.*, 10 November 1940.

[50]*Ibid.* Secretary of State, *Abstract of the Votes Polled in the General Election Held November 5, 1940* (Olympia: Government Printing Office). *Bellingham Herald*, 11 September 1940. Scott, "Arthur B. Langlie," 79–80.

[51]*Ibid.*, 79.

[52]*Seattle P.I.*, 10 November 1940. Scott, "Arthur B. Langlie," 78.

[53]*Seattle Times*, 13 November 1940. *Seattle P.I.*, 14 November 1940.

[54]Dill, *Where Water Falls*, 218.

[55]*Ibid. Spokesman-Review*, 21 October 1942.

[56]*Wenatchee Daily World*, 26 October 1942; 31 October 1942. Secretary of State, *Abstract of the Votes Polled in the Primary Election Held September 8, 1942* (Olympia: Government Printing Office). *Spokesman-Review*, 25 August 1942; 9 September 1942; 13 October 1942.

[57]*Spokesman-Review*, 7 October 1942. *Wenatchee Daily World*, November 1942.

[58]*Ibid.*, 5 November 1942; 4 November 1942. Secretary of State, *Abstract of the Votes Polled in the State of Washington at the General Election Held November 3, 1942* (Olympia: Government Printing Office).

[59]*Spokesman-Review*, 7 October 1942; 13 October 1942; 14 October 1942; 17 October 1942; 4 September 1942. *Wenatchee Daily World*, 14 October 1942.

[60]*Ibid.*, ? November 1942.

[61]Clarence Dill's speech before the Ephrata Chamber of Commerce, 6 December 1944, CDP. Dill, *Where Water Falls*, 220. Numerous letters in box 6, folder "Public Power," CDP, from and to Dill in the late forties and early fifties prove he led the effort in this period to arrange Canadian storage.

[62]*Wenatchee Daily World*, 8 January 1947.

[63]Clarence Dill to Warren Magnuson, 11 February 1948; Clarence Dill to Warren Magnuson, 22 June 1948; Warren Magnuson to Clarence Dill, 2 August 1948, MC.

[64]Clarence Dill to Warren Magnuson, 28 July 1948, MC.

[65]Warren Magnuson to Clarence Dill, 10 September 1948, MC.

[66]Warren Magnuson to Matthew Connelly, secretary to the president, 10 September 1948; Matthew Connelly to Warren Magnuson, 13 September 1948, MC.

[67]Clarence Dill to C.E. Webb, 30 December 1948, ABLC.

[68]*Spokesman-Review*, 10 January 1941. In this article the *Spokesman-Review*, seldom an admirer of Dill's, gives the ex-senator credit for advancing the Canadian storage proposal.

[69]*Wenatchee Daily World*, 7 January 1949. Clarence Dill to Hugh Mitchell, 11 January 1949, HMP.

[70]Clarence Dill to J.B. Thompson, 5 December 1950. Clarence Dill to William Warne, 8 January 1951, CDP.

[71]"Columbia's Storage Possibilities Would Develop Tremendous Energy," *Construction World* (July 1951): 20.

[72]Clarence Dill to Warren Magnuson, 10 September 1951; Oscar Chapman to Clarence Dill, 22 October 1951; Oscar Chapman to Clarence Dill, 19 January 1952, CDP. *Wenatchee Daily World*, 13 December 1951. Vanport, Oregon, was a planned community built during W.W.II to house workers from Henry Kaiser's shipyards. During the war it had a population of 35,000 people. Vanport was built on the lowlands near the Columbia River between Portland and Vancouver. In the flood of 1948 a dike gave way and Vanport was swept away never to be rebuilt. Sixteen people died in the flood. Gordon B. Dodds, *The American Northwest: A History of Oregon and Washington* (Arlington Heights, Ill.: Forum Press, 1986, 266, 275–76. Carlos A. Schwantes, *The Pacific Northwest: An Interpretive History* (Lincoln: University of Nebraska Press, 1989), 332.

[73]Clarence Dill to the commissioners of Grant County PUD No. 1, 22 December 1954, CDP. Dill, *Where Water Falls*, 222, 223.

[74]Proposal from Clarence Dill to the government of British Columbia, Canada for a fifty-fifty division of power to be produced from stored flood waters, 20 November 1957, CDP.

[75]*Spokesman-Review*, 8 October 1970; 27 April 1971.

[76]Clarence Dill to Gus Norwood, 26 September 1958, NPPAP.

[77]William Dittmer to Clarence Dill, 8 December 1958, CDP.

[78]*Wenatchee Daily World*, 5 January 1960; 17 August 1960; 19 October 1960; 21 October 1960.

[79]*Ibid.*, 12 January 1960; 20 October 1960; 23 October 1960.

[80]Dill's speech before the Senate Committee on Foreign Relations, 8 March 1961, CDP. *Wenatchee Daily World*, 24 March 1961. The Canadians found the treaty more susceptible to criticism. The problem lay with the conservative government of British Columbia under Premier W.A.C. Bennett. It should come as no surprise—given the drawn-out nature of the Canadian storage agreement to this time—that the disagreement between British Columbia and its own federal government caused a delay of nearly three years in finalizing the accord. Apparently, British Columbia wanted to sell its share of the power to the United States for cash, with which it would build the storage dams. The Canadian federal government offered to finance the project but Bennett would not hear of it. Eventually British Columbia got its way.

[81]*Wenatchee Daily World*, 10 July 1963; 16 December 1963; 22 January 1964; 11 June 1964; 13 September 1964; 17 September 1964. *Spokesman-Review*, 18 December 1972.

[82]Clarence Dill to Alfred Schweppe, 12 September 1961, CDP. Ken Billington, *People, Politics and Public Power* (Seattle: Washington Public Utility District Association, 1988), 432.

[83]Order modifying and adopting presiding examiners initial decision issuing license for project number 2144 (Boundary Dam), 10 July 1961; Affidavit of Clarence C. Dill concerning Robert Beezer versus the City of Seattle, No. 576444, Superior Court for the State of Washington, King County (1961); Beezer versus City of Seattle, No. 576444 (1963), CDP. Billington, *People, Politics, and Public Power*, 434. Contrary to Billington, the court did not consider the case frivolous or a lawyer's money-making scheme. In fact, the judge went out of his way to commend council for both parties.

[84]Billington, *People, Politics, and Public Power*, 432–435. *Spokesman-Review*, 27 April 1971; 12 June 1964.

Epilogue, pages 183–194

[1]*Wenatchee Daily World*, 23 March 1969.

[2]Ken Billington, *People, Politics, and Public Power* (Seattle: Washington Public Utility District Association, 1988), 435.

[3]Frank Freidel, *Franklin D. Roosevelt: Rendezvous with Destiny* (Boston: Little, Brown and Co., 1990), 163.

[4]Richard Lowitt, *The New Deal and the West* (Bloomington: Indiana University Press, 1984), 157.

[5]Murray Morgan, *The Dam* (New York: Viking Press, 1954), xviii.

[6]Stewart Holbrook, *The Columbia* (New York: Rinehart, 1956), 309.

[7]Donald Worster, *Rivers of Empire: Water, Aridity, and the Growth of the American West* (New York: Pantheon, 1985), 329–335.

[8]Holbrook, *The Columbia*, 303.

[9]*Ibid.*, 302–303.

[10]Wallace Stegner and Richard Etulain, *Conversations with Wallace Stegner on Western History and Literature* (Salt Lake City: University of Utah Press, 1983), 147.

[11]*Ibid.*, 163.

[12]Worster, *Rivers of Empire*, 228–229.

[13]*Ibid.*, 230.

[14]Stegner and Etulain, *Conversations with Wallace Stegner*, 175.

[15]*Ibid.*, 90–91.

[16]Richard White, *It's Your Misfortune and None of My Own: A New History of the American West* (Norman: University of Oklahoma Press, 1991, 405–406.

[17]Frank Freidel, "FDR in the Northwest: Informal Glimpses," *Pacific Northwest Quarterly* 76 (October 1985): 125.

[18]*Ibid.*, 126.

[19]Donald Reading, "New Deal Activity and the State, 1933–1939," *Journal of Economic History* 33 (December 1973): 796, 797, 805.

[20]*Ibid.*, 804.

[21]*Congressional Record* (17 April 1928), vol. 69, pt. 6, 6597, 6598, 6600, 6601. Dill was even convinced that vast trade with Asia was there for the taking in some not too distant future.

[22]Congress, House of Representatives, Committee on Irrigation and Reclamation, *Hearings before the Committee on Irrigation and Reclamation on H.R 7446*, 72nd Congress, 1st session, 3 June 1932, 202–203.

[23]Holbrook, *The Columbia*, 312.

[24]John Clive, *Not By Fact Alone: Essays on the Writing and Reading of History* (New York: Alfred A. Knopf, 1989), 106.

[25]Wallace Stegner, *Angle of Repose* (New York: Doubleday and Co., 1971), 126.

Bibliography

Selected Published Sources

Books

Allen, Howard W. *Poindexter of Washington: A Study in Progressive Politics.* Carbondale: Southern Illinois University Press, 1981.

Ashby, Leroy. *The Spearless Leader: Senator Borah and the Progressive Movement in the 1920's.* Urbana: University of Illinois Press, 1972.

Avery, Mary. *History and Government of the State of Washington.* Seattle: University of Washington Press, 1961.

Barnouw, Erik. *A History of Broadcasting in the United States.* New York: Oxford University Press, 1966.

Bellush, Bernard. *Franklin D. Roosevelt as Governor of New York.* New York: Columbia University Press, 1955.

Billington, Ken. *People, Politics, and Public Power.* Seattle: Washington Public Utility District Association, 1988.

Blair, Karen J. ed. *Women in the Pacific Northwest: An Anthology.* Seattle: University of Washington Press, 1981.

Burner, David. *The Politics of Provincialism: The Democratic Party in Transition, 1918–1932.* New York: Alfred A. Knopf, 1968.

_____. *Herbert Hoover: A Public Life.* New York: Alfred A. Knopf, 1979.

Burns, James M. *Roosevelt: The Soldier of Freedom.* New York: Harcourt Brace Jovanovich, Inc., 1970.

Carter, Paul. *The Twenties in America.* New York: Thomas Y. Crowell Co., 1968.

Clark, Norman. *The Dry Years: Prohibition and Social Change in Washington.* Seattle: University of Washington Press, 1965.

Clive, John. *Not by Fact Alone: Essays on the Writing and Reading of History.* New York: Alfred A. Knopf, 1989.

Cooper, John M. *Pivotal Decades: The United States, 1900–1920.* New York: W.W. Norton and Co., 1990.

Croly, Herbert. *The Promise of American Life.* New York: E.P. Dutton, 1963.

Dallek, Robert. *Franklin D. Roosevelt and American Foreign Policy, 1932–1945.* New York: Oxford University Press, 1979.

Davis, Stephen. *The Law of Radio Communication.* New York: McGraw Hill, 1927.

Davis, W. Jefferson. *Radio Law.* New York: Parker Stone and Baird, 1929.

Dawley, Alan. *Struggles for Justice: Social Responsibility and the Liberal State.* Cambridge: Belknap Press, 1991.

Dembo, Jonathan. "Dave Beck and the Transportation Revolution." In *Experiences in a Promised Land.* Ed. Thomas Edwards and Carlos A. Schwantes. Seattle: University of Washington Press, 1986.

Dill, Clarence C. *Radio Law*. Washington, D.C.: National Law Book Co., 1938.
_____. *Where Water Falls*. Spokane: Self published, 1970.
Dodds, Gordon B. *The American Northwest: A History of Oregon and Washington*. Arlington Heights, Ill.: Forum Press Inc., 1986.
Dyar, Ralph. *News for an Empire: The Story of the Spokesman-Review of Spokane, Washington, and of the Field It Serves*. Caldwell, Id.: Caxton Printers, 1952.
Emery, Walter B. *Broadcasting and Government: Responsibilities and Regulations*. East Lansing: Michigan State University Press, 1971.
Fahey, John. *The Inland Empire: Unfolding Years, 1879–1929*. Seattle: University of Washington Press, 1986.
Fargo, Lucille. *Spokane Story*. New York: Columbia University Press, 1950.
Farley, James. *Jim Farley's Story: The Roosevelt Years*. New York: Whittlesey House, 1948.
_____. *Behind the Ballots*. New York: Harcourt, Brace and Co., 1938.
Ferrell, Robert. *Woodrow Wilson and World War I, 1917–1921*. New York: Harper and Row, 1985.
Ficken, Robert E. *The Forested Land: A History of Lumbering in Western Washington*. Seattle: University of Washington Press, 1987.
_____. *Lumber and Politics: The Career of Mark E. Reed*. Seattle: University of Washington Press, 1979.
_____. *Rufus Woods: The Columbia River and the Building of Modern Washington*. Pullman: Washington State University Press, 1995.
Ficken, Robert E., and Charles P. LeWarne. *Washington: A Centennial History*. Seattle: University of Washington Press, 1988.
Fite, Gilbert. *George N. Peek and the Fight for Farm Parity*. Norman: University of Oklahoma Press, 1954.
Freidel, Frank. *Franklin D. Roosevelt: The Ordeal*. Boston: Little, Brown and Co., 1952–1973.
_____. *Franklin D. Roosevelt: Rendezvous with Destiny*. Boston: Little, Brown and Co., 1990.
_____. *Franklin D. Roosevelt: The Triumph*. Boston: Little, Brown and Co., 1952–1973.
Galenson, Walter. *The CIO Challenge to the AFL: A History of the American Labor Movement, 1935–1941*. Cambridge: Harvard University Press, 1960.
Gibson, George H. *Public Broadcasting: The Role of the Federal Government, 1912–1976*. New York: Praeger Publishing, 1977.
Gunns, Albert. *Civil Liberties in Crisis: The Pacific Northwest, 1917–1940*. New York: Garland, 1983.
Hardeman, D.B., and Donald Bacon. *Rayburn: A Biography*. Austin: Texas Monthly Press, 1987.
Head, Sydney. *Broadcasting in America*. Boston: Houghton Mifflin Co., 1956.
Heckscher, August. *Woodrow Wilson*. New York: Charles Scribner's Sons, 1991.
Hicks, John D. *Republican Ascendancy, 1921–1933*. New York: Harper and Row, 1960.
Hofstadter, Richard. *The Progressive Historians*. New York: Alfred A. Knopf, 1968.
_____, *The Age of Reform*. New York: Vintage, 1960 [1989].
Holbrook, Stewart. *The Columbia*. New York: Rinehart, 1956.
Horwitz, Robert B. *The Irony of Regulatory Reform*. New York: Oxford University Press, 1989.
Ickes, Harold. *The Secret Diary of Harold Ickes: The First 1000 Days*. New York: Simon and Schuster, 1953.

Johansen, Dorothy. "A Working Hypothesis for the Study of Migrations." In *Experiences in a Promised Land*. Ed. Thomas Edwards and Carlos A. Schwantes. Seattle: University of Washington Press, 1986.

Johnson, Jalmar. *Builders of the Northwest*. New York: Dodd and Mead Co., 1963.

Krasnow, Erwin, Lawrence Longley, and Terry Herbert. *The Politics of Broadcast Regulation*. New York: St. Martin's Press, 1982.

Larabee, Eric. *Commander in Chief: Franklin Delano Roosevelt, His Lieutenants and Their War*. New York: Harper and Row, 1987.

Larson, Cedric, and James Mock. *Words That Won the War: The Story of the Committee on Public Information, 1917–1919*. New York: Russell and Russell, 1939.

Leuchtenburg, William E. *Franklin D. Roosevelt and the New Deal*. New York: Harper and Row, 1963.

_____. *The Perils of Prosperity, 1914–1932*. Chicago: University of Chicago Press, 1958.

_____. *The Supreme Court Reborn*. New York: Oxford University Press, 1995.

Link, Arthur S. *Woodrow Wilson and the Progressive Era, 1910–1917*. New York: Harper Brothers, 1954.

_____. *Woodrow Wilson: Campaigns for Progressivism and Peace, 1916–1917*. Princeton: Princeton University Press, 1965.

Link, Arthur S., and Richard L. McCormick. *Progressivism*. Arlington Heights, Ill.: Harlan Davidson, 1983.

Lowitt, Richard. *George Norris: The Persistence of a Progressive, 1918–1933*. Urbana: University of Illinois Press, 1971.

_____. *The New Deal and the West*. Bloomington: Indiana University Press, 1984.

Lorenz, Carl. *Tom L. Johnson: Mayor of Cleveland*. New York: A.S. Barnes, 1911.

McKinley, Charles. *Uncle Sam in the Pacific Northwest: Federal Management of Natural Resources in the Columbia River Valley*. Berkeley: University of California Press, 1952.

McChesney, Robert. *Telecommunications, Mass Media, and Democracy: The Battle for Control of U.S. Broadcasting, 1928–1935*. New York: Oxford University Press, 1993.

McCoy, Donald. *Calvin Coolidge: The Quiet President*. New York: Macmillan Co., 1967 [1988].

Meany, Edmond S. *History of the State of Washington*. New York: Macmillan, 1950.

Merz, Charles. *The Dry Decade*. New York: Doubleday and Doran, 1931.

Miller, Nathan. *Theodore Roosevelt: A Life*. New York: William Morrow and Co., 1992.

Moley, Raymond. *After Seven Years*. New York: Harper Bros., 1939.

Morgan, Murray. *The Dam*. New York: Viking Press, 1954.

Peel, Roy, and Thomas Donnelly. *The 1932 Campaign: An Analysis*. New York: Farrar and Rinehart, 1935.

Peterson, H.C., and Gilbert C. Fite. *Opponents of War: 1917–1918*. Madison: University of Wisconsin Press, 1957.

Pitzer, Paul C. *Grand Coulee: Harnessing a Dream*. Pullman: Washington State University Press, 1994.

Rosen, Philip T. *The Modern Stentors: Radio Broadcasters and the Federal Government: 1920–1934*. Westport, Ct.: Greenwood Press, 1980.

Schlesinger, Arthur Jr. *The Crisis of the Old Order, 1919–1933*. Boston: Houghton Mifflin Co., 1957.

Schwantes, Carlos A. *The Pacific Northwest: An Interpretive History*. Lincoln: University of Nebraska Press, 1989.

Shideler, James H. *Farm Crisis, 1919–1923*. Westport, Ct.: Greenwood Press, 1976.

Spencer, Lloyd, and Lancaster Pollard. *A History of the State of Washington*. New York: American Historical Society, 1937.

Stegner, Wallace. *Angle of Repose*. New York: Doubleday and Co., 1971.

Stegner, Wallace, and Richard Etulain. *Conversations with Wallace Stegner on Western History and Literature*. Salt Lake City: University of Utah Press, 1983.

Sterling, Christopher H., and John M. Kittross. *Stay Tuned: A Concise History of American Broadcasting*. Belmont, Ca.: Wadsworth Publishing Co., 1990.

Stewart, Edgar I. *Washington: Northwest Frontier*. New York: Lewis Historical Publishing Co., 1957.

Stone, Alan. *Public Service Liberalism: Telecommunications and Transitions in Public Policy*. Princeton: Princeton University Press, 1991.

Sundborg, George. *Hail Columbia: The Thirty Year Struggle for Grand Coulee Dam*. New York: Macmillan, 1954.

Sweetman, Maude. *What Price Politics? The Inside Story of Washington State Politics*. Seattle: White and Hitchcock, 1927.

Tollefson, Gene. *BPA and the Struggle for Power at Cost*. Portland: Bonneville Power Administration, 1987.

Tucker, Ray. *Sons of a Wild Jackass*. Boston: L.C. Page and Co., 1932.

Woods, Rufus. *The 23 Years Battle for Grand Coulee Dam*. Wenatchee, 1942.

Worster, Donald. *Rivers of Empire: Water, Aridity, and the Growth of the American West*. New York: Pantheon, 1985.

Government Documents

Abstracts of the Votes Polled in the State of Washington at the General Elections (various years). Secretary of State. Olympia, Washington.

Abstracts of the Votes Polled in the State of Washington at the Primary Elections (various years). Secretary of State. Olympia, Washington.

Columbia Basin Survey Commission. *The Columbia Basin Irrigation Project*. State of Washington, 1920.

Interlocutory Decree of Divorce, Case No 97726, Superior Court of Spokane County, Spokane, Washington.

United States Army Corp of Engineers. *Columbia River and Minor Tributaries*. House Doc., no. 103, Government Printing Office, Washington D.C., 1934.

Washington State Department of Conservation and Development. *Columbia Basin Project*, by George W. Goethals. Department of Conservation and Development, 1922.

Newspapers

Almira Herald, Almira, Washington.
Bellingham Evening News, Bellingham, Washington.
Bellingham Herald, Bellingham, Washington.
Colville Examiner, Colville, Washington
Daily Olympian, Olympia, Washington.
Ellensburg Record, Ellensburg, Washington.
Evening Star, Ellensburg, Washington.
Everett Daily Herald, Everett, Washington.

Grange News, Seattle, Washington.
Grant County Journal, Ephrata, Washington.
Labor Journal, Everett, Washington.
New York Times, New York, New York.
New York Tribune, New York, New York.
Okanogan Independent, Okanogan, Washington.
Olympia Daily Recorder, Olympia, Washington
Omak Chronicle, Omak, Washington.
Oregonian, Portland, Oregon.
Oroville Gazette, Oroville, Washington.
Post-Intelligencer [P.I.], Seattle, Washington.
Republic Journal, Republic, Washington.
Seattle Star, Seattle, Washington.
Seattle Times, Seattle, Washington.
Seattle Union Record, Seattle, Washington.
Spokane Chronicle, Spokane, Washington.
Spokesman-Review, Spokane, Washington.
Tacoma News Tribune, Tacoma, Washington.
The Journal Herald, Delaware, Ohio.
The Labor World, Spokane, Washington.
Variety, Washington D.C.
Wenatchee Daily World, Wenatchee, Washington.

Periodicals

Arrington, Leonard. "The New Deal in the West: A Preliminary Statistical Inquiry." *Pacific Historical Review* 38 (August 1969).

Boening, Rose. "History of Irrigation in the State of Washington." *Washington Historical Quarterly* 9 (October 1918); 10 (January 1919).

Dill, Clarence C. "Safeguarding the Ether: The American Way." *Congressional Digest,* 12 (August-September 1933).

Freidel, Frank. "FDR in the Northwest: Informal Glimpses." *Pacific Northwest Quarterly* 76 (October 1985).

Godfrey, Donald. "Senator Dill and the 1927 Radio Act." *Journal of Broadcasting* 23 (Autumn 1979).

_____. "The 1927 Radio Act: People and Politics." *Journalism History* 14 (Autumn 1977).

Harding, Bruce. "Water from Pend Oreille: The Gravity Plan for Irrigating the Columbia Basin." *Pacific Northwest Quarterly* 52 (April 1954).

Kaiser, Benjamin. "May Arkwright Hutton." *Pacific Northwest Quarterly* 57 (April 1966).

Marple, Elliot. "Movement for Public Ownership of Power in Washington." *Journal of Land and Public Utility Economics* 7 (February 1931).

Mitchell, Bruce. "Rufus Woods and Columbia River Development." *Pacific Northwest Quarterly* 52 (October 1961).

Reading, Donald. "New Deal Activity and the State, 1933–1939." *Journal of Economic History* 33 (December 1973).

Richards, Kent. "In Search of the Pacific Northwest: The Historiography of Oregon and Washington." *Pacific Historical Review* 50 (November 1981).

Shepherd, James. "The Development of Wheat Production in the Pacific Northwest." *Agricultural History* 49 (January 1975).

Voeltz, Herman. "Genesis and Development of a Regional Power Agency in the Pacific Northwest, 1933–1943." *Pacific Northwest Quarterly* 53 (April 1962).

Unpublished Sources

Interviews

Dill, Clarence C. Interview by John Fahey, 24 April 1948. Copy in author's possession.

Public Manuscript Collections

Allen, Edward. Papers. University of Washington Library, Seattle Washington.

American Civil Liberties Union. Collection. University of Washington Library, Seattle, Washington.

Bagley, Clarence. Collection. University of Washington Library, Seattle, Washington.

Ballaine, John. Papers. University of Washington Library, Seattle, Washington.

Beals, Walter. Papers. University of Washington Library, Seattle, Washington.

Benson, Naomi. Collection. University of Washington Library, Seattle, Washington.

Bone, Homer. Papers. University of Washington Library, Seattle, Washington.

Bridges, Robert. Papers. University of Washington Library, Seattle, Washington.

Chadwick, Stephen J. Papers. University of Washington Library, Seattle, Washington.

China Club of Seattle. Papers. University of Washington Library, Seattle, Washington.

Coe, Earl. Collection. University of Washington Library, Seattle, Washington.

Cotterill, George. Manuscripts. University of Washington Library, Seattle, Washington.

Curtis, Asahel. Papers. University of Washington Library, Seattle, Washington.

Dill, Clarence C. Papers. Eastern Washington State Historical Society Archives, Spokane, Washington.

Freeman, Miller. Manuscripts. University of Washington Library, Seattle, Washington.

Gorrie, Jack. Papers. University of Washington Library, Seattle, Washington.

Gunn, Arthur. Collection. University of Washington Library, Seattle, Washington.

Haas, Saul. Papers. University of Washington Library, Seattle, Washington.

Houghton, Cluck, Coughlin, and Schubat. Papers. University of Washington Library, Seattle, Washington.

Humphrey, William. Collection. University of Washington Library, Seattle, Washington.

Ickes, Harold. Collection. Library of Congress. Washington, D.C.

Jackson, Henry. Papers. University of Washington Library, Seattle, Washington.

Jones, Wesley. Manuscripts. University of Washington Library, Seattle, Washington.

Langlie, Arthur B. Collection. University of Washington Library, Seattle, Washington.

Martin, Clarence. Papers. Washington State University Library, Pullman, Washington.

Magnuson, Warren. Collection. University of Washington Library, Seattle, Washington.

Matthews, Mark. Papers. University of Washington Library, Seattle, Washington.

Merrill and Ring Lumber. Collection. University of Washington Library, Seattle, Washington.

Meany, Edmund. Collection. University of Washington Library, Seattle, Washington.

Mitchell, Hugh. Papers. University of Washington Library, Seattle, Washington.

Myers, Guy. Papers. University of Washington Library, Seattle, Washington.

Northwest Public Power Association. Papers. University of Washington Library, Seattle, Washington.

O'Sullivan, James. Papers. Gonzaga University Library, Spokane, Washington.

Pitter, Edward. Papers. University of Washington Library, Seattle, Washington, Pitter.

Reclamation Bureau. Papers. National Archives, Washington, D.C.

Riley, Edith Dolan. Collection. University of Washington Library, Seattle, Washington.

Roosevelt, Franklin D. Collection. Franklin Delano Roosevelt Library, Hyde Park, New York.

Ross, J.O. Papers. University of Washington Library, Seattle, Washington.

Seattle Lighting Department. Papers. University of Washington Library, Seattle, Washington.

Seattle Port Commission. Papers. University of Washington Library, Seattle, Washington.

Smith, Joseph. Papers. University of Washington Library, Seattle, Washington.

St. Paul and Tacoma Lumber Co. Collection. University of Washington Library, Seattle, Washington.

Suzzallo, Henry. Papers. University of Washington Library, Seattle, Washington.

Testu, Jeannette. Papers. University of Washington Library, Seattle, Washington.

Washington Forest Resources College. Papers. University of Washington Library, Seattle, Washington.

Washington State Federation of Labor. Papers. University of Washington Library, Seattle, Washington.

Zioncheck, Marion. Papers. University of Washington Library, Seattle, Washington.

Theses and Dissertations

Bohrnsen, William. "A History of Grand Coulee Dam and the Columbia Basin Reclamation Project." M.A. thesis, University of Washington, 1942.

Cole, Robert L. "The Democratic Party in Washington State, 1919–1933: Barometer of Social Change." Ph.D. diss., University of Washington, 1972.

Cravens, Hamilton. "A History of the Washington Farmer-Labor Party, 1918–1924." M.A. thesis, University of Washington, 1962.

Forth, William. "Wesley L. Jones: A Political Biography." Ph.D. diss., University of Washington, 1962.

Godfrey, Donald. "A Rhetorical Analysis of the Congressional Debates on Broadcast Regulation in the United States." Ph.D. diss., University of Washington, 1975.

Gunns, Albert. "Roland Hartley and the Politics of Washington State." M.A. thesis, University of Washington, 1963.

Jordan, Myron. "The Kilowatt Wars: James D. Ross, Public Power, and the Public Relations Contest for the Hearts and Minds of Pacific Northwesterners." Ph.D. diss., University of Washington, 1991.

Krause, Fayette. "Democratic Party Politics in the State of Washington during the New Deal." Ph.D. diss., University of Washington, 1971.

Krause, Mary Lou. "Prohibition and the Reform Tradition." M.A. thesis, University of Washington, 1963.

Kreiss, James. "A County by County Analysis of Voting Trends in the State of Washington from 1920 to 1962." M.A. thesis, University of Washington, 1964.

Saltvig, Robert D. "The Progressive Movement in Washington." Ph.D. diss., University of Washington, 1966.

Scott, George. "Arthur B. Langlie: Republican Governor in a Democratic Age." Ph.D. diss., University of Washington, 1971.

Slatten, Terry. "Homer T. Bone, Public Power, and Washington State: Progressive Politics in the Mid 1920's." M.A. thesis, University of Washington, 198?.

Sleizer, Herman. "Governor Ernest Lister: Chapters of a Political Career." M.A. thesis, University of Washington, 1961.

Tjaden, Norman. "Populists and Progressives of Washington: A Comparative Study." M.A. thesis, University of Washington, 1950.

Vandeveer, Emmett. "History of Irrigation in Washington." Ph.D. diss., University of Washington, 1948.

Index

A reference to a continuous discussion over two or more pages is indicated by a span of page numbers, e.g., 10–13. *Passim* is used for a cluster of references in close but not consecutive sequence. Page numbers in *italics* locate illustrations.

_____. approval for: final approval for construction, 124; need for Presidential approval, 113–19; preliminary approval, 119, 122, 124, 170, 217nn62,67, 212n20; Presidential conferences on, 115–16, 121–25

_____. bids and contracts for: call for bids on, 118, 122, 128; construction bid opening, *130;* contract with Bureau of Reclamation, 121; legal basis for, 118; project construction contracts, 128; Six Companies bid, 128, 129

_____. construction of, 123, 124, 133, *134*; construction bill introduced in Congress, 101–02; construction of third powerhouse, 179, *182;* cooperative spirit in building of, 123; preliminary engineering work, 120–21, 122, 123; roadblocks to construction of, 123–24

_____. design of: Army Corps of Engineers plan, 103; gravity plan, 99–100, 119, 134; high dam proposal, 125, 126, 131, 133, 156, 161; high dam/low dam controversy, 126–28, 131–33, 215nn13,15; low dam proposal, 115–16, 117, 126, 215n15; as power dam, 118; power dam vs. reclamation and irrigation, 127; pumper plan, 99–101, 134; as reclamation dam, 43, 100, 113–24*passim*, 161, 215n13

_____. funding sources, 114–18, 120, 122, 170; arrangements for, 117, 118, 121–22, 126, 189–90; costs of, 115; preliminary engineering work funds, 120–21; RFC funds, 114–18; sale of electricity as cost recovery measure, 116–25*passim*

_____. project administration: 126; FPC and, 121; federal vs. state control of, 122, 126; as public power project, 114; PWA and, 119; role of Washington State Congressional delegation, 114, 123, 133, 216n25; state involvement with, 123, 125, 126

_____. public power and: formation of public power district, 117, 118, 121; increased generator capacity, 176, 179; power surplus concerns, 119

_____. reaction to project, 117; opposition to, 119, 122, 123, 126, 161; in Oregon, 117, 123, 216n22; political dynamics of, 127–28; private power interests and, 120, 125; Spokane opposition to, 119; support for, 122, 124; Washington Water Power Company (WWP) and, 119, 125, 217nn57,69

_____. regional benefits from, 134, 179, 185, 187–88, 190–91, 193; reasons to build project, 116; reclamation aspects of, 43, 100, 113–24*passim*, 161, 186–90*passim*, 215n13; role in Pacific Northwest unemployment relief, 115; role in World War II, 175, 190, 191; as tool for development of Pacific Northwest, 125, 190

Grand Coulee land scheme, 158, 163, 166, 218n88

Grange Movement, 48, 100–01, 170

Grant County PUD, 181, 191

Grant, Ulysses (U.S. President), 24

Grapes of Wrath, The (Steinbeck), 187

Graves, J.W. (atty., Spokane), 7

gravity plan. *See* Grand Coulee Dam

Grays Harbor County, 92, 172

Great Depression, 95, 102, 110, 111, 119, 155, 169; agricultural surpluses, 94, 95, 100, 113; banking crisis, 111, 113, 135; Civil Works Administration, 135; distractions from, 135–36; importance of radio, 135–36; importance of Will Rogers, 136; New Deal programs as remedy, 113, 146, 148, 155, 188–90, 224n22

Green, William (labor leader), 164, 166

Grier, C.E. (secret service agent), 129

Gunn, Arthur (Dill correspondent), 26

H

Hanford, Wash., 190–91

Harding, Warren G. (U.S. President), 2–3, 44, 47, 49, 108

Harper, S.O. (engineer), 127–28

Harrington, Wash., 33

Hart, Charles (journalist), 6

Hartley, Roland H. (governor, Wash.), 91

Hatfield, Henry D. (Sen., W. Virg.), 148

Haugen, Gilbert (Rep., Iowa), 61–65

Hay, Marion E. (governor, Wash.), 120

Hayden, Carl (Sen., Ariz.), 118

Hearst, William Randolph, 107, 109

Heflin, Thomas (Sen., Ala.), 58, 77

Heifner, Charles (politician), 9

Hicks, John (historian), 63

high dam proposal. *See* Grand Coulee Dam

Hill, Sam (Rep., Wash.), 101–02, 114, 115, 161

Hillyard, Wash., 16, 85

Holbrook, Stewart (historian), 185, 186, 219n100

Hoover Dam, 102

Hoover, Herbert (U.S. President), 170, 214n2; Columbia Basin Development, 102; Grand Coulee Dam, 100, 101, 102, 103, 117; management of radio, 67–72*passim*, 138, 152; Presidential election (1928), 88, 90, 93, 110; speech to Fourth National Radio Conference, 69–70; unpopularity of administration, 106, 111; veto of Radio Bill of (1933), 143

Hopkins, Harry (head, CWA), 126, 135

Horan, Walt (Rep., Wash.), 174–75